ISBN 978-1-330-94312-0
PIBN 10124463

FOREWORD

A few words may serve to make the aim of this book more plain to those who read it. A great part of what is written here was spoken to the students of divinity at Yale University in the spring of 1896, as one of the courses of "Lectures on Preaching" which have been given for some years on the Lyman Beecher Foundation. But I must frankly confess that a strong wish to say something which might reach beyond, or, better still, through, the immediate audience, and be of help to the wider circle of men and women who care for the vital problems of faith, drew me aside from the usual line of such lectures and gave this book a new purpose.

The question of how to preach is highly interesting to students for the ministry. But it has already been answered so fully and so ably by those who have preceded me in this course that I cannot hope to add anything of value to their various counsels. And after all, it is a technical question. The art of preaching, important and beautiful and powerful as it may be, is only a part of the larger art of life. Religion is the spiritual secret of this larger art of life. The force of religion to move and inspire the hearts of men lies not in the modes and forms of preaching, but in the Gospel, — the message which it brings to the human soul. The deep ques tion, the important question, the question of widest interest, is what to preach to the men and women of to-day, to cheer them, to uplift them, to lead them back to faith, and through faith to a brave, full, noble life. This is the question for which I have tried, at least, to point the way to an answer.

What is the word of spiritual life and power for the present age? Evidently it must be a real gospel, a word of gladness and a word of God.[1] It will not do to teach for doctrines the commandments of men. Tradition is powerless. Dry systems of dogma cannot quicken the soul. The preacher's message must come to him from a heavenly source, and take hold upon him with the charm of a divine novelty. It must be so fresh, so vivid, so original to his own heart that he cannot help wanting to tell it to the world.

[1] See Appendix, Note 1.

This wonderful sense of newness in the gospel is what makes men long to preach it and the world glad to hear it.

But it is no less plain that the message, in a certain sense, must also be old. It cannot be out of touch with the past. It must be in line with the upward movement of humanity through the ages. It must be in reverent harmony with the faith and hope and love which have already cheered and purified and blessed the best of human lives. An altogether new religion can hardly be an altogether true religion.

Now the solution of this apparent difficulty — the reconciling of the old and the new — lies in a personal view of the gospel of Jesus Christ. The effort to get such a view, for every age and for every man, results in a thrilling and joyful sense of new discovery of an old and changeless truth. One way in which this feeling of newness comes is through the necessity of clearing away the human accretions which have gathered about the gospel. Christianity always has been, and probably always will be, subject to obscuration and misunderstanding. It has been presented as a complex system of doctrine. In reality, it is a spiritual life. The arguments used to defend it have often become hindrances to its acceptance. The formulas framed to express it have often hidden Him who is its true and only centre. Christ is Christianity. To find God in Him, to trust and love God in Him, is to be a Christian. To preach Him, in the language of to-day, to the men of to-day, for the needs of to-day,[1] is to preach a gospel as new and as old as life itself.

This is the thing in which Christianity differs from all other religions. It has a Person at the heart of it; a Person who is as real as we are; a Person who carries in Himself the evidence of a spiritual world; a Person who has proved in myriads of souls His power to save men, not only from the evil of sin, but also from the gloom of doubt. He is the only steadfast Light shining through the deep, starless night of scepticism that has overspread our proud and unhappy modern world. To see Him is to be sure of God and immortality. Such a Person could not have lived if the universe were a mere product of matter and force. It would be easier to think that the floating clouds of sunset could beget out of their vaporous bosoms a solid and eternal mountain peak, than that the vain and vague

[1] See Appendix, Note 2.

dreams of spiritual life rising from a humanity born only of the dust, and fated to crumble altogether into dust again, could have produced such a firm and glorious reality as the character and life of Jesus of Nazareth. This is the foundation of faith, to believe that Christ is "the revelation of the true meaning and the realization of the true destination of every man; and that in Him as the personal incarnation and reproduction of the personal God in our personal selves, we and the whole creation shall come into our divine inheritance."[1]

We must get back from the confusions of theology to the simplicity that is in Christ. We must see clearly that our central message is not the gospel of a system, but the gospel of a Person. We must hold fast the true humanity of Jesus in order that we may know what is meant by His true divinity. We must recognize His supreme authority in the interpretation of the Bible itself. We must accept His revelations of human liberty and divine sovereignty. Above all, we must accept His great truth of election to service as our only salvation from the curse of sin, which is selfishness.

[1] W. P. Du Bose, S. T. D., *The Soteriology of the New Testament* (New York, 1892), p. 171.

If the following of this course should lead us to break with some time-honoured dogmas and definitions, let us only be careful to see to it that our sole desire and aim is to discern the truth as it is in Jesus more clearly and preach it more simply. If it should lead us to new modes of speech and forms of expression, let them grow only out of the earnest effort to bring religion more closely home to the real lives of men. Our age has its own character, its own perils, its own needs, its own hopes and aspirations. The only gospel that it is worth while to preach must stand in vital relation and speak with vital power to the present age.

This is the line that I have tried to follow in this book. I have added a full appendix of notes, chiefly from recent writers, with a twofold purpose. First, to make it clear by the sorrowful and confused confessions of modern doubt how much the age needs a gospel; and, second, to show how many men of all classes are moving in the same direction, — towards a renewal of faith. In truth if the evils and dangers of the age are great, its encouragements are even greater. The experiment of a secular unbelief has never been tried on such a large and splendid scale, with such blank and desperate failure. The longings and efforts of the world to attain a higher, happier existence for all men have never been more generous and ardent. With the materialism, the sensuality, the pride of our age, Christianity stands in conflict. With the altruism, the humanity, the sympathy of our age, Christianity must stand in loving and wise alliance. A simpler creed and a nobler life will prepare the way for a renaissance of religion greater and more potent than the world has known for centuries. It seems as if we stood on the brightening border of the new day. The watchword of its coming is the personal gospel of Jesus Christ, in whom we find the ideal man and the real God.

FOREST HILLS LODGE, FRANCONIA,
July 10th, 1896.

CONTENTS

I

AN AGE OF DOUBT

"Cleave ever to the sunnier side of doubt,
And cling to Faith beyond the forms of Faith!
She reels not in the storm of warring words,
She brightens at the clash of 'Yes' and 'No,'
She sees the Best that glimmers thro' the Worst,
She feels the Sun is hid but for a night,
She spies the summer thro' the winter bud,
She tastes the fruit before the blossom falls,
She hears the lark within the songless egg,
She finds the fountain where they wail'd 'Mirage'!"

TENNYSON, *The Ancient Sage.*

AN AGE OF DOUBT

The personal equation of the age.

THERE is one point in which all men resemble each other: it is that they are all different. But their differences are not fixed and immutable. They are variable and progressive. Types of character survive or perish, like the forms of animal life. Some predominate; others are subordinated.

Thus it comes to pass that underneath all the diversities of individual life, we may discern, not with the clearness of a portrait, but with the vague outlines of a composite photograph, the features of a *Zeitgeist*, a spirit of the time. Generations differ almost as much as the men who compose them. There is a personal equation in every age.

To know this is a necessity for the preacher. Even as the physician must apprehend the idiosyncrasy of his patient, and the teacher must recognize the quality of his pupil, so must the preacher be in touch with his age.

Literature as an index of life.

In endeavouring to arrive at this knowledge, contact with the world is of the first cousequence. For one who desires to make men and women what they ought to be, nothing can take the place of an acquaintance with men and women as they are. It seems to me that one of the best means of obtaining this acquaintance is through literature, — not that highly specialized and more or less technical variety of literature which is produced expressly for certain classes of readers, but literature in the broader sense, as it appeals to cultivated and intelligent people in general, including contemporary history and criticism, poetry and fiction, popular philosophy and diluted science. This kind of literature is the efflorescence of the Zeitgeist. It is at once a product, and a cause, of the temperament of the age. In it we see not only what certain men have written by way of comment on the movement of the times, but also what a great many men are reading while they move. It expresses, and it creates, a spirit, an attitude of mind. "I do not imagine," says a keen observer, "that I am announcing an altogether novel truth in affirming that literature is one of the elements of the ethical life, — the most important perhaps; for in the decline, more and more evident, of traditional and local influences, the book is taking its place as the great initiator."[1]

The value of general reading.

For this reason I believe that a course in modern novels and poetry might well be made a part of every scheme of preparation for the ministry. The preacher who does not know what his people are reading does not know his people. He will miss the significance of the current talk of society, and even of the daily comments of the newspapers, which are in fact only a cheap substitute for conversation, unless he has the key to it in the tone of popular literature. It is from this source that I have drawn many of the illustrations for this lecture. If they appear unfamiliar or out of place in a theological seminary, I can only say that they seem to me none the less, but perhaps the more, significant and valuable on that account. For I think that one of the causes by which, as John Foster wrote seventy years ago, "Evangelical Religion has been rendered unacceptable to persons of cultivated taste,"[2] has been a certain ill-disguised contempt on the part of

[1] Paul Bourget, *Essais de Psychologie Contemporaine*, Paris, 1895. See Appendix, note 3.

[2] John Foster, *Essays*, "On the Aversion of Men of Taste to Evangelical Religion," p. 188.

persons of orthodox opinions for what they are pleased to call, "mere *belles-lettres*." And though I do not fancy that there is any sympathy with that frame of mind in this place, yet the occasion seems opportune for saying in a definite way that the preacher who wishes to speak to this age must read many books in order that he may be in a position to make the best use of what Sir Walter Scott called "the one Book." He must keep himself in touch with modern life by studying modern literature, which is one of its essential factors.

I

A doubting age.

As soon as we step out of the theological circle into the broad field of general reading we see that we are living in an age of doubt.

I do not mean to say that this is the only feature in the physiognomy of the age. It has many other aspects, from any one of which we might pick a name. From the material side, we might call it an age of progress; from the intellectual side, an age of science; from the medical side, an age of hysteria; from the political side, an age of democracy; from the commercial side, an age of advertisement; from the social side, an age of publicomania.

But looking at it from the spiritual side, which is the preacher's point of view, and considering that interior life to which every proclamation of a gospel must be addressed, beyond a doubt it stands confessed as a doubting age.

The questioning spirit.

There is a profound and wide-spread unsettlement of soul in regard to fundamental truths of religion, and also in regard to the nature and existence of the so-called spiritual faculties by which alone these truths can be perceived. In its popular manifestations, this unsettlement takes the form of uncertainty rather than of denial, of unbelief rather than of disbelief, of general scepticism rather than of specific infidelity.[1] The questioning spirit is abroad, moving on the face of the waters, seeking rest and finding none.

It is not merely that particular doctrines, such as the inspiration of the Bible, or the future punishment of the wicked, are attacked and denied. The preacher who concentrates his attention at these points will fail to realize the gravity of the situation. It is not that a spirit of bitter and mocking atheism, such as Bishop Butler described at the close of the last century, has led people of discernment to set up religion "as a principal subject of

[1] See Appendix, note 4.

mirth and ridicule, as it were by way of reprisal for its having so long interrupted the pleasures of the world "[1] The preacher who takes that view of the case now will be at least fifty years too late. He will fail to understand the serious and pathetic temper of the age.

Respectful unbelief.

The questioning spirit of to-day is severe but not bitter, restless but not frivolous; it takes itself very seriously and applies its methods of criticism, of analysis, of dissolution, with a sad courtesy of demeanour, to the deepest and most vital truths of religion, the being of God, the reality of the soul, the possibility of a future life. Everywhere it comes and everywhere it asks for a reason, in the shape of a positive and scientific demonstration. When one is given, it asks for another, and when another is given, it asks for the reason of the reason. The laws of evidence, the principles of judgment, the witness of history, the testimony of consciousness, — all are called in question. The answers which have been given by religion to the most difficult and pressing problems of man's inner life are declared to be unsatisfactory and without foundation. The

[1] Joseph Butler, *The Analogy of Religion* (London, Bell & Daldy, 1858). "Advertisement," p. xxiv.

question remains unsolved. Is it insoluble? The age stands in doubt. Its coat-of-arms is an interrogation point rampant, above three bishops dormant, and its motto is *Query?*

II

Causes of scepticism.

If we inquire the cause of this general scepticism in regard to religion, the common answer from all sides would probably attribute it to the progress of science. I do not feel satisfied with this answer. At least I should wish to qualify it in such a way as to give it a very different meaning from that which is implied in the current phrase "the conflict between science and religion."

Science not hostile to religion.

Science, in itself considered, the orderly and reasoned knowledge of the phenomenal universe of things and events, ought not to be, and has not been, hostile to religion, simply because it does not, and cannot, enter into the same sphere. The great advance which has been made in the observation and classification of sensible facts, and in the induction of so-called general laws under which those facts may be arranged for purposes of study, has not even touched the two questions upon the answer to which the reality and nature of religion depend: first, the possible existence of other facts which physical science cannot observe and classify; and second, the probable explanation of these facts. What has happened is just this. The field in which faith has to work has been altered, and it seems to me enormously broadened. But the work remains the same. The question is whether faith has enough vital energy to face and accomplish it. For example, the material out of which to construct an argument from the evidences of final cause in nature has been incalculably increased by the discoveries of the last fifty years in regard to natural selection and the origin of species. The observant wanderer in the field of nature to-day no longer stumbles upon Dr. Paley's old-fashioned, open-faced, turnip-shaped watch lying on the ground. He finds, instead, an intricate and self-adjusting chronometer, capable not only of marking time with accuracy, but also of evolving by its own operation another more perfect and delicate instrument, with qualities and powers which adapt themselves to their surroundings and so advance forever. The idea of final cause has not been touched. Only the region which it must illuminate has been vastly enlarged. It remains to be seen whether faith can supply the illuminating power. Already we have the

The task of faith not changed, but enlarged.

promise of an answer in many books, by masters of science and philosophy, who show that the theory of evolution demands for its completion the recognition of the spiritual nature of man and the belief in an intelligent and personal God.[1]

The expansion of knowledge.

The spread of scepticism is often attributed to the growth of our conception of the physical magnitude of the universe. The bewildering numbers and distances of the stars, the gigantic masses of matter in motion, and the tremendous sweep of the forces which drive our tiny earth along like a grain of dust in an orderly whirlwind, are supposed to have overwhelmed and stunned the power of spiritual belief in man. The account seems to me incorrect and unconvincing. I observe that precisely the same argument was used by Job and Isaiah and the Psalmists to lead to a conclusion of faith. The striking disproportion between the littleness of man and the greatness of the stars was to them a demonstration of the necessity of religion to solve the equation. They saw in the heavens the glory of God. And if man to-day knows vastly more of the heavens, does not that put him in position to receive a larger and loftier vision of the glory?

[1] See Appendix, note 5.

Devout men of pure science.

We observe, moreover, that it is just in those departments of science where the knowledge of the magnitude and splendid order of the physical universe is most clear and exact, namely, in astronomy and mathematics, that we find the most illustrious men of science who have not been sceptics but sincere and steadfast believers in the Christian religion. Kepler and Newton were men of faith. The most brilliant galaxy of mathematicians ever assembled at one time and place was at the University of Cambridge in the latter half of this century. Of these "Sir W. Thomson, Sir George Stokes, Professors Tait, Adams, Clerk-Maxwell, and Cayley — not to mention a number of lesser lights, such as Routh, Todhunter, Ferrers, etc. — were all avowed Christians."[1] Surely it needs no further proof to show that the pursuit of pure science does not necessarily tend to scepticism.

The arrogance of science falsely so-called.

No, we must look more closely and distinguish more clearly in order to discover in the scientific activities of the age a cause of the prevailing doubt. And if we do this I think we shall find it in the fallacy of that kind of science which mistakes itself for omniscience.

[1] George John Romanes, M.A., LL.D., F.R.S., *Thoughts on Religion* (Chicago, 1895), p. 147.

"What we see is the pretence of certain sciences to represent in themselves all human knowledge. And as outside of knowledge there is no longer, in the eyes of science thus curtailed, any means for man to come in contact with the realities, we see the pretence advanced by some that all reality and all life should be reduced to that which they have verified. Outside of this there are only dreams and illusions. This is indeed too much. It is no longer science, but scientific absolutism."[1]

"The history of the natural sciences," said Du Bois-Reymond in 1877, "is the veritable history of mankind." "The world," says another, "is made of atoms and ether, and there is no room for ghosts." M. Berthelot in the preface to his *Origines de l'alchimie*, modestly claims that "the world to-day is without mysteries"; meaning thereby, I suppose, that there is nothing in existence, from the crystallization of a diamond to the character of a saint, which cannot be investigated and explained by means of a crucible, a blow-pipe, a microscope, and a few other tools.

An immense assumption.

This is simply begging the question of a spiritual world in the negative. It is an im-

[1] Charles Wagner, *Youth*, translated from the French by Ernest Redwood (New York, 1893), p. 28.

mense and stupefying assumption. It is a claim to solve the problems of the inner life by suppressing them. This claim is not in any sense necessary to the existence of science, nor to any degree supported by the work which it has actually accomplished. But it is made with a calm assurance which imposes powerfully upon the popular mind; and, being made in the name of science, it carries with it an appearance of authority borrowed from the great service which science has rendered to humanity by its discoveries in the sphere of the visible.

Results of this assumption.

The result of this *petitio principii* in the minds of those who accept it fully and carry it out to its logical conclusion, is a definite system of metaphysical negation which goes under the various names of Naturalism, Positivism, Empiricism, and Agnosticism. Its result in the minds of those who accept it partially and provisionally, but lack the ability or the inclination to formulate it, is the development of a sceptical temper. Its result in the minds of those who are unconsciously affected by it, through those profound instincts of sympathy and involuntary imitation which influence all men, is an attitude,—more or less sincere, more or less consistent and continuous, — an attitude of doubt. The spirit of the age tacitly divides all the various beliefs which are held among men into two classes. Those which are supported by scientific proof must be accepted. Those which are not thus supported either must be rejected, or may safely and properly be disregarded as matters of no consequence.

III

The mirror of literature and the shadow of doubt.

Now this general scepticism, in all its shades and degrees, from the most clear, self-conscious, and aggressive, to the most vague, diffused, and deprecatory, is reflected in the productions of current literature. Never was literary art more perfect, more accomplished, more versatile and successful than in the present age. Never have its laws been more widely understood and its fascinations more potently exercised. Never has it evoked more magical and charming forms to float above an abyss of disenchantment and nothingness.

In the lay sermons and essays of Huxley and Tyndall and Frederic Harrison and W. K. Clifford, scepticism appears militant and trenchant. These knights-errant of Doubting Castle are brilliantly equipped as men of war; and even when they fall foul of each other, as they often do, the ground of the conflict is an accusation of infidelity to the principles of unbelief, and its object is to drive the adversary back into a more complete and consistent negation.

Over the fragmentary but majestic life-philosophies of Carlyle and Emerson, lying in the disarray of stones hewn for a temple yet unbuilt, imaginative scepticism hangs like a cloud. Over Carlyle, it is the shadow of a noonday tempest, full of darkness and tumult and muttering thunder. Over Emerson, it floats like a cumulus of evening vapours, luminous and beautiful, alluringly transfigured

> "In the golden lightning
> Of the sunken sun." [1]

In the vivid and picturesque historical studies of Renan and Froude, scepticism is at once ironical and idealistic, destructive and dogmatic. In the penetrative and intelligent critiques of Scherer and Morley, it adheres with proud but illogical persistence to the ethical consequences of the faith with which logic has broken: like a son disinherited, but resolved to maintain the right of possession by the strong arm.

[1] Shelley, "Ode to a Skylark."

Fiction gloomy.

In the novels of unflinching and unblushing naturalism,—like those of Zola and Maupassant and the later works of Thomas Hardy, scepticism speaks with a harsh and menacing accent of the emptiness of all life and the futility of all endeavour. In the psychological romances of Flaubert and Bourget and Spielhagen, George Eliot and Mrs. Humphry Ward, it holds the mirror up to human nature to disclose a face darkened with inconsolable regret for lost dreams. Far apart as *Madame Bovary* and *Cosmopolis*, *Problematische Naturen* and *Middlemarch* and *Robert Elsmere* may be in many of their features, do they not wear the same expression,—the cureless melancholy of disillusion?

Fiction in its more superficial form, dealing only with the manners and customs of the social drama, and relying for its interest mainly upon local colour and the charm of incident narrated with vivacity and grace, betrays its scepticism by a serene, unconscious disregard of the part which religion plays in real life.[1] In how many of the lighter novels of the day do we find any recognition, even between the lines, of the influence which the idea of God or its absence, the practice of prayer or its neg-

[1] See Appendix, note 6.

lect, actually exercise upon the character and conduct of men? Take, for example, *Trilby*,[1] as the type of a clever book carelessly written for the thoughtless public of a passing moment. It is incredibly credulous in regard to the dramatic possibilities of hypnotism. It is pitifully in adequate in its conception of the actual potencies of religion; and it uses Christianity chiefly as a subject for caricature in the style of the illustrated newspapers, which are called comic.

Poetry despondent.

Poetry has always been the most direct and intimate utterance of the human heart. And it is in poetry that we hear to-day the voice of scepticism most clearly, "making abundant music around an elementary nihilism, now stripped naked."[2] Listen to its sonorous chantings as they come from France in the verse of Leconte de Lisle, celebrating the sombre ritual of human automata before the altar of the unknown and almighty tyrant, who agitates them endlessly for his own amusement. Listen to its delicate and decadent lyrics, as Charles Baudelaire sings his defeat in life and his thirst for annihilation.

> "Morne esprit, autrefois amoureux de la lutte,
> L'Espoir dont l'éperon attisait ton ardeur

[1] George Du Maurier, *Trilby* (Harpers, 1895).

[2] Paul Desjardins, *Le Devoir Present* (Paris, 1892), p. 65.

Ne veut plus t'enfourcher. Couche toi sans pudeur,
Vieux cheval dont le pied à chaque obstacle butte.

Résigne-toi, mon cœur, dors ton sommeil de brute.

Et le Temps m'engloutit minute par minute
Comme la neige immense un corps pris de roideur:
Je contemple d'en haut le globe en sa rondeur
Et je n'y cherche plus l'abri d'une cahute!

Avalanche, veux tu m'emporter dans ta chute?"[1]

Turn to England and hear its musical confession in the cool, sad, melodious tones of Matthew Arnold, no enemy of faith, but her disenchanted lover.

"Forgive me, masters of the mind,
At whose behest I long ago
So much unlearned, so much resigned —
I come not here to be your foe;
I seek these anchorites not in ruth,
To curse and to deny your truth;

Not as their friend, or child, I speak
But as on some far northern strand,
Thinking of his own gods, a Greek,
In pity and mournful awe might stand
Before a fallen Runic stone,
For both were faiths, and both are gone."[2]

There is a poem by Tennyson (who never broke with faith, though he felt the strain of

[1] Charles Baudelaire, *Fleurs du Mal* (Paris, 1888), p. 205. "Le goût du Néant."

[2] Matthew Arnold, *Poems* (New York, Macmillan, 1878), p. 337. "Stanzas from the Grande Chartreuse."

doubt), in which he describes with intense dramatic sympathy the finality of scepticism in the human soul. It is called "Despair." There is another poem, called "Sea Dreams," in which he gives a vision of the rising tide of doubt as it threatens to undermine and overwhelm the beliefs of the past. The woman is telling her husband the dream which came to her in the night as she watched by their sick child.

A picture of the sea of doubt.

"But round the North, a light,
A belt, it seem'd, of luminous vapour, lay,
And ever in it a low musical note
Swell'd up and died; and, as it swell'd, a ridge
Of breaker issued from the belt, and still
Grew with the growing note, and when the note
Had reach'd a thunderous fulness, on those cliffs
Broke, mixt with awful light (the same as that
Living within the belt) whereby she saw
That all those lines of cliffs were cliffs no more,
But huge cathedral fronts of every age,
Grave, florid, stern, as far as eye could see,
One after one: and then the great ridge drew,
Lessening to the lessening music, back,
And passed into the belt and swell'd again
Slowly to music: ever when it broke
The statues, king, or saint, or founder, fell;
Then from the gaps and chasms of ruin left
Came men and women in dark clusters round,
Some crying, 'Set them up! they shall not fall!'
And others, 'Let them lie, for they have fall'n.'
And still they strove and wrangled: . . .
. . . and ever as their shrieks

Ran highest up the gamut, that great wave
Returning, while none mark'd it, on the crowd
Broke, mixt with awful light, and show'd their eyes
Glaring, and passionate looks, and swept away
The men of flesh and blood, and men of stone,
To the waste deeps together." [1]

The pity of it.

It was but a dream, dispelled from the mind of her to whom it came in the night-watches by the crying of her little child, and soon forgotten in the sweet reality of human love. Only a dream, but how many souls have felt the vague sadness, the haunting, helpless pity and fear of a like vision, looking out upon the landscape of man's inner life, and seeing the ancient landmarks slowly melted or swiftly swept away, the shrines of memory shaken and removed, the fair images of immortal desire and aspiration dissolving and disappearing in the onward waves, silently creeping, or surging with mysterious and inarticulate music out of the waste deep of doubt, —

"The unplumbed, salt, estranging sea." [2]

Who can think of the sharp anguish and dull grief that have fallen upon innumerable hearts through the loss of their most precious faiths;

[1] Tennyson's *Poetical Works* (Macmillan, 1890), p. 138.

[2] Matthew Arnold, "To Marguerite." *Poems* (Macmillan, 1878), p. 184.

who can think of the gray, formless, ever-moving, yet immovable flood of mordant gloom that has covered so many once bright and fertile fields of human hope and endeavour, so many once secure and peaceful homes of human trust and confidence, — who can think of these things, even though his own standpoint be still untouched, his own faith-dwelling founded upon an untrembling rock far above the tide, without a sorrowful perturbation of spirit and a deep, inward sense of compassionate distress and dread? We stand upon the shore, but we stand beside the sea. And we look out upon it, as Émile Littré sadly wrote,[1] like the women of Troy, whom the Roman poet pictured gazing at its mighty currents and engulfing waves:

"*Pontum adspectabant flentes.*"

IV

Sympathy with doubt.

It is with no careless and exaggerating hand, it is in no unsympathetic and condemning spirit, that I have tried to draw this picture of the sceptical age in which we live. Its faults, its perils, are mine and yours. The preacher who assumes a supercilious and damnatory attitude

[1] Émile Littré, *Conservation*, *Révolution*, Positivisme, *Remarques*, p. 430.

towards the doubts of the present time can do little to relieve, and may do much to increase them. If we desire to be true ministers to a doubting age, we must put ourselves in the position of Maurice, who said, "I wish to confess the sins of the time as my own."[1] So far as current scepticism has its source in evil, it flows from faults of which we all partake, — the pride of intellect, the haste of judgment, the preference of the seen to the unseen, the impatience of ignorance, the vain demand of perfection in the finite comprehension of the infinite, and the disloyalty of reason to conscience.

Lessons of encouragement.

But indeed this is not the point of view from which we speak. This lecture is not an indictment. It is a diagnosis. Doubt, as we are thinking of it, is not a crime, but a malady. And if we are to have any hope or power of staying its progress and healing its ravages, we must not only be sympathetic in our understanding of it, but we must also look through it, earnestly and patiently, to see whether there are not some favourable symptoms, some signs of enduring vitality, some promises of returning health and strength in the spirit of the age.

Of these it seems to me that there are three,

[1] *The Life of Frederick Denison Maurice* (New York, Scribners, 1884), vol. ii., p. 235.

so evident and so important, that we ought not to overlook them. First, the acknowledged discontent and pain of unbelief; second, the practical recoil of some of the finest minds from the void of absolute scepticism; third, the persistent desire of many doubting spirits to serve mankind by love, self-sacrifice, and ethical endeavour. In other words, I would read the lesson of encouragement in the sufferings of doubt, in the doubts of doubt, and in the splendid moral inconsistencies of doubt.

Pessimism.

Begin, then, with pain, which is not only a warning of disease, but also a sign of life. The pessimism which goes hand in hand with scepticism in this nineteenth century is a cry of suffering. The closely reasoned philosophies of Schopenhauer and Hartmann, with their premisses of misery and conclusions of despair, are only the scientific statement of a widely diffused sentiment of dissatisfaction and despondency in regard to life.[1] Their spread, like that of some apparently new disease, is due to the fact that they give a name to something from which men have long suffered.

eerfu scepticism almost extinct.

It seemed at one time as if the course of modern scepticism was to be free from sadness, a painless malady. At the beginning of the

[1] James Sully, *Pessimism*, pp. 2, 3. See Appendix, note 7.

century the tone of infidelity was jubilant and triumphant. Percy Bysshe Shelley walked into the inn at Montanvert and wrote his name in the visitors' book, adding "democrat, philanthropist, atheist,"—as if it were a record of victory and a title of glory. This cheerful type of scepticism still survives, here and there, in a few men who insist that the process of disenchantment is pleasant and joyous, and that the optimism which belonged to faith may remain while the faith itself disappears. It is like the smile of the famous cat, in the child's story-book, which broadened and brightened while the cat faded, until finally the animal was gone and nothing but the grin was left.

The sorrow of losing faith.

But for the most part modern doubt shows a sad and pain-drawn face, heavy with grief and dark with apprehension. There is an illustration of this change in the life of George Eliot. In her girlhood she passed suddenly, by an unconditional surrender, out of a warm faith in Evangelical Christianity into the coldest kind of rational scepticism. She writes of the dull, and now forgotten, book which wrought this change, Charles Hennell's *Inquiry concerning the Origin of Christianity*, with strange and almost fantastic merriment: "Mr. Hennell ought to be one of the happiest of men that he has done such a life's work. I am sure if I had written such a book I should be invulnerable to all the arrows of all the gods and goddesses. The book is full of wit to me. It gives me that exquisite kind of laughter which comes from the gratification of the reasoning faculties."[1] But the arrows which she despised struck home, ere life was ended, to her own heart.

"I remember," writes Mr. F. W. H. Myers, "how at Cambridge I walked with her once in the Fellows' Garden of Trinity, on an evening of rainy May, and she, stirred somewhat beyond her wont, and taking as her text the three words which have been used so often as the inspiring trumpet-calls of men, — the words God, Immortality, Duty, — pronounced, with terrible earnestness, how inconceivable was the first, how unbelievable was the second, and how peremptory and absolute the third. Never, perhaps, had sterner accents affirmed the sovereignty of impersonal and unrecompensing law. I listened and night fell; her grave, majestic countenance turned towards me like a Sibyl's in the gloom; it was as though she withdrew from my grasp, one by one, the two scrolls of promise, and

[1] *George Eliot's Life, as related in her Letters* (New York, Harpers), vol. i., p. 119.

left me the third scroll only, awful with inevitable fate."[1]

The sad aspect of life.

An inevitable fate, seen through the gloom of falling night, — that indeed is the aspect of life which the literature of doubt displays to us. A gray shadow of melancholy spreads over the questioning, uncertain, disillusioned age; languid sighs of weariness breathe from its salons and palaces. Bitter discontent mutters in its workshops and tenements. "Never, I believe," says Paul Desjardins, "have men been more universally sad than in the present time." And then he adds, with keen insight, "Our misery lies in feeling that we are less men than we were sixty years ago."[2] Human life has been unspeakably impoverished and narrowed by the loss of faith. Comedy has become tragic, and tragedy has grown mean and sordid.[3] Men have lost the sound of a Divine voice in the story of their existence and learned to listen to it as

> "a tale
> Told by an idiot, full of sound and fury
> Signifying nothing."

[1] R. H. Hutton, *Modern Guides of English Thought* (London, Macmillan, 1887), p. 262.

[2] *Le Devoir Present*, pp. 17, 19.

[3] See the plays of Ibsen: *Ghosts, A Doll's House, The Wild Duck*, etc.

Love itself, the great purifier and ennobler, has been transformed in the subtle analysis of sexual passion, from the sea-born Venus, pure and radiant with immortal youth, to a dirt-engendered goddess, concealing her secret ugliness with illusory and artificial charms, and presiding with malignant power over the lower currents of man's being, — a veritable Cloacina of human life.[1]

The meanness of man.

The thought of "the grandeur and misery of man," as Pascal conceived it, was painful but elevating. The conception of the insignificance and misery of man as scepticism presents it, is painful and dispiriting. Born of blind force and unconscious matter, quickened by some mysterious cruelty to a consciousness of his own origin and a foreboding of his inexplicable and fruitless destiny, he "drees his weird," between two fathomless abysses of gloom, as one who is indeed weary and heavy-laden. The music with which he accompanies his march towards the blank and dismal bourn, rolls and clashes through the literature of every land with deep and mournful discords, as if man had at last invented that strange organ of

[1] Bourget, *Psychologie Contemporaine*, pp, 5, 8. See Appendix, note 8.

expression which a satirist has called "the *Misérophon.*"[1]

The nausea of existence.

"This philosophy," says Stendhal, commenting upon the last reflections of his hero in *Rouge et Noir*, "was perhaps true, but it was of such a nature as to make one long for death." And then the critic from whom I have quoted these words, adds his own commentary. "Do you perceive, at the close of this work, the most complete which the author has left, the breaking of the tragic dawn of pessimism? It rises, this dawn of blood and tears, and, like the clearness of a new-born day, it overspreads with crimson hues the loftiest spirits of our age, those whose thoughts are at the summit, those to whom the eyes of the men of to-morrow lift themselves, — religiously. I am come in this series of psychological studies to the fifth and last of the personages whom I propose to analyze. I have examined a poet, Baudelaire; a historian, Renan; a romancer, Flaubert; a philosopher, Taine; I have just examined one of these composite artists in whom the critic and the imaginative writer are closely united; and I have found in these five Frenchmen of

[1] Anton Bettelheim, article in *Cosmopolis*, January, 1896. See Appendix, note 9.

such importance, the same philosophy of disgust with the universal nothingness."[1]

Melancholia. If we turn to Russia, which has given us some of the most brilliant and influential, though undisciplined, writers of modern fiction, do we not hear, in an accent harsher and more formidable, the same conclusions, the same cries of nausea over the inextricable confusion and vain efforts of human life? If we turn to England, do we not see the same cloud of melancholy, less threatening, less angry, but no less dark, rising from the chasm which doubt has made between man's inner life and the world as scientific positivism pictures it? How mournful is the voice in which W. K. Clifford proclaims, "The Great Companion is dead!" How dark with silent, passionate grief is that lonely wood in which "Robert Elsmere" feels himself going blind to the dearest visions of his former faith.[2] How black the air in which "Jude the Obscure" breathes out the last throbbings of his insurgent heart in curses upon his sordid and desperate fate![3] Let a

[1] Paul Bourget, *Psychologie Contemporaine*, p. 321.

[2] Mrs. Humphry Ward, *Robert Elsmere* (Macmillan, 1888), vol. ii., chap. xxvi.

[3] Thomas Hardy, *Jude the Obscure* (Harpers, 1896).

poet, with that sublime insight of genius which endures even amid the ruins created by its own destructive passion, speak the last word of doubt, — the epitaph of *The City of Dreadful Night.* The portentous figure of "Melancholia" sits enthroned above her vast metropolis.

> "The moving Moon and stars from east to west
> Circle before her in the sea of air;
> Shadows and gleams glide round her solemn rest.
> Her subjects often gaze up to her there:
> The strong to drink new strength of iron endurance,
> The weak, new terrors; all, renewed assurance
> And confirmation of the old despair."[1]

Pain gives an argument of hope.

But why despair, unless indeed because man, in his very nature and inmost essence, is framed for an immortal hope? No other creature is filled with disgust and anger by the mere recognition of its own environment and the realization of its own destiny. This strange issue of a purely physical evolution in a profound revolt against itself is incredibly miraculous. Can a vast universe of atoms and ether, unfolding out of darkness into darkness, produce at some point in its progress, and that point apparently the highest, a feeling of profound disappointment with its par-

[1] James Thomson, *The City of Dreadful Night*, xxi. 12.

tially discovered processes and resentful grief at its dimly foreseen end? To believe this would require a monstrous credulity! Atheism does not touch this difficulty. Agnosticism evades it. There are but two solutions which really face the facts. One is the black, unspeakable creed that the source of all things is an unknown, mocking, malignant Power, whose last and most cruel jest is the misery of disenchanted man.[1] The other is the hopeful creed that the very pain which man suffers when his spiritual nature is denied, is proof that it exists, and part of the discipline by which a truthful, loving God would lead man to Himself. Let the world judge which is the more reasonable faith. But for our part, while we cling to the creed of hope, let us not fail to "cleave ever to the sunnier side of doubt," and see in the very shadow that it casts the evidence of a light behind and above it. Let us learn the meaning of that noble word of St. Augustine: *Thou hast made us for Thyself, and unquiet is our heart until it rests in Thee.*

[1] "It must have been an *ill*-advised God, who cou*l*d fa*ll* upon no better amusement than the transforming of Himself into such a hungry wor*l*d as this, which is utter*l*y miserab*l*e and worse than none at all." — David *F*riedrich Strauss, quoted in *The British Quarterly Review*, January, 1877, p. 146.

The renaissance of faith.

Yes, the inquietude of the heart which doubt has robbed of its faith in God, is an evidence that scepticism is a malady, not a normal state. The sadness of our times under the pressure of positive disbelief and negative uncertainty has in it the promise and potency of a return to health and happiness. Already we can see, if we look with clear eyes, the signs of what I have dared to call "the reaction out of the heart of a doubting age towards the Christianity of Christ and the faith in Immortal Love."[1]

Pagan poets, full of melancholy beauty and vague regret for lost ideals, poets of decadence and despondence, the age has born, to sing its grief and gloom. But its two great singers, Tennyson and Browning, strike a clearer note of returning faith and hope. "They resume the quest, and do not pause until they find Him whom they seek."[2] Pessimists like Hartmann work back unconsciously, from the vague remoteness of pantheism, far in the direction, at least, of a theistic view of the universe. His later books — *Religionsphilosophie* and

[1] *The Poetry of Tennyson* (New York, Scribners, 1889), p. xiii.

[2] Vida D. Scudder, *The Life of the Spirit in the Modern English Poets* (Houghton, Mifflin, & Co., 1895), p. 333.

Selbstersetzung des Christenthums — breathe a different spirit from his *Philosophie des Unbewussten*.[1] One of the most cautious of our younger students of philosophy has noted with care, in a recent article, the indications that "the era of doubt is drawing to a close."[2] A statesman, like Signor Crispi, does not hesitate to cut loose from his former atheistic connections and declare that "the belief in God is the fundamental basis of the healthy life of the people, while atheism puts in it the germ of an irreparable decay." The French critic, M. Edouard Rod, declares that "only religion can regulate at the same time human thought and human action."[3] Mr. Benjamin Kidd, from the side of English sociology, assures us that "since man became a social creature, the development of his intellectual character has become subordinate to the development of his religious character," and concludes that religion affords the only permanent sanction for progress.[4] A famous biologist, Romanes,

[1] James Orr, *The Christian View of God and the World* (New York, Randolph, 1893), pp. 456, 457. See Appendix, note 10.

[2] *The Methodist Review*, January, 1896. "The Return to Faith," by Prof. A. C. Armstrong, Jr.

[3] Edouard Rod, *Les Idees Morales du Temps Present* (Paris, 1894), p. 304.

[4] Benjamin Kidd, *Social Evolution* (London, 1894), p. 245.

who once professed the most absolute rejection of revealed, and the most unqualified scepticism of natural, religion, thinks his way soberly back from the painful void to a position where he confesses that "it is reasonable to be a Christian believer," and dies in the full communion of the church of Jesus.[1]

All along the line, we see men who once thought it necessary or desirable to abandon forever the soul's abode of faith in the unseen, returning by many and devious ways from the far country of doubt, driven by homesickness and hunger to seek some path which shall at least bring them in sight of a Father's house.

The indomitable conscience.

And meanwhile we hear the conscience, the ethical instinct of mankind, asserting itself with splendid courage and patience, even in those who have as yet found no sure ground for it to stand upon. There is a sublime contradiction between the positivist's view of man as "the hero of a lamentable drama played in an obscure corner of the universe, in virtue of blind laws, before an indifferent nature, and with annihilation for its denouement,"[2] and the doctrine that it is his supreme duty to sacrifice himself for the good of humanity. Yet many

[1] *Thoughts on Religion*, p. 196.

[2] Madame L. Ackermann, *Ma Vie* (Paris, 1885), p. xviii.

of the sceptical thinkers of the age do not stumble at the contradiction. They hold fast to love and justice and moral enthusiasm even though they suspect that they themselves are the products of a nature which is blind and dumb and heartless and stupid. Never have the obligations of self-restraint, and helpfulness, and equity, and universal brotherhood been preached more fervently than by some of the English agnostics.

The new crusade in France.

In France a new crusade has risen; a crusade which seeks to gather into its hosts men of all creeds and men of none, and which proclaims as its object the recovery of the sacred places of man's spiritual life, the holy land in which virtue shines forever by its own light, and the higher impulses of our nature are inspired, invincible, and immortal. On its banner M. Paul Desjardins writes the word of Tolstoi, "*Il faut avoir une âme;* it is necessary to have a soul," and declares that the crusaders will follow it wherever it leads them. "For my part," he cries, "I shall not blush certainly to acknowledge as sole master the Christ preached by the doctors. I shall not recoil if my premisses force me to believe, at last, as Pascal believed."[1]

[1] *Le Devoir Present,* 45.

The new crusade in America.

In our own land such a crusade does not yet appear to be necessary. The disintegration of faith under the secret processes of general scepticism has not yet gone far enough to make the peril of religion evident, or to cause a new marshalling of hosts to recover and defend the forsaken shrines of man's spiritual life. When the process which is now subtly working in so many departments of our literature has gone farther, it may be needful to call for such a crusade. If so, I believe it will come. I believe that the leaders of thought, the artists, the poets of the future, when they stand face to face with the manifest results of negation and disillusion, which really destroy the very sphere in which alone art and poetry can live, will rise to meet the peril, and proclaim anew with one voice the watchword, "It is necessary to have a soul! And though a man gain the whole world, if his soul is lost, it shall profit him nothing." But meanwhile, before the following of the errors of France in literature and art has led us to that point of spiritual impoverishment where we must imitate the organized and avowed effort to recover that which has been lost, we see a new crusade of another kind: a powerful movement of moral enthusiasm, of self-sacrifice, of altruism, even among those who profess to be out of sympathy with Christianity, which is a sign of promise, because it reveals a force that cries out for faith, and for Christian faith, to guide and direct it.

The cry for a gospel of leadership.

Never was there a time when the fine aspirations of the young manhood and young womanhood of our country needed a more inspiring and direct Christian leadership. The indications of this need lie open to our sight on every side. Here is a company of refined and educated people going down to make a college settlement among the poor and ignorant, to help them and lift them up. They declare that it is not a religious movement, that there is to be no preaching connected with it, that the only faith which it is to embody is faith in humanity. They choose a leader who has only that faith. But they find, under his guidance, that the movement will not move, that the work cannot be done, that it faints and fails because it lacks the spring of moral inspiration which can come only from a divine and spiritual faith. And they are forced to seek a new leader who, although he is not a preacher, yet carries within his heart that power of religious conviction, that force of devotion to the will of God, that faith in the living and supreme Christ, which is in fact the centre of Christianity. All around the circle of human doubt and despair, where men and women are going out to enlighten and uplift and comfort and strengthen their fellow-men under the perplexities and burdens of life, we hear the cry for a gospel which shall be divine, and therefore sovereign and unquestionable and sure and victorious. All through the noblest aspirations and efforts and hopes of our age of doubt, we feel the longing, and we hear the demand, for a new inspiration of Christian faith.

The signs of the times.

These are the signs of the times. Surely we must take note of them, surely we must labour and pray to understand their true significance, if we are to say anything to our fellow-men which shall be worth our saying and their hearing.

Renan made a strange remark not long before his death: "I fear that the work of the Twentieth Century will consist in taking out of the waste-basket a multitude of excellent ideas which the Nineteenth Century has heedlessly thrown into it." The sceptic's fear is the believer's hope. Once more the fields are white unto the harvest. The time is ripe; ripe in the sorrow of scepticism, ripe in the return of aspiration, ripe in the enthusiasm of humanity, for a renaissance of the spiritual life. Blessed are they who are come to the kingdom for such a time as this, if indeed they believe and preach a living, saving Gospel for this Age of Doubt.

II

THE GOSPEL OF A PERSON

Subtlest thought shall fail and learning falter
  Churches change, forms perish, systems go,
But our human needs, they will not alter
  Christ no after age shall e'er outgrow.

Yea, Amen! O changeless One, Thou only,
  Art life's guide and spiritual goal,
Thou the Light across the dark vale lonely,
  Thou the eternal haven of the soul.

—John Campbell Shairp.

II

THE GOSPEL OF A PERSON

How shall we serve the present age?

The prevalence and the quality of modern doubt, with its discontent and sadness, its self-misgivings and reactions, its moral inconsistencies and fine enthusiasms, bring the preacher who is alive and in earnest, face to face with the most important question of his life. What can I do, what ought I to do, as a preacher, to meet the strange, urgent, complicated needs of such a time as this?

First of all, as a man,—and every preacher ought to be a man, though not every man is bound to be a preacher—as a man, it is necessary to lead a clean, upright, steadfast, useful life, purged from all insincerity, and lifted above all selfishness, and especially above that form of religious selfishness which is the besetting peril of those who feel themselves rich in faith in the midst of a generation that has been made poor by unbelief. Never has there been a time when character and conduct counted for more than they do to-day. A life on a high level, yet full of helpful, healing sympathy for all life on its lowest levels, is the first debt which we owe to our fellow-men in this age.

But beyond this, is there not something personal and specific which the conditions of the present demand from us, as men who have not only the common duty of living, but also the peculiar vocation of speaking directly and constantly to the inner life of our brothers? We want some distinct and definite message, which is to be clearly formed in our thought and feeling and utterance, as the central, guiding, dominating force in all our efforts to realize the fine aspiration of the old hymn:

> "To serve the present age,
> My calling to fulfil, —
> Oh, may it all my powers engage
> To do my Master's will!"

Proposed remedies insufficient.

Now the moment we look at the problem in this light, we see that there are various lines of activity open to us, and along all of these lines men are making promises and prophecies of usefulness and success. The cures which are suggested for the malady of the age are many and diverse. Of some of them we need speak only in passing, to recognize that for us, at least, they are unsuitable.

Reaction to barbarism.

Herr Max Nordau, for example, in his curious and chaotic book, *Degeneration*, diagnoses the sickness of modern times as the result, not of a loss of faith, but of a fatal increase of nervous irritability produced by the strain of an intricate civilization. He declares that the malady must run its course, but that in time it will be healed by the restorative force of "*misoneism*, that instinctive, invincible aversion to progress and its difficulties that Lombroso has studied so much and to which he has given this name."[1]

The name is certainly not a pretty one, nor do I think that, after the first feeling of pleasure in learning to pronounce a newly imported word has passed, the contemplation of its meaning will afford us any profound sense of satisfaction or hope. The picture of mankind as a magnified Jemmy Button, returning from his temporary residence in England to his native *Terra del Fuego*, and flinging away his gloves and patent-leather shoes, to relapse into a peaceful and contented barbarism, is not inspiring. Who is there that would care to devote his life to the hastening of such a result? Who but the veriest quack, himself affected by the hysteria of the age, would think of curing

[1] Max Nordau, *Degeneration* (New York, 1895), p. 542.

the convulsions of St. Vitus' dance in an overstrained humanity by throwing the patient into the stupor of typhoid fever?

Psychical research.

Another and very different method of dealing with the malady of the times is suggested by those who believe that Science itself, in the immense future advance which is predicted for it, will supply the antidote for the scepticism which has accompanied its previous course. New discoveries will be made which will support the proposition: *Il faut avoir une âme.* New arguments will be constructed which will give us a scientific demonstration of the unseen universe and the future life. It is in this spirit that Mr. F. W. H. Myers calls attention to the phenomena of mesmerism and hypnotism and telepathy, and suggests that the need of the age is a more cordial and general interest in the investigations of the Society of Psychical Research.[1] I do not think, for one, that these investigations are to be slighted or despised. They may be of great value. But it is difficult to believe that this is the source to which the preacher is to look either for his inspiration or his message. For, in the first place, it is highly improbable that science is about to make any such aston-

[1] See Appendix, note 11.

ishing advance, either in methods or results, as some men anticipate. The best authorities admit this, and warn us that there are "limitations in the nature of the universe which must circumscribe the achievements of speeulative research."[1] Mr. Myers himself makes the same admission, and says that so far as our discoveries are confined to the physical side of things, there is no ground whatever for sanguine hope. Moreover, in the second place, whatever work may be done in this direction must be accomplished, not by preachers, but by scientists. The average preacher has no particular vocation, and no adequate qualification, for the task. Neither by temperament nor by training is he fitted to judge of these matters. Now and then you will find a rare exception; but as a rule nothing could be of less value than the scientific sermons of preachers who have only a bowing acquaintance with science. If the cure of modern scepticism is to be accomplished by the further progress of physical investigation, at least we must confess that this enterprise is not for us.

But there are two other ways of deal ing with current doubt which demand closer attention. One of them is the philosophic

[1] See Appendix, note 12.

Thorough-going rationalism.

method of a *reductio ad absurdum.* The logic of rationalism is applied to its own premisses in order to show that they are unfounded and unverifiable. The result of this attack, as it has been made with a relentless and masterly hand by the Hon. Arthur James Balfour in his *Defence of Philosophic Doubt*, is to exhibit the startling fact that "the universe as represented to us by science is wholly unimaginable, and that our conception of it is what in Theology would be termed purely anthropomorphic "[1] The evidence for the existence of a world composed of atoms and ether is no more conclusive, the account which science gives of their nature and qualities is no more coherent, than the evidence and account which faith gives of a world created by a personal God and inhabited by immortal souls. Pure agnosticism is thus forced into the service of Christianity and used to destroy all *a priori* objections to it. Giant Doubt is brought low by turning his own weapons against himself, even as Benaiah, the son of Jehoiada, slew the Egyptian "with his own spear."[2]

The value of this service of philosophy is

[1] *A Defence of Philosophic Doubt* (Macmillan, 1879), pp. 284, 285, 287–289. See Appendix, note 13.

[2] 1 *Chron.* xi. 23.

considerable. The Christian preacher ought not to be ignorant of its actual results, for they are such as to encourage him in preserving his independence against the tyrannous claims of positivism; nor unfamiliar with its methods, for they are fitted to train and discipline his mind by hard exercise and exact work. But it must be remembered that only a mighty man of valour, one who, like Benaiah, ranks above the host, and above the thirty captains of the host, can hope to play a leading part in this enterprise of "carrying the war into Africa." It must be remembered also that the reduction of scientific naturalism to an absurdity falls far short of the establishment of religious faith as a verity. Grateful for all that philosophy can do, and is doing, to clear the way, the preacher must have a principle, an impulse, a line of action which will carry him beyond the negative result of making unbelief doubtful, to the positive result of making belief credible.

Theological fortification

At this point our attention is called to another way of dealing with current scepticism, — the dogmatic method, which relies for the defence of faith upon the construction of a complete and consistent system of doctrine in regard to God and man, the present world and the future life. Faith, in other words, is to be established by fortification, surrounded and entrenched with banquette and parapet, scarp and ditch and counterscarp of iron-worded proof, defended on every side by solid syllogisms, and impregnable against all assaults of unbelief. It is foolish not to recognize the great work which has been done along this line by wise and strong men in the past. Those who affect to despise it and make light of it, are simply ignorant of some of the loftiest achievements of the human intellect. The works of Augustine and Anselm and Thomas Aquinas, of John Calvin and Richard Hooker and John Owen, of Ralph Cudworth and William Chillingworth, of Richard Baxter and Samuel Clarke and Joseph Butler, of Jonathan Edwards and Charles Hodge and W. G. T. Shedd, are massive works. They impose a sense of wonder upon every thoughtful observer.

anged conditions.

But concerning the attempt to conquer modern doubt by a system of dogmatic theology, certain things must be remembered. The conditions of warfare change from age to age. The vast fortresses of solid stone whose possession was once regarded as the security of nations, are not ranked so high as they were a hundred years ago. The earthwork, the rifled cannon, the iron-clad ship, the torpedo, have wrought great changes. Deductive logic is just as strong as it ever was, but somehow or other men are not as much impressed by it. Induction is the method of to-day: and that is a subtle, evasive, mobile method. It cannot be shut in by a ring of fortresses. Already the dogmatic systems in which the inductive method is ignored or subordinated (whether made long ago, or constructed yesterday as modern antiques) are out of date. They are good for the men who are within them, but on the outside world they have no more effect than Windsor Castle would have in protecting England from a foreign invasion.

The future of theology.

We feel sure that theology, in time, must and will vindicate its claim to be considered as an essential factor in the intellectual life of man, by adapting itself to the changed conditions, and producing even mightier works by the new methods than those which it produced by the old. Already we see the promise of a renaissance of dogmatics in such books as Mulford's *The Republic of God*, Harris' *The Self-Revelation of God*, Orr's *The Christian View of God and the World*, and Fairbairn's *The Place of Christ in Modern Theology*. But we must remember that even those who anticipate and

Great things demanded of the new theologian.

predict this reconstruction of the old truth on the new lines most enthusiastically, recognize that it must be a long and difficult task, and that the man who is to be a master-builder must have a magnificent equipment. How exhilarating at the first sight, but at the second sight how overwhelming and discouraging, are the demands of the age upon him who would fain be an epoch-making theologian, as they are stated, for example, in Mr. Balfour's *Foundations of Belief*, or in Dr. George A. Gordon's inspiring book *The Christ of To-day*.[1] Truly it appears that such a man must realize the supposition of St. Paul: he must speak with the tongues of men and of angels, and have the gift of prophecy, and understand all mysteries and all knowledge. Who is sufficient for these things? It will take a long time for the best of us to learn all this. Perhaps the most of us may never go so far. Meantime, whether we are labouring towards that goal, or despairing of it, we need something divinely simple and divinely true that we can preach at once, directly, joyfully, fervently to the heart of the age.

A view of the world, a *Welt-anschauung*, is desirable, perhaps in the long run necessary, for the mind of man; but there is another thing

[1] See Appendix, note 14.

which is more desirable and of prior necessity, and that is a standpoint of practical conviction from which to obtain such a view. It may be but a foothold, only a single point of contact, but we must have it, and it must be solid as a fact. A complete and consistent theology is a consummation most devoutly to be wished for; but before it can come there must be something else, — a living, active power of faith in the soul. This power, as we believe, already exists in every human being. But there is only one thing that can awaken it and call it into action, and that is *a gospel*, a message clear as light, which in its very essence is a force to quicken and stir the soul.

A starting-point for faith is the first necessity.

We look out upon the world and we see that some men have had such a gospel without being in any sense finished and systematic theologians. St. Paul and St. Peter and St. John had it. St. Chrysostom and St. Francis of Assisi and Savonarola had it. John Wesley and George Whitfield had it. In different ages and under different conditions these preachers had the primal message which moves men to believe. And in our own age, under our own conditions, a like message has been proclaimed with power. Père Lacordaire preached such a message in Notre Dâme, and Canon Liddon in

Preaching with power.

St. Paul's, to listening thousands. Bishop Brooks made it thrill like a celestial music through the young manhood of America; and Dwight L. Moody has spoken it with vigorous directness in every great city that knows the English tongue. In many things, in ecclesiastical relation, in theological statement, in dress, in manner, in language, these preachers are unlike. One thing only is the same in all of them, and that is the source of their power. Their central message, the core of their preaching, is the piercing, moving, personal gospel of Jesus of Nazareth, the Son of God and Saviour of mankind. This, in its simplest form; this, in its clearest expression; this presentation of a person to persons in order that they may first know, and then love and trust and follow Him — this is pre-eminently the gospel for an age of doubt.

I

The Gospel of Christ.

The adaptation of our central message, thus conceived and thus expressed, to meet the peculiar needs of a time of general scepticism, is the theme of this lecture. I do not say that this is the whole of Christianity. I do not say that when the preacher has delivered this message in this form he has fulfilled all of his duties. He may have to bear testimony against errors of thought and vices of conduct; he is certainly bound to give encouragement and guidance to new efforts of virtue and new enterprises of benevolence in every field. But his first and greatest duty, the discharge of which is to give him influence over doubting hearts and strength for all his other work, is simply to preach Christ.

The gospel of a fact.

This gospel meets the needs of the present time because it is the gospel of a fact.

Personality is a fact. Indeed we may say that it is the aboriginal fact; the source of all perception; the starting-point of all thought· the informing and moulding principle of all language. "All human observation implies that the mind, the 'I,' is a thing in itself, a fixed point in a world of change, of which world of change its own organs form a part. It is the same, yesterday, to-day, and to-morrow. It was what it is, when its organs were of a different shape and consisted of different matter from their present shape and matter. It will be what it is, when they have gone through other changes."[1]

[1] Sir James Fitzjames Stephen, *Liberty, Equality, Fraternity*. Quoted by Hutton, *Contemporary Thought*, I., p. 114. See Appendix, note 15.

Personality is the foundation.

This fact of a rational, free, conscious, persistent self is the foundation of all sensation and of all reflection; it is the basis of physics as well as of metaphysics. By contrast it gives us our first notion of matter; by resistance, our first notion of force; by operation, our first notion of causality. It is a necessary assumption even in the philosophies of agnosticism, positivism, and materialism. They cannot move a step without it.

"They reckon ill who leave *me* out."

To deny personality is to deny the possibility of any kind of knowledge and reduce the universe to a blank.[1]

Moreover, it is not only true that the recognition of our own personality lies at the root of perception and reasoning. It is also true that contact with other personalities, conscious, intelligent, free, and persistent like ourselves, is the gateway through which we reach the reality of all external things. To a solitary mind the outward world may be only a dream. But the moment two minds come into contact and communication, it becomes at least a permanent possibility of sensation. By comparison and contrast with the sensations and experiences of

[1] See Appendix, note 16.

others, we verify our own. If it were not for this the whole universe would dissolve around us like the baseless fabric of a vision. The subtle analysis of modern science, transforming the apparently solid elements into invisible atoms, and these atoms into vortex rings in the impalpable and immeasurable ether, throws us back, more and more, upon personality, subjective and objective, as the only thing that remains sure and immutable.

Persons are realities.

Persons, then, are the most real and substantial objects of our knowledge. They touch us at more points, they affect us in more ways and with greater intensity, they fit more closely into the faculties and powers of our own being, than anything else in the universe. A person who has influenced us or our fellow-men leaves a more profound, positive, permanent, and real impression than any other fact whatsoever. We live as persons in a world of persons, far more truly than we live in a world of phenomena or laws or ideas.

Now, in an age that is characterized, as some German writer has said, by "a hunger for facts," the gospel of a person, if it is rightly apprehended and preached, ought to have peculiar power because it is a factual gospel. We can come to those who are under the benumbing spell of universal doubt and say: Here is a fact, a personality, real and imperishable. It is not merely a doctrine that was believed in Palestine eighteen hundred years ago. It is some one who was born and lived among men. It is not merely a theory of God and the soul and the future life that sprang up in the East in the first century and has strangely spread itself over the world. This religion is historical in every sense of the word, as the actual fulfilment of an ancient hope, and the starting-point of a new life.[1]

The reality of Christ.

The person of Jesus Christ stands solid in the history of man. He is indeed more substantial, more abiding, in human apprehension, than any form of matter, or any mode of force. The conceptions of earth and air and fire and water change and melt around Him, as the clouds melt and change around an everlasting mountain peak. All attempts to resolve Him into a myth, a legend, an idea, — and hundreds of such attempts have been made, — have drifted over the enduring reality of His character and left not a rack behind. The result of all criticism, the final verdict of enlightened common-sense, is that Christ is historical. He is such a person as men could not have imagined if they

[1] See Appendix, note 17.

would, and would not have imagined if they could. He is neither Greek myth, nor Hebrew legend.[1] The artist capable of fashioning Him did not exist, nor could he have found the materials. A non-existent Christianity did not spring out of the air and create a Christ. A real Christ appeared in the world and created Christianity. This is what we mean by the gospel of a fact.

II

The gospel of a force.

And here we come at once into sight of the second quality of this gospel which is peculiarly fitted to meet the needs of a doubting age.

If it be true that a person is a fact, it is no less true that a person is a force. The world moves by personality. All the great currents of history have flowed from persons. Organization is powerful; but no organization has ever accomplished anything until a person has stood at the centre of it and filled it with his thought, with his life. Truth is mighty and must prevail. But it never does prevail actually until it gets itself embodied, incarnated, in a personality. Christianity has an organization. Christianity has a doctrine. But the force of Christianity, that which made it move

[1] See Appendix, note 18.

and lent it power to move the world, is the Person at the heart of it, who gives vitality to the organization and reality to the doctrine. All the abstract truths of Christianity might have come into the world in another form, — nay, the substance of these truths did actually come into the world, dimly and partially through the fragmentary religions of the nations, more clearly and with increasing, prophetic light through the inspired Scriptures of the Hebrews; but still the world would not stir, still the truth could not make itself felt as a universal force in the life of humanity until

> "The Word had breath, and wrought
> With human hands the creed of creeds,
> In loveliness of perfect deeds,
> More strong than all poetic thought."[1]

I think we must get back, in our conception of Christianity and in our preaching of it, to this primary position. The fount and origin of its power was, and continued to be, and still is, the Person Christ.

Christ was His own gospel.

This was the secret of His ministry. He Himself was the central word of His own preaching. He offered Himself to the world as the solution of its difficulties and the source

[1] Tennyson, *In Memoriam*, xxxvi.

of a new life. He asked men simply to believe in Him, to love Him, to follow Him. He called the self-righteous to humble themselves to His correction, the sinful to confide in His forgiveness, the doubting to trust His assurance, and the believing to accept His guidance into fuller light.[1] To those who became His disciples He gave doctrine and instruction in many things. But to those who were not yet His disciples, to the world, He offered first of all Himself, not a doctrine, not a plan of life, but a living Person. This was the substance of His first sermon when He stood up in the synagogue at Nazareth and having read from the Book of Isaiah the prophecy of the Great Liberator, declared unto the people "This day is this Scripture fulfilled in your ears."[2] This was the attraction of His universal invitation, "Come unto Me, all ye that labour and are heavy laden and I will give you rest."[3] This was the heart of His summary of His completed work when He said, "I, if I be lifted up from the earth, will draw all men unto Me."[4]

[1] Henry Latham, *Pastor Pastorum* (New York, James Pott & Co., 1891), pp. 273–275.

[2] St. Luke iv. 16–21.

[3] St. Matt. xi. 28.

[4] St. John xii. 32.

We are not considering, at this moment, the tremendous implications of such a personal self-assertion, unparalleled, I believe, in the founder of any other religion. We pass by for the present that famous and inevitable alternative, ***Aut Christus Deus, aut homo non bonus est.***[1] The point, now, is simply this. As a matter of history, setting aside all question of the divine inspiration and authority of the Gospels, taking them merely as a trustworthy report of a certain sequence of events,[2] it is plain that the force which started the religion of Jesus was the person Jesus. Christ was His own Christianity. Christ was the core of His own gospel.

The life of the Church flowed from Christ.

Read on through the other books of the New Testament, the Acts and the Epistles, and you will see that they are just the record of the operation of this force in life and literature. It was this that sent the apostles out into the

[1] See Appendix, note 19.

[2] The evidence for the historic trustworthiness of the Gospels may be found summed up in its modern form in Dr. Salmon's *Introduction to the New Testament*, fourth edition (New York, Young & Co., 1889); in Bishop Lightfoot's *Essays on "Supernatural Religion"* (Macmillan, 1889); in Beyschlag's *New Testament Theology* (Edinburgh, T. & T. Clark, 1895), pp. 29–31, 216–221 of volume i.; and in Prof. George P. Fisher's *Grounds of Theistic and Christian Belief* (Scribners, 1883).

world, reluctantly and hesitatingly at first, then joyfully and triumphantly, like men driven by an irresistible impulse. It was the manifestation of Christ that converted them,[1] the love of Christ that constrained them,[2] the power of Christ that impelled them.[3] He was their certainty[4] and their strength.[5] He was their peace[6] and their hope.[7] For Christ they laboured and suffered;[8] in Christ they gloried;[9] for Christ's sake they lived and died.[10] They felt and they declared that the life that was in them was His life[11] They were confident that they could do all things through Christ which strengthened them.[12] The offices of the Church — apostle, bishop, deacon, evangelist, — call them by what names you will — were simply forms of service to Him as Master;[13] the doctrines of the Church were simply unfoldings of what she had received from Him as Teacher;[14] the worship of the Church, as distinguished from that of the Jewish Synagogue and the Heathen Temple, was the adoration of Christ as Lord.[15]

Now it was precisely this relation of the

[1] Gal. i. 16.
[2] 2 Cor. v. 14.
[3] 2 Cor. xii. 9.
[4] 2 Tim. i. 12.
[5] 2 Tim. ii. 1.
[6] Eph. ii. 14.
[7] Col. i. 27.
[8] Phil. iii. 8–10.
[9] Gal. vi. 14.
[10] 2 Cor. iv. 5, 11.
[11] Gal. ii. 20.
[12] Phil. iv. 13.
[13] Eph. iv. 8–12.
[14] 1 Cor. xi. 1, 23; xv. 3.
[15] Phil. ii. 11; 1 Cor. xii. 3.

The influence of r st an t came from r st.

early Church, in her organization and doctrine and worship, to the person Christ, held fast in her memory as identical with the real Jesus who was born in Bethlehem and crucified on Calvary, conceived in her faith as still living and present with His disciples, — it was this personal animation of the Church by Christ that gave her influence over men. Contrary to all human probability, against the prejudice of the Hebrews who abhorred the name of a crucified man, against the prejudice of the Greeks and Romans who despised the name of a common Jew, she made her way, not by concealing, but by exalting and glorifying, the name of Jesus Christ. Indeed, it seems as if her career of conquest was actually delayed until that name was taken up and written upon her banners. It was in Antioch, where the disciples were first called Christians,[1] that the missionary enterprise of the Church began, and it was from that centre, with that title, that she went out to her triumph.

The magic of Christ's name.

The name of Christ was magical; not as a secret and unintelligible incantation, but as the sign of a real person, known and loved. It enlightened and healed and quickened the heart of an age which, like our own, was dark

[1] Acts xi. 26; xiii. 1–3.

and sorrowful and heavy with doubt. It was the charm which drew men to Christianity out of the abstractions of philosophy,[1] and the confusions of idolatry darkened with a thousand personifications but empty of all true personality. The music of that name rang through all the temple of the Church, and to its harmonies her walls were builded. The acknowledgment of that name was the mark of Christian discipleship. To confess that "Jesus is the Christ" was the way to enter the Church. The symbolism of that name was the mark of Christian worship. The central rites of the Church were baptism into Christ and communion with Christ. Fidelity to His name was the crown of Christian martyrdom. Unnumbered multitudes of men and women and children went down to death because they would not deny the Christ. Whatever the early Church was and did, beyond a doubt her character and her activity were but the resultant of the personal influence that flowed from Jesus Christ.[2]

When we turn to follow the history of Christianity through the later centuries down to the

[1] See Justin Martyr, *Dialogue with Trypho*, chap. viii.

[2] George B. Stevens, *The Pauline Theology*. See Appendix, note 20.

The personal power of Christ continues.

present time, we see that the same thing is true. The temporal power of the Bishop of Rome doubtless grew out of the union of the Church with the Empire. The immense wealth and secular authority of ecclesiastics may be traced to social and political causes. But the inward, vitalizing, self-propagating power of Christianity as a religion has always come from the person of Jesus who stands at the heart of it. The attraction of its hymns and psalms and spiritual songs, the beauty of its holy days and solemn ceremonies, were derived from Him who is the central figure in praise and prayer. The renaissance of Christian Art sprang from the desire to picture to the imagination the visible, adorable form and face of Him whom speculative theology had so often concealed or obscured. The penetrating and abiding fragranee of Christian literature resides in those books, like *The Imitation of Christ*, in which the sweetness of His character is embalmed forever. The potency of Christian preaching comes from, and is measured by, the clearness of the light which it throws upon the personality of Jesus. Read the roll of those in every age whom the world has acknowledged as the best Christians, kings and warriors and philosophers, martyrs and heroes and labourers in every noble cause,

rist is the charm of Christianity.

the purest and the highest of mankind, and you will see that the test by which they are judged, the mark by which they are recognized, is likeness and loyalty to the personal Christ. Then turn to the work which the Church is doing to-day in the lowest and darkest fields of human life, among the submerged classes of our great cities, among the sunken races of heathendom, and you cannot deny that the force of that work to enlighten and uplift, still depends upon the simplicity and reality with which it reveals the person of Jesus to the hearts of men. Christianity as a missionary religion would be fatally crippled if you took out of it the familiar story of Jesus and His love.

The testimony of a doubter.

"Mr. Darwin," says Admiral Sir James Sullivan, "had often expressed to me his conviction that it was utterly useless to send missionaries to such a set of savages as the Fuegians, probably the very lowest of the human race. I had always replied that I did not believe any human beings existed too low to comprehend the simple message of the Gospel of Christ. After many years he wrote to me that the recent account of the mission showed that he had been wrong and I right . . . and he requested me to forward to the Society an enclosed cheque for £5, as a testimony of his interest in their good work."[1]

The force which breaks the inertia of unbelief.

Observe, we are not constructing an argument. We are only tracing a force, — the force that flows from the person of Jesus Christ. The more closely, the more powerfully we can feel it in ourselves and in others, the more confidently we can come to a doubting age and say: Here is this force, intense, persistent, far-reaching. It has moved all kinds of men, from the highest to the lowest. What do you make of it? What will you do with it? Is it not the only thing that can lift and move you out of your doubt? For scepticism is just the inertia of the soul which stands poised between contrary and mutually destructive theories. From that state of impotence there is but one deliverance, and that is by force, the force of life embodied in a person.

III

The gospel of a real spiritual world.

But the force which proceeds from the person of Jesus is not mere power, blind and purposeless. It moves always in a certain direction. It has a quality in it which produces certain

[1] Alfred Barry, *Some Lights of Science on the Faith* (London, Longmans, 1892), p. 116.

results. And one of these results is an immediate and overwhelming sense of the reality and nearness of spiritual things. This is the third point of adaptation in the gospel of the personal Christ to the needs of a sceptical age. It carries with itself an evidence of things not seen, a substance of things hoped for.

The mystery of Jesus.

An aura of wonder and mystery surrounded Jesus of Nazareth in His earthly life. All who came in contact with Him felt it; in love, if they desired to believe; in repulsion, if they hated to believe. In His presence, faith in the invisible, in the soul, in the future life, in God, revived and unfolded with new bloom and colour. In His presence hypocrisy was silenced and afraid, but sincere piety found a voice and prayed. This effluence of His character breathes from the whole record of His life. It was not merely what He said to men about the eternal verities that convinced them. It was something in Himself, an atmosphere surrounding Him, and a silent radiance shining from Him, that made it easier for them to believe in their own spiritual nature and in the Divine existence and presence. He drew out of their fallen and neglected hearts, by some celestial attraction, spontaneous, gentle, irresistible, a new efflorescence of faith and hope and love. Where He came a spiritual springtide flowed over the landscape of the inner life. Blossoms appeared in the earth and the time for the singing of birds was come.

The effect of His presence.

Faith was not imposed on doubting hearts by an external and mechanical process. It grew in the warmth that streamed from Him. It was not merely that men were at their best in His company, except, indeed, those who were at their worst through sullen resistance and malignant alarm at His power. It was that men were conscious of something far better than their best, a transcendent force, an influence from the unfathomable heights above them. And to withstand it they must sink below themselves, make new falsehoods and new negations to bind them down, grapple themselves more closely to the base, the earthly, the sensual. But if they yielded to that influence, it lifted and moved their thoughts inevitably upward. It was not merely what He told them of His own sight of spiritual things. It was what they saw reflected in His face and form of that loftier, wider outlook. He was like one standing on a high peak, reporting of the sunrise to men in the dark valley. They heard His words. But they saw also upon His countenance the glow of dawn, and dazzling all about Him the incommunicable splendours of a new day.

This was the effect of the personality of Jesus, as He stood amid the shadows and uncertainties of human life; an effect strangely overlooked and ignored, often even beclouded and hidden, in much that has been written about Him by theologians and historians. I do not dream that I can put it into words. But I know that it can be felt as a reality in the Gospels. And I turn back to one who saw Him face to face, one who touched His hand and leaned upon His bosom, for the expression of the soul-uplifting, faith-begetting wonder of the person of Christ: *The Word was made flesh and dwelt among us, and we beheld His glory, the glory as of the only-begotten of the Father, full of grace and truth.*[1]

The influence of His picture.

Nor has this effect vanished from the world with the removal of the bodily presence of Jesus. It has perpetuated itself by its own vital power, increasing rather than diminishing. It still flows from the picture of His life which is preserved in the Gospels, from the image of His character as it is formed in the minds of men. Eliminate, if you please, what is called the miraculous element. Make what

[1] St. John i. 14.

allowance you will for the enthusiasm and unguarded utterance of His disciples. There still remains that enthusiasm itself to be reckoned with, an enthusiasm which was kindled by Him alone. There still remains the figure of the person of Christ, who never can be expressed in terms of matter and force, who never can be explained by natural and historical causes, who carries us by His own inherent mystery into the presence of the spiritual, the divine, the supernatural.

Christ unique.

Something of this spiritual light, I will admit, — nay, I will maintain with joyous and firm conviction, — comes from every human personality, even the lowliest, in so far as it refuses to be summed up in terms of sense perception, in so far as it gives evidence, by its affections and hopes and fears, of elements in man that are not of the dust. But in Christ this light is transcendent and unique, because He manifestly surpasses the ordinary attainments of humanity, because He cannot be accounted for by the laws of heredity and environment. The more closely we apply these laws, the more clearly He shines out above them.[1]

"The learned men of our day," says M.

[1] J. S. Mill, Essays on *Religion*, p. 253.

Pierre Loti in his latest book, *La Galilée*, "have endeavoured to find a human explication of His mission, but they have not yet reached it. . . . Around Him, none the less, there still glows a radiance of beams which cannot be comprehended."[1]

Christ solitary.

Historically He appears alone, as no great man has ever appeared before or since. Heroes, teachers, and leaders of men have always been seen as central stars in larger constellations, surrounded by lesser but kindred lights. Plato shines in conjunction with Socrates and Aristotle; Cæsar with Pompey and Crassus; Luther with Melanchthon and Calvin; Shakespeare with Beaumont and Fletcher and Ben Jonson; Napoleon surrounded with his brilliant staff of marshals and diplomats; Wordsworth among the mild glories of the Lake poets. In every case, if you search the neighbourhood of a great name, you will find not a blank sky, but an encircling galaxy. But Jesus Christ stands in an immense solitude. Among the prophets who predicted Him, among the apostles who testified of Him, there is none worthy to be compared or conjoined with Him. It is as if the heavens were swept bare of stars; and suddenly, un

[1] Pierre Loti, *La Galilée* (Paris, 1895), p. 93.

expected, unaccompanied, the light of lights appears alone, in supreme isolation.

Christ sin-'ess.

Nor is there anything in His antecedents, in His surroundings, to explain His appearance and radiance. There was nothing in the soil of the sordid and narrow Jewish race to produce such an embodiment of pure and universal love.[1] There was nothing in the atmosphere of that corrupt and sensual age to beget or foster such a character of stainless and complete virtue. Nor was His own life, — I say it reverently, — judged by purely human and natural laws, calculated to result in such an evident perfection as all men have wonderingly recognized in Him. The highest type of human piety, the excellence of a beautiful soul, has never been reached among men without repentance and self-abasement. But Jesus never repented, never abased Himself in shame and sorrow before God, never asked for pardon and mercy. Alone, among His followers who kneel at His command to confess their unworthiness and implore forgiveness, He stands upright and lifts a cloudless face to heaven in the inexplicable glory

[1] Amory H. Bradford, *Heredity and Christian Problems* (New York, Macmillan, 1895), p. 266. See Appendix, note 21.

of piety without penitence. Moral perfection of this kind is not only without a parallel; it is also without an approach. Men have never attained to it, and there is no way for them to climb thither. We can only look up to that perfection, serene, sinless, unsurpassable, and feel that here we are in sight of something which cannot be expressed except by saying that it is the glory of eternal spirit embodied in a person.

IV

The gospel of a Saviour

But the force which resides in the person of Jesus is not exhausted in the production of this profound impression of its own spiritual and transcendent nature. It goes beyond this result of a vivid sense of the reality of the unseen. It has in itself a purifying, cleansing power, a delivering, uplifting, sanctifying power. The Gospel of Christ is the gospel of a person who saves men from sin.[1] And herein it comes very close to the heart of a doubting age.

The great and wonderful fact of this experience, which can neither be questioned nor fully explained, is not involved in the theo logical speculations which have gathered about

[1] See Appendix, note 22.

it. The person of Jesus stands out clear and simple as a powerful Saviour of sinful men and women. In His presence, the publican and the harlot felt their hearts dissolve with I know not what unutterable rapture of forgiveness. At His word, the heavy-laden were mysteriously loosed from the imponderable burden of past transgression. He suffered with sinners, and even while He suffered He delivered them from the sharpest of all pains, — the pain of conscious and unpardoned evil. He died for sinners, according to His own word; and ever since, His cross has been the sign of rescue for humanity. Whatever may be the nature of that sublime transaction upon Calvary· whatever the name by which men call it, — Atonement, Sacrifice, Redemption, Propitiation; whatever relations it may have to the eternal moral law and to the Divine righteousness, — its relation to the human heart is luminous and beautiful. It does take away sin. Kneeling at that holy altar, the soul at once remembers most vividly, and confesses most humbly, and loses most entirely, all her guilt. A sense of profound, unutterable relief, a sacred quietude, diffuses itself through all the recesses of the troubled spirit. Looking

The power of Christ's cross.

unto Christ crucified, we receive an assurance of sin forgiven, which goes deeper than thought can fathom, and far deeper than words can measure.

> "We may not know, we cannot tell
> What pains He had to bear,
> But we believe it was for us
> He hung and suffered there.
>
> "He died that we might be forgiven,
> He died to make us good;
> That we might go at last to heaven,
> Saved by His precious blood."

This is not theory, this is not philosophy, this is not theology. It is veritable fact. The person Jesus, living with men, dying for men, has actually made this impression of pardon for the past and hope for the future, upon the heart of mankind. And from pure love of Him — a love which is first of all and most of all a sense of gratitude for this immeasurable service — have blossomed, often out of the very abysses of sin and degradation, the saintliest and sublimest lives that the world has ever seen.

Now this, as I know from my own experience, is the gospel for doubting men, and for an age of doubt; the gospel of a Person who is a fact and a force, an evidence of the unseen, and a Saviour from sin. Can we preach it? Will we preach it? Then one thing is necessary for us, a thing which might not be necessary, perhaps, if our message were of another kind.

All knowledge, of the world, of human nature, of books, will be helpful and tributary; all gifts, of clear thought, of powerful speech, of prudent action, will be valuable and should be cultivated; but one thing will be absolutely and forever indispensable.

To know Christ, the one thing needful.

If we are to preach Christ we must know Christ, and know Him in such a sense that we can say with St. Paul that we are determined not to know anything save Jesus Christ and Him crucified.[1] We must study Him in the record of His life until His character is more real and vivid to us than that of brother or friend. We must imagine Him with ardent soul, until His figure glows before our inward sight, and His words sound in our ears as a living voice. We must love with His love, and sorrow with His grief, and rejoice with His joy, and offer ourselves with His sacrifice, so truly, so intensely that we can say, as St. Paul said, that we are crucified by His cross and risen in His resurrection.[2] We must trace the power

[1] 1 Cor. ii. 2. [2] Gal. ii. 20.

of His life in the lives of our fellow-men, following and realizing His triumphs in souls redeemed and sins forgiven, until we know the rapture that thrilled the breast of a St. Bernard, a St. Francis, a Thomas à Kempis, a Samuel Rutherford, a Robert McCheyne; the chivalrous loyalty that animated a Henry Havelock, a Charles Kingsley, a Frederick Robertson, a Charles Gordon; the deep devotion that strengthened a David Brainerd, a Henry Martyn, a Coleridge Patteson. We must become the brothers of these men through brotherhood with Christ. We must kindle our hearts in communion with Him, by meditation, by prayer, and by service, which is the best kind of prayer. No day must pass in which we do not do something distinctly in Jesus' name, for Jesus' sake. We must go where He would go if He were on earth. We must try to do what He would do if He were still among men. And so, by our failure as well as by our effort, by the very contrast between our incompleteness and His perfection, the image of our Companion and our saving Lord will grow radiant and distinct within us. We shall know that potent attraction which His person has exercised upon the hearts of men, and feel in our breast that overmastering sense of loyalty to Him, which alone can draw us to follow Him through life and death.

> "If Jesus Christ is a man,—
> And only a man,—I say
> That of all mankind I cleave to Him,
> And to Him will I cleave alway.
>
> "If Jesus is a God,—
> And the only God,—I swear
> I will follow Him through heaven and hell,
> The earth, the sea, and the air."[1]

[1] Richard Watson Gilder, "Song of a Heathen, sojourning in Galilee, A.D. 32."

III

THE UNVEILING OF THE FATHER

"He, who from the Father forth was sent,
Came the true Light, light to our hearts to bring;
The Word of God, — the telling of His thought;
The Light of God, — the making visible ·
The far-transcending glory brought
In human form with man to dwell;
The dazzling gone — the power not less
To show, irradiate, and bless;
The gathering of the primal rays divine,
Informing Chaos to a pure sunshine!"

— George MacDonald.

III

THE UNVEILING OF THE FATHER

A sceptic's account of the spread of Christianity.

In the famous fifteenth chapter of *The Decline and Fall of the Roman Empire*, that painstaking historian and superficial sceptic, Edward Gibbon, Esq., introduces an account of the rise and spread of the Christian Religion. He attributes its remarkable triumph over the established religions of the earth to a series of causes which he ironically describes as secondary, and uniformly treats as primary. He exhibits them as in themselves sufficient to explain the peculiarly favourable reception of the Christian faith in the world, and sets aside the question of a possible divine origin as unnecessary. With serene self-satisfaction he traces the rapid growth of the Christian Church to the five following causes: I. *The Zeal of the Christians*, derived from the Jews, — but purified from that narrow and unsocial spirit which, instead of inviting, had deterred the Gentiles from embracing the law of Moses.

II. *The Doctrine of a Future Life*, improved by every additional circumstance which could give weight and efficacy to that important truth. III. *The Miraculous Powers* ascribed to the primitive Church. IV. *The Pure and Austere Morals* of the Christians. V. *The Union and Discipline of the Christian Republic*, which gradually formed an increasing and independent state in the heart of the Roman empire.[1]

The shallowness of this view.

Now this is a very fair, we may even say a brilliant, example of the kind of work which was done by the shallow and complacent seepticism of a century ago. But the moment we subject it to the more searching analysis of the scepticism of the present age, it dissolves into a thin and incoherent absurdity. For it is evident that, so far from giving an explanation of the growth of Christianity, Gibbon is simply describing some of the phenomena which accompanied that growth. What, for example, is "the zeal of the Christians" but an unilluminating name for a contagious and irresistible enthusiasm which spread through the world in connection with faith in Christ? What is

[1] Edward Gibbon, Esq., *A History of the Decline and Fall of the Roman Empire* (London, John Murray, 8th Edition, 1854), vol. ii., p. 152.

"the union and discipline of the Christian republic" but a description, without explanation, of the organic unfolding of a new, mysterious principle of fellowship. These alleged "causes," more closely examined, are in fact the very things that require to be accounted for. Instead of clearing up the mystery, they increase it.

The "explanation" needs to be explained.

By a singular fatality of language, the sceptical historian has embodied in the statement of his position the demonstration of its insufficiency. In each of his causes, and in the relation that subsists between them, he has practically suggested a difficulty which demands another and a higher solution of the whole problem. Examine his words carefully.

Questions which demand an answer.

By what means, human or divine, was the zeal of the Christians 'purified from the narrow and unsocial spirit of the Jews'? The natural history of sects and schisms teaches us that their invariable tendency is to intensify rather than to eliminate bigotry and exclusiveness. Through what influence was the doctrine of a future life 'improved by every additional circumstance that could give it weight and efficacy'? The inevitable course of its human development under the guidance of abstract philosophy has been towards vagueness, coldness, and uncertainty; under the guidance of concrete superstition, towards puerility and crass sensualism. On what grounds were miraculous powers ascribed to the early Church? They must have been ascribed truly or falsely. If truly, there must have been some basis of fact for them to rest upon. If falsely, the Christians themselves were either ignorant, or cognizant, of the falsehood. Take the former supposition, and you present yourself with the inexplicable theory that what Pliny the Younger called *superstitio prava immodica*, and imagined would be easily and certainly extirpated, was able to hold its own against all the assaults of learning and philosophy. Take the latter supposition, and you are forced to the incredible assumption that a conscious deception was the fountain of highest and strongest moral force that the world has ever felt.[1] How then did the "pure and austere morals of the Christians" come into existence? From a lie, or from a truth? If from a truth, what was the nature of that truth, in what form was it expressed, and how did it win credence?

[1] Carlyle, *Heroes and Hero-Worship*, sect. ii.: "A false man found a religion? Why, a false man cannot even build a brick house! If he do not know and follow *truly* the properties of mortar, burnt clay, and what else he works in, it is no house that he makes, but a rubbish heap."

And, finally, how did "the Christian republic" succeed in maintaining and increasing itself as an independent state in the heart of the Roman empire? Every other attempt to do this particular thing, by secret philosophic doctrine, or by open political organization, failed, and was violently crushed by imperial power, or silently dissolved and absorbed by imperial statesmanship. How was it that this one invisible fellowship, this one visible organization, lived, and spread, and stood out at last, serene, complete, and magnificent, when the time-worn ruins of the empire crumbled around it?[1]

The answer is Christ.

The answer to these questions is found in the person of Christ. This is not a matter of choice. It is a matter of necessity. For if He was, as all candid observers will admit, the originator and animator of Christianity, then to stop short of Him in our inquiry as to the causes of its existence and progress is to stop half-way, as if one should account for the flow of the Nile, after the fashion of the ancient geographers, by attributing it to the melting of the snows on the Mountains of the Moon, instead of tracing it to its great fountain in the Albert Nyanza.

Christ stands above and behind the Church, and all these secondary causes which have been

[1] See Appendix, note 23.

Christ, the reator of Christianity.

enumerated to account for her growth and power flow directly from Him. He it was who purified and humanized the zeal of Christians, so that they emerged from the narrowest of races to preach the broadest and most universal of all religions. He it was who cleared and enlarged their view of immortality, so that it became at once important and efficacious, the only doctrine of a future life that has exercised a direct and uplifting influence upon the present life. He it was who endowed the Church with whatever powers she possessed. He it was who cleansed and ennobled her moral ideals and gave her the only pattern and rule of virtue which has been universally acknowledged as self-consistent, satisfactory, and supreme. He it was who cemented her union and strengthened her discipline to such an indestructible solidarity, that the tie which bound the individual soul to Him was regarded as superior to all earthly relations, and the fellowship which that common tie created, surpassed and survived all fellowships of race, of culture, of nationality.

These are simple historical facts. In stating them we make no assumptions and propound no theories. It is not necessary to take anything for granted or to adopt any particular theological or philosophical system, in order to see clearly and beyond the possibility of mistake that all the force and influence of Christianity in the world have, as a matter of fact, flowed directly from Jesus Christ and from the faith which He has inspired in the hearts of men.

Who, then, is Christ?

The one question of supreme importance, then, if we would understand what Christianity really means, is, Who is this person who stands at the centre of it and fills it with life and strength? What did the first Christians see in Him that made them believe in Him so absolutely and implicitly and gave them power to do such mighty works? What has the church seen in Him through the ages that has bound her to Him as her living Lord and Master? And what are we to see in Him if He is to be in deed and in truth the theme of our gospel? *What think ye of Christ?*

The inevitable question.

This question, you see, is vital and inevitable. If we are to have a Christianity which is real and historical, we must get into line with history. If we are to have behind us the power which comes from actual achievements of our gospel in the world, we must understand the relation which it has always held to the person of Christ. If we are to be in any sense the followers of the first Christians, and to share the joy and peace and power of their religion, we must take the view which they took, of Jesus of Nazareth.[1]

The historic answer.

Now, the object of this lecture may be stated in a single sentence. It is to show that the first Christians saw, and that the Church has always seen, in Jesus Christ a real incarnation of God; a true and personal unveiling of the Father; God in Christ, reconciling the world unto Himself. In other words, not only must we find in Jesus Christ the centre of Christianity, but we must also behold an actual divinity as the centre of life in Jesus Christ.

I

rist's Godhood slowly revealed.

We are not to suppose that faith in Christ began with a clear and definite conception of His divinity. On the contrary, it is evident from the whole gospel record that the idea that Christ was divine gradually developed and un folded in the minds of those who knew and loved and trusted Him. The idea of an incarnation was foreign to the Hebrew mind. There was no race in the world that held so strongly to the thought that God was solitary, unsearchable, and incommunicable. They believed that even His true name could not be pronounced by human lips, and that it was impossible for

[1] See Appendix, note 24.

human eyes really to behold His glory. And the very strength of this ancestral faith of theirs, standing as it must have done directly in the way of belief in an incarnation, is an evidence of the tremendous power and unquestionable reality of the experience which forced the disciples, by slow degrees, to believe firmly and unhesitatingly in the divinity of Christ.

The gradual process of faith.

The process by which this result was accomplished lies open to our thought in the New Testament. We must go back to the point indicated in the second lecture. It was the impression made upon the disciples by Christ's own manifestation of Himself, His character, His actions, and His words, evidently consistent and unique, which led them at last to see in Him the object of divine faith and worship. He was not a mere man. That was evident and undeniable. He was higher than men; holier than men; He possessed an excellence and a power which made them feel in His presence that He was more than they were. What then was He? There were but two directions in which their faith could move. The alternative was sharply set before the disciples on that memorable day at Cæsarea Philippi, when Christ asked them first, "Whom do men say that I, the Son of man, am?" and then, "But whom say ye that I am?" There were but two lines open to them. One was the line of popular superstition, which led them back into the past to see in Christ only the ghost of John the Baptist, or Elias, or one of the prophets come to life again. The other was the new line of Christian faith which led them forward to see in Jesus "the Christ, the Son of the living God."[1]

The new line of Christian belief.

New? Of course it was new! It had to be new, in order to fit the facts, which were such as had never been seen before. And just because it was so new it had to unfold itself by degrees to the fulness of conscious apprehension of all that it involved.

What it meant to be the Christ.

It is evident that the disciples did not know at first what was meant by the Christhood, the Messiahship, the fulfilment of all ancient prophecy and sacred ritual in Jesus. But they learned the lesson as they kept company with Him. They heard Him speak with an authority which none of the prophets had ever claimed. Recognizing a divine inspiration in the Old Testament Scriptures, He distinctly set Himself above them as the bringer of a new and better revelation. He accomplished, interpreted, and revised them. "Ye have heard how it hath been said by them of old time"— by whom?

[1] St. Matt. xvi. 13–16.

By the lawgivers and prophets and psalmists whom Christ recognized as His own forerunners and foretellers. "But I say unto you, love your enemies, bless them that curse you, and pray for them that despitefully use you."[1]

A new power to reveal truth.

Suppose that this were all; suppose that the Sermon on the Mount were the whole of the New Testament, what should we behold in it? Not merely the amazing revelation of a morality more pure and perfect than any other the human heart has conceived, proceeding from the lips of an unlearned Nazarene peasant of the first century, but the absolutely overwhelming sight of a believing Hebrew placing Himself above the rule of His own faith, a humble teacher asserting supreme authority over all human conduct, a moral reformer discarding all other foundations, and saying, "Every one that heareth these sayings of mine and doeth them, I will liken him unto a wise man which built his house upon a rock."[2] Nine and forty times, in the brief and fragmentary record of the discourses of Jesus, recurs this solemn phrase with which He authenticates the truth: *Verily, I say unto you.* And every time that the disciples heard it they must have gotten a new idea of what it meant to be the Christ.

[1] St. Matt. v. 43, 44. [2] St. Matt. vii. 24.

A new relation to humanity.

Think also of the significance which the favourite Messianic title used by Jesus to describe Himself must have had to their minds. He called Himself "the Son of man."[1] Why? Was it because He was merely human? If that was all, surely it would not need to be asserted and emphasized again and again. Imagine any other man, the highest and the holiest, insisting upon the reality of his human life, dwelling upon it, repeating the assertion of it over and over. But this title was, in fact, the claim to a peculiar and supreme relation to the human race. Christ was not *a* son of man, but *the* Son of man, one who, in the luminous words of Irenæus, *recapitulavit in se ipso longam hominum expositionem.*[2] And as such He assumed on earth and in His prevision of heaven a position which no mere man could rightly take. "The Son of man hath power on earth to forgive sins."[3] "The Son of man is Lord also of the Sabbath."[4] "When the Son of man shall come in His glory, and all the holy

[1] In St. Matthew, 30 times; in St. Luke, 25 times; in St. Mark, 14 times. See Appendix, note 25.

[2] Irenæus, *Adv. Hær.*, iii. 18. 1: "He summed up in himself the long unfolding of humanity." The Syriac version of this passage is equally beautiful and significant: "He *commenced afresh* the long line of men."

[3] St. Matt. ix. 6.

[4] St. Mark ii. 28.

angels with Him, then shall He sit upon the throne of His glory; and before Him shall be gathered all nations, and He shall separate them one from another, as a shepherd divideth the sheep from the goats."[1]

A supreme authority to judge the world.

Consider what this implied. It was a declaration that Jesus expected, and was willing, to take into His own hands the task of discriminating between the good and the bad in the unsearchable confusions and complexities of the human heart, and of determining, without hesitation, without misgiving, without redress, the final destinies of the untold myriads of men; "an office," it has been well said, "involving such spiritual insight, such discernment of the thoughts and intents of the heart of each one of the millions at His feet, such awful, unshared supremacy in the moral world, that the imagination recoils in sheer agony from the task of seriously contemplating the assumption of these duties by any created intelligence."[2] When the disciples heard their Master declare that He would fulfil this office of Judge of the World, they must have begun to feel what it meant to be the Christ.

[1] St. Matt. xxv. 31, 32.

[2] H. P. Liddon, *The Divinity of Our Lord* (London, 1885), p. 176.

What it meant to be the Son of God.

Nor do I suppose that they realized at first the full intention of that second phrase in which their view of Jesus was expressed. *The Son of the living God,*—that also was an idea to be gradually apprehended and unfolded. And think what light must have fallen upon it from the conduct of Jesus as they followed Him from day to day. The more closely they knew Him, the more deeply they felt His sinless purity and sovereign virtue. There was a certainty, an independence, a freedom from all effort and from all restraint in His goodness, such as no other good man has ever shown. He had the deepest knowledge of the evil of sin, yet no shadow or stain of it fell upon His own soul. He was on terms of closest intimacy—an intimacy such as no saint ever dared to assume—with God. He conversed with the Father in a friendship which was utterly without fear or regret or misgiving.

r st's own words.

Now when the disciples saw this, it must have put them upon deep thoughts, and the guidance to these thoughts was given by Christ's own words about Himself. He put Himself side by side with the Divine activity. "My Father worketh hitherto and I work."[1] The Jews who heard Him say this, sought to kill Him,

[1] St. John v. 17.

because He had not only broken the Sabbath, but said also that God was His Father, making Himself equal with God. And if the Jews thought this, what did His own disciples think? He claimed a Divine origin and mission: "I came forth from the Father." [1] "My Father sent me." [2] He claimed a Divine knowledge and fellowship: "No man knoweth the Father save the Son." [3] "O righteous Father, the world hath not known Thee, but I have known Thee." [4] He claimed to unveil the Father's being in Himself: "He that hath seen me hath seen the Father. I am in the Father and the Father in me." [5]

The inevitable conclusion.

To what conclusion must such conduct and such words as these lead the disciples in their interpretation of the true meaning of the title "the Son of God"? A conclusion which Jesus Himself, if He was as wise and good as all men admit, must inevitably have foreseen. A conelusion which He Himself, if He had been only a holy man, better than His disciples but of the same nature, would certainly have guarded against and prevented at any cost. A conelusion which is expressed in the attitude of

[1] St. John xvi. 28.
[2] St. John xii. 49.
[3] St. Matt. xi. 27.
[4] St. John xvii. 25.
[5] St. John xiv. 9, 11.

Thomas, kneeling at the feet of Christ and crying, "My Lord and my God"[1] A conclusion which is finally and definitively embodied in the action of the apostles going out into the world to disciple all nations, and to baptize them "into the name of the Father, and of the Son, and of the Holy Ghost."[2]

II

The disciples believed that Christ was Divine.

There cannot be any question as to the state of mind which this action implied. It was the deep conviction, not necessarily reasoned out and formulated, but lying at the very root of conduct, that Jesus Christ the Son was the unveiling of His Father God, and that the Holy Spirit who came upon the disciples was the Spirit of the Father and the Son. The part which the resurrection played in the clarifying and confirming of this conviction was important. But we must not misunderstand the meaning of the resurrection. It was not in any sense a new and different revelation of God, imagined or actually received. Whatever the form in which Jesus appeared to the disciples during the forty days that followed His death, He was recognized as the same Jesus; and the one effect of His appearance was

[1] St. John xx. 28. [2] St. Matt. xxviii. 19.

simply to confirm and deepen the truth of what He had said and done while He was with them. And with this confirmation the truth took shape and substance as an active and enduring power in human faith and life and worship.

There is no more room for doubt that the early Christians saw in Christ a personal unveiling of God, than that the friends and followers of Abraham Lincoln regarded him as a good and loyal American citizen of the white race.[1] And even if we could find no direct and definite statement of either of these views, the evidence that men held them could be clearly and certainly read in the facts of history.

The early Church worshipped Christ.

Divine honours were paid to Christ in the primitive Church. The first common prayer of the disciples, when they were assembled to choose an apostle in the place of the traitor Judas, was addressed to Christ.[2] The Christians were distinguished both from the Jews and from the heathen as those who called upon the name of the Lord Jesus Christ.[3] The dying martyr Stephen showed what was meant by this phrase in his prayer, "Lord Jesus, receive my spirit."[4] Saul of Tarsus, when he was con-

[1] See Appendix, note 26.

[2] Acts i. 24. See Alford *in loc.*

[3] Acts ix. 21; 1 Cor. i. 2.

[4] Acts vii. 59.

vinced by that strange experience on the road to Damascus that Jesus was not an impostor, but the Christ, at once addressed Him in prayer, "Lord, what wilt thou have me to do?"[1] And Ananias, who received Saul into the Church, asked guidance and direction from the same Lord.[2] Peter baptized the multitudes on the day of Pentecost in the name of Jesus Christ.[3] John wrote of prayer to the Son of God as a familiar ground of confidence in Christian experience.[4] The apostolic benediction was: "The grace of our Lord Jesus Christ, and the love of God, and the communion of the Holy Ghost be with you all."[5] The whole current of adoration and devotion in the New Testament leads up naturally and without surprise to the magnificent words of St. Paul, in which he speaks of "Christ, who is over all, God blessed forever."[6]

It should be frankly recognized that the first Christians assigned a certain subordination to the Son in relation to the Father; but it must be admitted with equal candour that this subordination was not in any sense a separation,

[1] Acts ix. 6. [2] Acts ix. 13. [3] Acts ii. 38.
[4] I John v. 13–15. [5] 2 Cor. xiii. 14.
[6] Rom. ix. 5. *Cf.* Stevens, *The Pauline Theology*, p. 201, for a succinct statement of the grounds on which this interpretation of the text is preferred.

and that it really implied and involved a unity between them which made it possible and natural and inevitable for the disciples to pay an adoration to the Son with the Father, which, if it had been offered to, or claimed by, the greatest and best of the apostles, would have been instantly repudiated by the whole Church as not only absurd but radically blasphemous.

It is an easy matter to trace the worship of Christ in the later development of Christianity. There are two sources of evidence: the Christian hymns and liturgies; the heathen attacks and the apologies which they evoked.

The testimony of the hymns.

The earliest hymns of the Greek Church, the "Thanksgiving at lamplighting," "Shepherd of tender youth," "The Bridegroom cometh," the "Hymn to Christ after Silence," celebrate the praise of the Lord Jesus. Syriac poetry, through its great poet, Ephrem Syrus, takes up the same strain of adoration to the Son of God, and its undying music may still be heard among the mountains of Armenia where the unspeakable Turk is exterminating a whole race for loyalty to the name of Christ. Latin hymnody, from its earliest origin in translations from the Greek like the *Gloria in Excelsis* and the *Te Deum*, through its splendid unfolding in the poetry of Hilary of Poictiers, Ambrose of Milan, and

Gregory the Great, to its sweet culmination in the two Bernards, him of Clairvaux and him of Cluny, repeats the same burden :

> "O Jesus, Thou the glory art
> Of angel worlds above ;
> Thy name is music to my heart,
> Enchanting it with love."

In every land and language, in German, in French, in English, the most precious and potent melodies of the Church are fragrant with the name of Christ.

The testimony of the early liturgies.

The early liturgies bear the same testimony to the pre-eminence of the Lord Jesus in the doxologies and supplications of Christian faith. The Apostolical Constitutions,[1] the liturgy of St. James,[2] the liturgy of St. Mark,[3] the liturgy of St. Adæus and St. Maris,[4] unquestionably preserve the spirit of the early Christian worship; and they all are witnesses to the fact that the Christians prayed directly to Christ. Indeed, it lies upon the very surface of history that the growth of Christianity, as manifested

[1] *Apost. Const.*, Book VIII., chap. vii.

[2] *The Divine Liturgy of St. James*, iii.: "Sovereign Lord Jesus Christ, O Word of God," etc.

[3] *The Divine Liturgy of the Holy Apostle and Evangelist Mark*, v., xxii., etc.

[4] *Liturgy of the Blessed Apostles, composed by St. Adæus and St. Maris*, xiv.

in a spreading worship, was not simply the increase of those who were willing to adore God on the authority of Christ. It was distinctly and essentially the diffusion of an inward force which impelled men to blend the name of Christ with the name of God in their prayers, and to worship the Son with the Father. The beautiful Prayer of St. Chrysostom, which closes the Litany and the Morning and Evening Prayers of the Protestant Episcopal Church, is addressed to Christ, "who dost promise that when two or three are gathered together in Thy name, Thou wilt grant their requests."[1] There is not in the world to-day a single great liturgy, Greek, Roman, Armenian, French, German, Scotch, or English, which does not contain ascriptions of divine glory, and petitions for divine grace, addressed to Jesus Christ.

The testimony of the heathen.

Heathen writers of very early date assure us that this was the practice of Christians from the beginning. The younger Pliny reported to the Emperor Trajan that the people called Christians were accustomed to assemble before daybreak and "sing a hymn of praise responsively to Christ, as it were to God."[2] In the

[1] St. Matt. xviii. 20.

[2] A.D. 112. See the chapter on "Pliny's Report and Trajan's Rescript" in Ramsay, *The Church in the Roman Empire* (New York, Putnam, 1893), pp. 196 ff.

public trials that followed there was never any denial of this statement. It was admitted alike by those who apostatized under the pressure of persecution and by those who remained faithful to the name of Christ. The Emperor Hadrian wrote to Servian that of the population of Alexandria "some worshipped Serapis, and others Christ." Lucian, the pagan satirist, says in his biography of Peregrinus Proteus: "The Christians are still worshipping that great man who was crucified in Palestine."[1]

r st ans despised for worshipping hrist.

In all the apologies for the Christian religion which were put forth during the persecutions under Hadrian, and his successors Antoninus Pius and Marcus Aurelius, there was no attempt to refute the universal charge that the Christians worshipped Christ.[2] As if to confirm this evidence by one of those indications which are all the more significant because they are so slight and so clearly unpremeditated, there still exists a rude caricature, scratched by some careless hand upon the walls of the

[1] *Luciani Samosatensis Opera.* (Ed. Leipsic, 1829), Tomus iv., p. 173.

[2] *The First Apology of Justin Martyr,* chap. xiii.: "Our teacher of these things is Jesus Christ; and that we reasonably worship Him, having learned that He is the Son of the true God Himself, and holding Him in the second place, and the prophetic Spirit in the third, we will prove."

Palatine Palace in Rome not later than the beginning of the third century, representing a human figure with an ass's head hanging upon a cross, while a man stands before it in the attitude of worship. Underneath is this ill-spelled inscription, —

"Alexamenos adore his God."[1]

Thus the songs and prayers of believers, the accusations of persecutors, the sneers of seeptics, and the coarse jests of mockers all join in proving beyond a doubt that the primitive Christians paid divine honour to the Lord Jesus. I do not see how any man can be in touch with Christianity as a living form of worship in the world, unless he knows the reality and appreciates the force of this unquestionable fact.

III

Christ was a new theology.

Nor will it be possible to understand the intellectual and moral teachings of the Christian religion, as they are recorded in the New Testament, unless we put ourselves at the focal point from which, as a matter of history, these teachings were first conceived and then un-

[1] *Das Spott-Crucifix der Römischen Kaiser Paläste*, Ferdinand Becker (Gera, 1876). *Das Spott-Crucifix vom Palatin*, Franz Xaver Kraus (Freiburg, 1872).

folded. This point was the vision of an unveiling of the being and mind of God in Christ.[1] It was not merely that Jesus said certain things about God which men had not known, or had forgotten. It was that they saw in the coming of Christ a personal revelation of the Divine Being. And this revelation touched and transformed every possible sphere of thought and feeling in regard to the problems of religion. The personality of God was made distinct and luminous, not only by the recognition of an eternal Fatherhood in His nature, but by the light of the knowledge of His glory shining in the face of a person.[2] The righteousness of God was disclosed in a new aspect by the thought that He had sent His own Son in the likeness of sinful flesh, and for sin to condemn sin in the flesh.[3] The goodness of God was confirmed and made sufficient for all possible human needs by the conviction that He who spared not His own Son, but freely delivered Him up for us all, would also with Him freely give us all things.[4] The saving will and power of God were apprehended through the vision of Him in Christ reconciling the world to Himself.[5] The everlasting

[1] See Appendix, note 27. [2] 2 Cor. iv. 6.
[3] Rom. viii. 3. [4] Rom. viii. 32. [5] 2 Cor. v. 19.

and inseparable love of God became the sure ground of hope only when it was seen embodied in Christ Jesus our Lord.[1] The true meaning of filial obedience to God and of union with God was interpreted in the light of conformity to the image of His Son.[2] And the immense significance of immortality was comprehended in the possession of a life hid with Christ in God.[3]

God was seen through Christ.

Now the window through which men caught sight of these truths was, and could have been, nothing else than faith in a real incarnation of God in Christ. The personal, moral, sympathetic view of God which distinguished the early Church was seen only through that opening.[4] She saw the Divine Being beaming with a new radiance, she saw the wide landscape of human duty and destiny illuminated and transfigured, she saw a new heaven and a new earth, when she saw in Christ all the fulness of the Godhead dwelling bodily.[5] And it was in the

[1] Rom. viii. 39. [2] Rom. viii. 29. [3] Col. iii. 3.

[4] *First Epistle of St. Clement*, chap. xxxvi. : "By Him we look up to the heights of heaven. By Him we behold, as in a glass, His immaculate and most excellent visage. By Him are the eyes of our heart opened. By Him our foolish and darkened understanding blossoms up anew towards the light." Bp. Lightfoot's Edition. (Macmillan, 1890.)

[5] See appendix, note 28.

strength and enthusiasm of this vision, that she concentrated all her moral and intellectual energies on the one point of keeping that window open, and maintaining against direct assault and secret dissolution the real and personal Deity of Christ.

IV

Christian doctrine grew around the Deity of Christ.

I am careful to put the statement in this form because I believe that it alone corresponds with the facts, and because it is only by getting our minds into this position that we can hope to understand the course, the meaning, and the force of Christian doctrine. The early Christians looked at God through Christ: they did not look at Christ through a preconceived idea and a logical definition of God. The true development of theology, to put the matter plainly, was not abstract, it was personal and practical. The doctrine of the Trinity came into being to meet an imperious necessity.[1] That necessity was the defence of the actual worship of Christ, the actual trust in Christ as the Unveiler of the Father, which already existed at the heart of Christianity. It was recognized instinctively that the loss of this trust, the silencing of this worship,

[1] See Appendix, note 29.

meant the death of Christianity by heart-failure. Every speculation which threatened this result, every theory of human nature or of divine nature which seemed to separate the personality of Christ from the personality of God, was regarded by the Church as dangerous and hostile. Every attempted statement of theological dogma which appeared to obscure or to imperil the reality and the eternal validity of the unveiling of the Father in the Son, was resented, and a counter statement of theological dogma was framed to meet it. This was the intellectual conflict of Christianity in the first centuries: a struggle for life centring about the actual Deity of Christ.

The conflict with heresy.

As we trace the progress of this conflict, its vital importance emerges more and more clearly. Often, I suppose, we cannot help feeling a sense of sympathy with the earnest purpose and the personal character of those men who were called heretics. Often we are conscious of a certain distrust for the metaphysical and exegetical arguments, and of a grave repugnance for the physical and political methods, which were used by the orthodox to enforce their definitions. Athanasius was not an altogether lovely person. Some of the early Church Councils were almost as disorderly and as cruel as some of the regiments that fought in the war to defend the American Union and free the slave. But the question is not one of the manner of defence or attack. It is a question of the reality and significance of the cause attacked and defended. And here we see that Athanasius with all his faults was on the right side, and Arius with all his virtues was on the wrong side. Through all the confusion of metaphysical dispute about the exact meaning of substance and subsistence, nature and personality, ideal existence and real existence, — terms which, as I conceive them, must change their significance as the methods of human philosophy change, and must always represent imperfectly a mystery which is for us unsearchable and indefinable, — through all this confusion one fact shines out clear and distinct. The unveiling of the Father in Christ was, and continued to be, and still is, the Palladium of Christianity. All who have surrendered it, for whatever reason, have been dispersed and scattered. All who have defended it, in whatever method, have been held fast in the unity of the faith and of the knowledge of the Son of God.[1]

The Palladium of Christianity.

[1] Eph. iv. 13.

The doctrine of the Trinity constructed to defend the Deity of Christ.

This point of view must condition the attitude of our minds towards the doctrine of the Trinity. No Christian man can be hostile or indifferent to it when he remembers its history. It may have been too much elaborated by minds over-curious in metaphysical distinctions. It may have been put in a position of undue preeminence by theologians whose energies were all absorbed in its construction and in the contemplation of the work of their own reason in the service of Christianity. But in spite of all excesses and errors, it stands as an enduring monument of the loyalty of the faith to its central conviction. In all its forms, from the sharply tri-personal Trinity of Athanasius, to the essentially tri-modal Trinity of Augustine, the great service which it has rendered is not abstract nor philosophical. It is practical. It has protected the conviction that the real nature of God is revealed in Christ; it has justified the consciousness that the Spirit of Christ, animating the Christian life, is the Spirit of God; it has preserved the sense of real communion with God in Christ which is the nerve of Christian worship.

And yet the doctrine of the Trinity is not the gospel, nor is it the foundation of the gospel. It cannot be preached as a saving message to the

The doctrine of the Trinity subordinate to the gospel.

souls of men, except in that form in which we find it in Phillips Brooks' noble *Sermon for Trinity Sunday*, and Dr. George A. Gordon's powerful discourse on *The Trinity the Ground of Humanity*. It is the effort to apprehend a relation of the Being of God to the conscious experience of man; a truth exhibited in the course of revelation and recognized in its mysterious unfolding both before and after all efforts to symbolize it in theological language; in brief, it is the reaching out of the human mind, conscious of its limitations and conditions, towards a vision and worship of the Father in the Son through the Spirit. The doctrine of the Trinity is not the Palladium. It is the defence. I will confess that in its broad outlines it seems to me necessary and satisfactory. I will confess that no other answer to the profound questions which inevitably arise out of the contact between the idea of God, and the experience of real life in all its manifoldness, appears to me half so reasonable or complete as that which asserts that "the various fundamental forms of society on the earth, the essential relationships of humanity, have their Archetype, their Eternal Pattern and Causal Source, in the nature of the Infinite."[1] I will confess that the form of

[1] Gordon, *The Christ of To-day*, p. 101.

this answer which contemplates the existence of these eternal relationships in the Divine nature as most clearly and positively personal, is more conclusive to my mind than any other. But if other men think otherwise on this point, we are not therefore divided from each other, or from the Christian faith. The question is one of metaphysics. It is not a question of religion. All modes of defining the Trinity as a doctrine must be kept subordinate to the purpose for which it exists. All attempts to express it are valuable only in so far as they help us to keep in view the unveiling of the Divine nature which centres in Him who was manifested in the flesh, justified in the Spirit, seen of angels, preached among the nations, believed on in the world, received up in glory.[1]

V

The gospel of the Incarnation adapted to this age.

Now wherein is a message like this, the gospel of a personal unveiling of God in the person of Christ, adapted to the needs of the present age?

1. It seems to me first of all that the course of modern thought has prepared the way for it by destroying the *a priori* objections to the In-

[1] 1 Tim. iii. 16.

Philosophy has cleared the way for it.

carnation. Shallow agnosticism makes two assumptions which are contradictory. It assumes that man is unable to attain to the knowledge of God; and that it is impossible for God to reveal Himself to man. But if we cannot know Him, how can we know that He cannot reveal Himself? This would be in effect the most intimate kind of knowledge. To take it for granted that an Incarnation of God is impossible or incredible is to profess a most per feet and exclusive understanding of the Divine nature. "At one time," says Mr. Romanes, "it seemed to me impossible that any proposition, verbally intelligible as such, could be more violently absurd than that of the Incarnation. Now I see that this standpoint is wholly irrational. . . . 'But the Incarnation is opposed to common sense.' No doubt: utterly so; but so it ought to be if true. Common sense is merely a rough register of common experience. But the Incarnation, if it ever took place, whatever else it may have been, was not a common event. 'But it is derogatory to God to become man.' How do you know? Besides, Christ was not an ordinary man. Both negative criticism and the positive effects of His life prove this; while if we for a moment adopt the Christian point of view for the sake of argument, the whole ***raison d'être*** of mankind is bound up in Him. Lastly there are considerations ***per contra***, rendering an Incarnation antecedently probable."[1]

2. Now these considerations to which Romanes alludes are not foreign to the intellectual atmosphere of our age; they are native to it; they are in fact the offspring of the times, born of the spirit which now leads the best thoughts of men.

Evolution points towards it.

The whole doctrine of development, as it is conceived by the deepest and clearest minds, looks forward to the discovery of an Incarnation which shall be at once the crown and the completion of the process of natural evolution. If nature is an orderly and progressive manifestation of an Unseen Power; if each successive step in this manifestation realizes and exhibits something higher and more perfect, to which all that has gone before has pointed, and in which the potentialities of all previous developments are not only summed up, but raised to a new power; if the mechanical structure of inorganic substances contains a prophecy (only to be interpreted after the event) of organic life, and organic life is a basis for instinct and the elementary processes of intellect,

[1] *Thoughts on Religion*, p. 186.

and the rude forms of thought and feeling in the lower animals foreshadow the unfolding of reflective reason and moral consciousness in man,—then surely this reflective reason and this moral consciousness, in themselves confessedly imperfect, must be only the foundation for a fuller and more perfect manifestation of that Unseen Power out of whose depths all preceding manifestations have come forth. And if the universal verdict of human science and philosophy is correct in assuming that the lower must precede the higher, and that organie life is above inorganic life, and that reason is above instinct, and that virtue is above automatic action, then it is to be expected that the complete manifestation of that Unseen Power which makes for Reason and Righteousness will neither be omitted nor intruded before its time. It cannot come too soon, without violating the order of evolution. It cannot fail to come, without destroying the significance of evolution.

Personality the final revelation.

But in what form can it come except in one which at once sums up all that has gone before it, and advances to a new level? If the universe contains an unveiling of the might, and wisdom, and reasonableness, and righteousness, of its Primal Cause, then certainly it must contain at last an unveiling of His personality. This is the only thing that remains to be added. This is the only thing that embraces all the rest and raises it to a new power. The highest category known to our minds is that of self-conscious life. Without the conception of a personal God, man's view of the universe must remain forever incomplete, incoherent, and unreasonable. Without the revelation of a personal God, the process of evolution as the unfolding of the real secret of the universe must remain unfinished and futile. Philosophy as well as religion pushes us forward to this conclusion. Personality is the ultimate reality. Personality must be the final revelation. But a person can be unveiled only in a personal form. Therefore all the presumptions of reason are in favour of an Incarnation of the Deity, not outside of nature, but in nature, to consummate and crown that visible evolution whereby the invisible things of Him from the creation of the world are clearly seen.[1] And all the processes of intelligence are satisfied, and rest and repose in the conviction that the Word, which was in the beginning with God and which was God and by whom all things were made, finally became flesh and dwelt among us, revealing His glory, the glory

[1] See Appendix, note 30.

as of the only-begotten of the Father, full of grace and truth.[1]

The gospel of the Incarnation is historically consistent.

3. Moreover, this view of Christ is adapted to the present age because it is historically consistent. We have seen that it underlies the very existence and growth of the Christian Church. The testimony of eighteen centuries to the impossibility of explaining the personality of Christ on humanitarian grounds is in itself an evidence of His divinity.

Lincoln was right when he said: "You can fool some of the people all of the time, and all of the people some of the time, but you cannot fool all of the people all of the time." A thousand attempts to account for the life of Christ without admitting His divinity have been made. Not one of them has succeeded in winning the assent and approbation of any great mass of men for any great length of time. They have hardly survived the lives of those who have invented them. Each new naturalistic theory of Christ has discredited and demolished its predecessors. And if any one of them is alive and finds credence to-day, it is only because it is the latest, and it is but

[1] See Lyman Abbott, *The Evolution of Christianity* (Houghton, Mifflin & Co., 1894), "Christ is not the product of evolution, but the producer," pp. 240–242.

waiting for its successor (as the theory of Socinus waited for the theory of Strauss, and the theory of Strauss for the theory of Renan) to be its judge and destroyer.

The impregnable rock of Christianity.

Meantime historic Christianity, which beholds God incarnate in Christ, stands as a rock around which the tides of opinion ebb and flow. The Church has changed in some things, but not in this. It has modified, enlarged, diminished, or abandoned some articles of faith, but not this. If it be an error, it is such an error as the world has never seen anywhere else; for it has not only stood firm through the fiercest and most persistent storm of criticism that has ever been directed against any human opinion, but it has also been the foundation of the strongest and saintliest lives that humanity has ever known. If it be a truth, it must be for every Christian preacher the central truth. For it is certain that this age of ours, with its ruthless critical spirit, with its keen historical sense, will never respect the intelligence, though it may acknowledge the good intentions, of a man who professes to speak in the name of Christianity without proclaiming, as the core of his message, the Divine Christ.

4. And this gospel meets the need of our times because it is the satisfaction of humanity.

The incarnation satisfies the human heart.

More urgent and painful even than the questions of the intellect in regard to the being and nature of God, are the misgivings of the heart in regard to His relations to us. If He is that remote and inaccessible Sovereign

> "Who sees with equal eyes, as Lord of all,
> A hero perish or a sparrow fall,"

what possible answer can we find in Him to the longings and desires of our souls for a Divine love? what possible support can we find in Him for our struggles against outward temptation and indwelling evil? what possible sympathy can we find in Him for our hopes and aspirations and upward strivings, out of the quicksands of heredity and environment, towards liberty and light? The religion of the Incarnation is the only one that brings us near to Him, assures us of our kinship with Him, and of His infinite, practical, helpful love for us. This faith alone bridges the chasm that divides the eternal self-existent Spirit from our finite, despondent, earthbound souls. This faith alone gives us any knowledge of the things that we most need to know about Him. Deism is like a message written in an inscrutable hieroglyph which conveys no clear meaning to the mind. Theism is like a message which is intelligible to the intellect, but unsatisfactory to the heart, because it has no personal address and no signature. Christianity is a personal message, signed by the hand of a Father, and conveyed to us by the hand of the Son.[1]

Christ is God with us.

The comparison is imperfect. It falls far short of the truth. In Christianity the messenger is the message. The love which sent and the love which delivered it are the same. Christ is Immanuel, God with us. The gospel of the Incarnation does not profess to remove all intellectual perplexities in regard to the existence of God and our own souls. It professes simply to establish such a conscious relation between our souls and God that our ethical needs shall be satisfied at once; and thus it shall be infinitely easier, either to dissolve, or to endure, our intellectual perplexities. This relation is possible only in Christ. And it is possible in Him only when we receive Him as the unveiling of the Father. This requires an act of faith. But it is a faith which is simpler in its form, more natural in its method, and more profound in its spiritual results than any other. For in the last analysis it is just an act of personal confidence in a person. And this does not demand perfect knowledge, but absolute trust.

[1] See Appendix, note 31.

The Deity of Christ is the strength of our gospel.

To imagine that we can adapt our preaching to this age of doubt by weakening, concealing, or abandoning the truth of the Deity of Christ is to mistake the great need of our times. It is to seek to commend our gospel by taking away from it the chief thing that men really want, — an assurance of sympathy and kinship with God. "One of the great marks of the youth of to-day," says Ernest Lavisse, — "I speak of thinking youth, — is a longing for the Divine."[1] This longing is to be met not by slighting, but by emphasizing, not by clouding, but by clarifying, not by withdrawing, but by advancing, the true Deity of our Lord Jesus Christ. Let us take up the words of the ancient creed: "*We believe in one Lord Jesus Christ, the Son of God, only-begotten of the Father, that is of the substance of the Father, God of God, Light of Light, very God of God, begotten, not made, being of one substance with the Father: by Whom all things were made which are in heaven and earth: Who, for us men and for our salvation, came down, and was incarnate, and was made man, and suffered, and rose the third day, and ascended into the heavens, and shall come to judge the quick and the dead.*"[2]

[1] Ernest Lavisse, *La Génération de 1890.*

[2] Symbolum Nicænum, *The Creeds of Christendom*, Vol. ii. (Harpers, 1882).

IV

THE HUMAN LIFE OF GOD

"Behold Him now where He comes!
Not the Christ of our subtle creeds,
But the light of our hearts, of our homes,
Of our hopes, our prayers, our needs;
The brother of want and blame,
The lover of women and men,
With a love that puts to shame
All passions of mortal ken.

* * * * * *

"Ah no, thou life of the heart,
Never shalt thou depart!
Not till the leaven of God
Shall lighten each human clod·
Not till the world shall climb
To thy height serene, sublime,
Shall the Christ who enters our door
Pass to return no more."

— Richard Watson Gilder,
The Passing of Christ.

IV

THE HUMAN LIFE OF GOD

A great truth in eclipse.

NEARLY fifty years ago, Horace Bushnell, the most mystical of logicians, or the most logical of mystics, delivered before Yale University a magnificent discourse upon *The Divinity of Christ.* In that fine work of genius, wrought out of darkness and light, mystery and clearness, like an intricate carving of ebony and gold, I find these words: "Christ is in such a sense God, or God manifested, that the unknown term of His nature, that which we are most in doubt of, and about which we are least capable of any positive affirmation, is the human."[1]

This sentence, it seems to me, is not of light, but of darkness. It does not represent that illuminating and harmonious kind of truth which comes directly from the divine revelation of Christ. It belongs rather to that obscured

[1] Horace Bushnell, *God in Christ* (New York, Scribners, 1887), p. 123.

Theology has lost sight of Christ's humanity.

and discordant manner of presenting truth which is the consequence of studying it too much at second-hand and too little at first-hand, too much in the speculations and reasonings of men and too little in the facts of life wherein it was first manifested. Whatever may be said of this sentence as a statement of the result of dogmatic theology,—and in this sense I, for one, do not question its accuracy,—when we consider its plain meaning as an expression of Christian experience and faith, one thing is clear: It is utterly out of touch with the experience and faith of the first disciples. It is in sharp and striking discord with the consciousness of the primitive Church. For if there is anything in regard to which the New Testament makes positive and undoubting affirmation, it is the complete, genuine, and veritable humanity of Christ. If there is any fact which stands out luminous and distinct in the experience of the early Christians, it is that they saw in Christ, not merely a myste rious manifestation of the Divine in a form cal culated to beget new doubts, and under conditions which must remain inscrutable and incomprehensible, but something utterly different. They saw the mystery reduced to terms of simplicity, the revelation levelled to the direct apprehension of man, the unveiling of the Father under conditions which were so familiar that they dissolved doubts and difficulties. They saw in Christ the human life of God.

How shall the vision be restored?

The object of this lecture is, first, to trace very briefly the way in which this view of Christ has been beclouded so that His humanity has appeared doubtful and less capable of positive affirmation; second, to show how the primitive view of His person and life may be, and in the history of Christian faith often has been, recovered and restored to its pristine brilliancy and beauty; and third, to try to express, though but imperfectly, the meaning and importance of this view for the present age.

I

Obscuration by formulas

Definition is dangerous. Necessary it may be; useful it undoubtedly is; but our recognition of these qualities ought not to make us forget or deny the peril which the process certainly involves. And this is the nature of the danger: the definition has an inherent tendency to substitute itself for the thing defined. The terms in which a fact is expressed creep into the place of the fact itself. The reality is removed insensibly to a remote distance behind the verbal symbols which represent it. The way of access to it is blocked, and its influence is restricted by the forms of expression invented to define it.

An illustration from the history of Art.

I do not know where we can find a more vivid illustration of this process than that which is given, in many ways, in the history of art. The first effort of the artist is to represent something that he has seen or imagined. Out of this effort and the work which it produces, grow certain methods and habits of representing landscape and architecture and the human figure. Out of these habits grow rules and formulas, not only for the hand but also for the eye. On these formulas schools are founded. In these schools the example of masters comes to have an authority which overshadows and limits the vision of facts as well as the repre sentation of them.[1] The Japanese artists, of certain schools, actually reproduce that infan tile condition of sight in which all things appear flat, in a single plane without perspective. The Giotteschi of Italy carried their disregard of anatomy to such a point that joints and articulations vanished from the human figure.

[1] See Appendix, note 32.

Representations of Christ.

Now this same process of limitation by formulas may be observed, on the ideal side, in the course of religious art. The first pictures of Christ, traced in colour upon the walls of the Catacombs, or carved in stone upon the sarcophagi,of the Christian dead, do not give us indeed the very earliest conception of Him; for the Christian art of the first two centuries, if it ever existed, has long since perished. But that which remains, dating from the third and fourth centuries, bears witness to an idea of the Christ which was simple and natural and humane. He appears as a figure of youthful beauty and graciousness; the good Shepherd bearing a lamb upon His shoulders; the true Orpheus drawing all creatures and souls by the charm of His amiable music.[1] These are only symbolie representations, yet they evidence a conception of Him which was still in touch with the facts. A little later we find an effort to conceive and depict Him with more realism. His face appears in pictures which resemble the description given in the spurious Epistle of Lentulus: "A man of dignified presence, with dark hair parted in the middle and flowing down, after the custom of the Naza-

[1] So in the paintings from the Catacombs of *S. Agnese* and *S. Callisto.*

renes, over both shoulders; His brow clear and pure; His unfurrowed face of pleasant aspect and medium complexion; His mouth and nose faultless; His short, light beard parted in the middle; His eyes bright and lustrous."[1]

Tradition petrifies Christian Art.

But when we pass on to the creations of so-called Byzantine art, we find ourselves face to face with an utterly different view of the Christ. His countenance now stares out in glittering mosaic from the walls of great churches, huge, dark, threatening, a dreadful and forbidding face. The fixed and formal lines are repeated and deepened by artist after artist. Every feature of naturalness is obliterated; every feature that seemed to express awfulness is exaggerated and emphasized. The wide-set eyes, the long narrow countenance, the stern, inflexible mouth, — in this ocular definition the man Christ Jesus has vanished, and we see only the immense, immutable, and terrible Pantokrator, who cannot be touched with the feeling of our infirmities.[2]

When we turn to the intellectual life of the Church out of which this type of art grew, we

[1] This is the *imago Christi* which we see in the painting from the Catacomb of *S. Ponziano*.

[2] See the mosaic of Christ in the Church of St. Paul outside the walls, near Rome.

Dogmas darken the view of Christ.

see there the process explained. The early Greek Fathers, like Irenæus, went directly to the Holy Scriptures for their view of the person of Christ, and frankly accepted all the features of the living, lovely portrait there disclosed.[1] They recognized without reserve the reality of Christ's human growth in wisdom and stature and in favour with God and men; the actual limitations of Christ's human knowledge as expressed in the questions that He asked and in His profession of ignorance in regard to the time of His second advent; the intimacy of His sympathy with us in temptation, suffering, and death. But with the development of theological definition this direct view of Christ was modified, obscured, and at last totally eclipsed. Instead of looking at God through His revelation in Christ, the Fathers began to look at Christ through a more and more abstract, precise, and inflexible statement of the metaphysical idea of God. It became necessary to harmonize the Scripture record of the life of Jesus with the theories of the divine nature set forth in the decrees of councils and defined with amazing particularity in the writings of theologians. In the effort to accomplish this, two main lines of thought were followed. One line abandoned the belief in

[1] See Appendix, note 33.

The hiding of the face of Jesus.

Christ's real and complete humanity, and reduced His human life to a tenuous and filmy apparition. The other line distinguished between His humanity and His Divinity in such a way as to divide Him into two halves, either of which appears virtually complete without the other, and both of which are united, not in a single and sincere personality, but in an outward manifestation and a concealed life, covering in some mysterious way a double centre of existence. It is only fair to say that the extreme results of these two lines of thought were condemned by the Church in the heresies of Doketism and Apollinarianism, Eutychianism and Nestorianism. But it is equally fair to say that the influence of these theories was by no means checked nor extirpated. They continued to make themselves felt powerfully and perniciously; now in the direction of dissolving the humanity of Christ into a mere cloud enveloping His Deity; and again in the direction of dividing and destroying the unity of His person in the definitions of a dual nature.

Bending the Bible to fit definitions.

It is not necessary, nor would it be possible, for us to trace this process in detail through all its complexities and self-contradictions. It will be enough to give two or three specimens of the kind of work to which it led in dealing with two essential features of the picture of Christ which is given to us in the Gospels: His human limitation of knowledge, and His human growth in wisdom, stature, and grace. Both limitation and growth are unexempt conditions of manhood. Both are unquestionably attributed to Christ in the New Testament. Both are explicitly denied by theologians. Ephrem Syrus, commenting upon the *Diatessaron* of Tatian, says: "Christ, though He knew the moment of His advent, yet that they might not ask Him any more about it, said, *I know it not.*"[1] Chrysostom, in his explanation of St. Matthew xxiv. 36, paraphrases Christ's words in this extraordinary fashion: "For if thou seek after the day and the hour thou shalt not hear them of me, saith He; but if of times and preludes, I will tell thee all exactly. *For that indeed I am not ignorant of it*, I have shown by many things.—I lead thee to the very vestibule; and if I do not open unto thee the doors, this also I do for your good."[2] John of Damascus, defending the orthodox faith, declares that

[1] *Evang. Concordant. Expos.* (Aucher and Moesinger, Venice, 1876), p. 16.

[2] St. Chrysostom, *Homilies on the Gospel of St. Matthew*, lxxvii. 2. *The Nicene Fathers* (New York, Christian Literature Co., 1888), vol. x.

"Christ is said to advance in wisdom and stature and grace, because He grows in fact in stature, and through His growth in stature brings out into exhibition the wisdom which already existed in Him. . . . But those who say that He really grew in wisdom and grace as receiving increase in these, deny that the flesh was united to the word from the first moment of its existence."[1] Peter Lombard does not explicitly adopt, but quotes with evident approval, the opinion that the person of the eternal Word put on a human body and soul as a robe, in order that He might appear suitably to the eyes of mortals, yet in Himself He was not changed by this incarnation, but remained one and the same, immutable.[2]

A very full and clear exhibition of the darkness and unreality in which the patristic and mediæval theologians involved the person of Christ may be found in Professor A. B. Bruce's great book on *The Humiliation of Christ*,[3] and in Canon Charles Gore's two admirable volumes on *The Incarnation*,[4] from which I have

[1] John Damascene, *De Fide Orthod.*, Lib. iii. chap. xxii.

[2] Peter Lombard, *Sentt.*, Book iii., Dist. vi. § 6.

[3] Prof. Alexander Balmain Bruce, *The Humiliation of Christ* (New York, Armstrongs, 1887).

[4] Canon Charles Gore, *The Incarnation of the Son of God*, Bampton Lectures, 1891 (New York, Scribners, 1891). *Dis-*

taken some illustrations after verifying them. Professor Bruce sums up the matter by saying: "The effect, though not the design, of theories of Christ's person has been to a large extent to obscure some of these elementary truths,— the unity of the person, or the reality of the humanity, or the divinity dwelling within the man, or the voluntariness and ethical value of the state of the humiliation. That is, certainties have been sacrificed for uncertainties, facts for hypotheses, faith for speculation."[1]

The manhood of Jesus vanishes.

Canon Gore, in his Bampton Lectures, adroitly uses the Jesuit theologian De Lugo as a man of straw through whom he may safely and vigorously attack the false conceptions of Christ's person which are still current, and to a considerable degree dominant, in dogmatic theology. He says that De Lugo depicts a Christ "who, if He was, as far as His body is concerned, in a condition of growth, was, as regards His soul and intellect, from the first moment and throughout His life in full enjoyment of the beatific vision. Externally a wayfarer, a *viator*, inwardly He was throughout a *comprehensor*, He had already attained. . . . It is denied that He can be strictly called

sertations on Subjects connected with the Incarnation (New York, Scribners, 1895). [1] *The Humiliation of Christ*, p. 192.

'the servant of God' even as man, in spite of the direct use of that expression in the Acts of the Apostles. He is spoken of at the institution of the Eucharist as offering sacrifice to His own Godhead."[1]

Modern examples of false Christology.

Canon Gore condemns this picture by De Lugo as in striking contradiction to that which the New Testament presents. But the point which I wish to make clear and distinct, is that, in spite of this contradiction, the picture has not been frankly and finally discarded in Christian theology. It still exercises an obscuring and perverting influence upon the vision of Christ. It still produces, by imitation, representations of Him in which definitions dominate facts, and formulas hide or obliterate realities. We do not need to go back to the seventeenth century, nor abroad to the Jesuits, for our examples. We may turn to Archdeacon Wilberforce's book on *The Incarnation*, and find him representing the body of Christ as miraculous in its freedom from sickness, its power over animals, its exemption from the necessity of death, and its inherent power of communicating life to others.[2] In regard to the mind of

[1] *The Incarnation*, p. 164.

[2] Archdeacon Wilberforce, *The Doctrine of the Incarnation* (New York, Young, 1885), pp. 60–65.

Christ, he says that "since it would be impious to suppose that our Lord had pretended an ignorance which He did not experience, we are led to the conclusion [astonishing conclusion!] that what He partook, as man, was not actual ignorance, but such deficiency in the means of arriving at truth as belongs to mankind."[1] We may turn to the *Dogmatic Theology* of Dr. W. G. T. Shedd and read: "Jesus Christ as a theanthropic person was constituted of a divine nature and a human nature. The divine nature had its own form of experience, like the mind in an ordinary human person; and the human nature had its own form of experience, like the body in a common man. The experiences of the divine nature were as diverse from those of the human nature as those of the human mind are from those of the human body. Yet there was but one person who was the subject-ego of both of these experiences. At the very time when Christ was conscious of weariness and thirst by the well of Samaria, He also was conscious that He was the eternal and only-begotten Son of God, the second person in the Trinity. This is proved by His words to the Samaritan woman: 'Whosoever drinketh of the water that I shall give

A double consciousness.

[1] *Ibid.*, p. 71.

him shall never thirst; but the water that I shall give him shall be in him a well of water springing up into everlasting life. I that speak unto thee am the Messiah.' The first-mentioned consciousness of fatigue and thirst came through the human nature in His person; the second-mentioned consciousness of omnipotence and supremacy came through the divine nature in His person. If He had not had a human nature, He could not have had the former consciousness; and if He had not had a divine nature, He could not have had the latter. Because He had both natures in one person, He could have both."[1] We may turn to Canon Liddon's magnificent work on *The Divinity of our Lord* and find him writing: "Christ's Manhood is not of Itself an individual being; It is not a seat and centre of personality; It has no conceivable existence apart from the act whereby the Eternal Word in becoming Incarnate called It into being and made It His Own. It is a vesture which He has folded around His person; It is an instrument through which He places Himself in contact with men and whereby He acts upon humanity."[2]

His manhood a vesture.

[1] W. G. T. Shedd, *Dogmatic Theology* (New York, Scribners, 1888), vol. ii., pp. 307, 308.

[2] H. P. Liddon, *The Divinity of our Lord and Saviour Jesus Christ*, Bampton Lectures, 1866 (London, Rivingtons, 11th edition, 1885), p. 262.

The human Christ is lost.

And so, if we accept this picture of Christ, the manhood of Jesus fades, retreats, grows dim and shadowy. It wavers like a veil. It dissolves like mist. It descends again mys terious and impenetrable, illusory and impersonal, to envelop Him whom we love and adore in its strange and unfamiliar folds. We grope after Him, but we can touch nothing but the hem of His mystic robe. We long for Him, but He approaches us, and comes into contact with us, only through an instrument. He is not what He seems. The Son of God behind that veil is beyond our reach. The Son of man, whom human eyes beheld and human hands touched, is not the real, living, veritable Saviour, but only the form, the garment, of an inscrutable life. And if, in our dire confusion, our reasoning faith still succeeds in holding fast to the Eternal Logos, our confiding faith is maimed and robbed by the loss of that true, near, personal, loving, sympathizing Jesus, who was born of a woman, suffered under Pontius Pilot, was crucified, dead, and buried. He is gone from us, as certainly as if the Pharisees had spoken truth when they said that His disciples came by night and stole Him away. The thing of which we are most in doubt, and about which we are least capable of any positive affirmation, is the humanity of Christ. We are left with a perfectly orthodox doctrine of two natures, but we no longer have a clear and simple gospel of One Person to preach to the doubting souls of men.[1]

II

The cry of the heart for a human Saviour.

But the heart of Christendom has never rested content with this distant, vague, nucertain view of the real manhood of our Lord. There has always been a protest against it. There has always been an effort to escape from it.

The worship of the Virgin Mary.

We can see a strange and indirect but indubitable evidence of this deep inward dissatisfaction, in the rise and growth of an impassioned devotion to the human mother of Jesus. The worship of the Virgin Mary was a reprisal for the obscuration of the humanity of her Son. In the thought of her true womanly tenderness and affection, her real and unquestionable sorrows, her simple and familiar joys, her intimate, genuine, unfailing sympathy with all that makes our mortal life a bitter, blessed reality to us, the souls of the lowly and the lonely found that peace and consolation

[1] See Appendix, note 34.

which they could no longer find in the contemplation of the distant Second Person of the Trinity through the telescope of theology. That which Jesus Himself was to John and Peter, to the household of Bethany, to the penitent publican, and to the woman which was a sinner, Mary became to the baffled and confused faith of a later age, — an approachable mediator of the divine mercy, a helper who could really understand and feel the need of those who cried for help, a warm and living image of the Eternal Sympathy in flesh and blood. In the light of mediæval dogmatics Mariolatry appears not without its justification. And for my part, I should not wish to be bound to the Christology of Peter Lombard and Thomas Aquinas, without finding the compensation which their followers found in personal devotion and confidential trust, flowing instinctively and irresistibly towards the blessed Virgin.

The search after Jesus.

But, after all, this was only a substitute for the real thing. It gave to faith the image of a lovely and adorable humanity in closest union with God; but it did not give back the old vision of the human life of God. And so through all the ages we see men turning, now in solitary thought, now in great companies, to seek that vision. The renaissance of Christian art, with its beautiful pictures of the infancy of Jesus, with its piercing and pathetic representations of the sufferings of Jesus, bears witness to the eagerness of that search. The revivals of Christian life, seen in such diverse yet cognate forms as the rise of the "Poor Men of Lyons" and the foundation of the "Brotherhood of St. Francis" are evidences of the same movement back to Christ. Peter Waldo outside of the Church, and Francis of Assisi within the Church, were awakened by the same vision of Jesus, "a man of sorrows and acquainted with grief," and were inspired by the same desire to make His real human life the pattern of all piety and the example of all goodness. The Reformation, which was at once and equally an intellectual and a spiritual protest against the arrogance of current theology and the coldness of religious life, supplies no better watchword to express its great motive than the saying of Erasmus: "I could wish that those frigid subtleties either were completely cut off, or were not the only things that the theologians held as certain, and that *the Christ pure and simple might be implanted deep within the minds of men.*"[1]

The spirit of the Reformation.

[1] Erasmus, quoted in Gore, *Dissertations*, etc., p. 180, Epistle 207.

Modern Biblical scholarship, with its splendid apparatus of linguistic and historical learning, proceeding in part, at first, from a sceptical impulse, has developed in our generation, either through the conversion of sceptics in the process of research, or through the awakening of believers to the necessities of their faith, into a reverent and eager quest for the historic Christ, the Jesus of the Gospels, the Lord of the primitive Church, that we may see Him as the first Christians saw Him, in the integrity of His person and the sincerity of His life, and receive from Him what they received,—a faith that dissolved doubts and an inspiration that conquered difficulties. Back to the New Testament of our Lord and Saviour Jesus Christ,—back to the facts that lie behind the definitions, back to the Person who embodies the truth, back to the record and reflection of that which the apostles "heard, and saw with their eyes, and looked upon, and their hands handled of the word of life,"—this, and this only, is the way that leads us within sight of

"Back to Christ!"

> "the heaven-drawn picture
> Of Christ, the living Word."

Now it is a marvellous thing, and one for which we can never be grateful enough, that

The Bible gives us a Kinsman-Redeemer.

when we come to the New Testament in this spirit, we find in it exactly what we need; not an abstract formula, not a collection of definitions, but the graphic reflection of a Person seen from a fourfold point of view, and the simple record of manifold human experience under the direct and dominant influence of that Person. And the one fact that emerges clear and triumphant from the reflection and the record, is that the writers of the New Testament never were in doubt of the human nature of Christ and never hesitated to make the most positive affirmations in regard to it.

The Christ of the Gospels.

The Christ of the Gospels is bone of our bone, flesh of our flesh, mind of our mind, heart of our heart. He is in subjection to His parents as a child. He grows to manhood. His character is unfolded and perfected by discipline. He labours for daily bread, and prays for Divine grace. He hungers, and thirsts, and sleeps, and rejoices, and weeps. He is anointed with the Spirit for His ministry. He is tempted. He is lonely and disappointed. He asks for information. He confesses ignorance. He interprets the facts of nature and life with a prophetic insight. But He makes no new disclosure of the secrets of omniscience. There is no hint nor indication that He is leading a double life, reigning consciously as God while He is suffering apparently as man. His personality is simple and indivisible. The glory of what He is and does, lies not only in its perfection, but in the hard conditions of its accomplishment. Superhuman in His origin, as the only-begotten Son of God; superhuman in His office and work, as the revealer of the Father and the redeemer of mankind; in His earthly existence the Christ of the Gospels enters without reserve and without deception into all the conditions and limitations which are necessary to give to the world, once and forever, the human life of God.[1]

The Christ of the Epistles.

When we turn to the Epistles to see how this view of Christ was affected by the recognition of His divine glory and power as one who had been raised to the right hand of God and made head over all things to the Church, two things strike us with tremendous force. First, the identity of His person was not lost, nor the continuity of His being broken: the exalted Christ is none other than "this same Jesus."[2] Second, the reality and absoluteness of His humiliation are emphasized as the ground and cause of His exaltation.

How vividly these two things come out, for

[1] See Appendix, note 35. [2] Acts i. 11.

St. Paul's view.

example, in the writings of St. Paul. It has been well said that "the Christ whom Paul had seen was the risen Christ, and the conception of Him in His glorified character is the one which rules his thoughts and forms the starting-point of his teaching."[1] Corresponding to this present glory, Paul assumes an eternally pre-existent glory of Christ as the image of the invisible God, the medium and end of creation.[2] Now it is of this Person, divinely glorious in the past as the One who is before all things and in whom all things consist,[3] divinely glorious in the present as the One who is far above every name that is named, not only in this world but in that which is to come,[4]— it is of this Person that Paul writes, in words so strong that they touch the very border of the impossible: "For our sakes, *He beggared Himself* that we through His beggary might be enriched."[5] And again: "He, existing in the form of God, did not consider an equal state with God a thing to be selfishly grasped and held, but *emptied Himself*, and took the form of a slave, being made in the likeness of man."[6] These powerful expressions, "self-

[1] Stevens, *The Pauline Theology*, p. 206.
[2] Col. i. 16. [3] Col. i. 17. [4] Eph. i. 21.
[5] 2 Cor. viii. 9. [6] Phil. ii. 6, 7.

beggary," "self-emptying," seem to be directly designed to break up the conventional moulds in which dogmatic theology has attempted to cast the truth and let it harden. They bring back a vital warmth and motion into the facts of the Incarnation. Once more it glows and flows. Once more we see that it is not a mere exhibition of being but a process of becoming. The idea of self-beggary mightily overflows the mere statement that a human nature was added and united to the divine nature; for that would have been no impoverishment but an enrichment.[1] The idea of self-emptying shatters the narrow dogma that the Son of God suffered no change in Himself when He became man. It was a change so absolute, so immense, that it can only be compared with the vicissitude from fulness to emptiness. He laid aside the existence-form of God, in order that He might take the existence-form of man. Whatever right He had to an equal state of glory with God, that right He did not cling to, but surrendered, in order that He might become a servant. And upon this real self-emptying there followed a real self-humiliation, wherein, being found in fashion as a man, He became obedient unto death, even the death

The Kenosis.

[1] See Appendix, note 36.

of the cross.[1] It was on account of this,—and bv "this" we must understand the entire actual operation of the self-denying, self-humbling, self-sacrificing mind of Christ,—it was for this reason, St. Paul declares, that "God highly exalted Him, and gave unto Him the name which is above every name."[2] And I know not how to interpret such language with any reality of intelligence, unless it means that the present glory of the Son of God is in some true sense the result of His having become man and so fulfilled the will of God.

The Epistle of Christ's brotherhood.

This view, which St. Paul condenses into a single pregnant "wherefore," is expanded in the Epistle to the Hebrews. The object of this Epistle is to show the superiority of the priesthood and sacrifice of Christ, which are substantial and enduring, to the priesthood and sacrifice of the old dispensation, which were shadowy and transient. But the method which the writer follows is not to deny, but to assert the verity of Christ's humanity. Without this He could not be the true priest nor offer the true sacrifice. "In all things it behoved Him to be made like unto His brethren."[3] "For we have not an high priest which cannot be touched

[1] Phil. ii. 8. [2] Phil. ii. 9. [3] Heb. ii. 17.

with the feeling of our infirmities: but was in all points tempted like as we are, yet without sin."[1] "Though He were a Son, yet learned He obedience by the things which He suffered, and being made perfect, He became the author of eternal salvation unto all them that obey Him"[2] This complete incarnation, this thorough trial under human conditions, this perfect discipline of obedience through suffering, was a humiliation. But it was in no sense a degradation. On the contrary, it was a crowning of Christ with glory and honour in order that He might taste death for every man. "For it became Him, for whom are all things, and by whom are all things, in bringing many sons to glory, to make the captain of their salvation perfect through suffering."[3] If the Epistle to the Hebrews teaches anything, it certainly teaches this. The humanity of Jesus was not the veiling but the unveiling of the divine glory. The limitations, temptations, and sufferings of manhood were the conditions under which alone Christ could accomplish the greatest work of the Deity, — the redemption of a sinful race. The seat of the divine revelation and the centre of the divine atonement was and is the human life of God.

The glory of condescension.

[1] Heb. iv. 15. [2] Heb. v. 8, 9. [3] Heb. ii. 9, 10.

III

A summary of conclusions.

Here, then, we may pause for a moment and try to sum up the conclusions to which the New Testament leads us in regard to the person of Christ.

Current theology at fault.

I am sincerely anxious not to be misunderstood. On the one hand, I would not conceal for a moment my conviction that current theology has failed, very often and very largely, to do justice to the meaning of the Incarnation on the human side, and that we *must* go back to the image of Jesus Christ as it is reflected in the Gospels to purify, and refresh, and simplify our faith. We should not suffer any reverence for ancient definitions of doctrine, however well founded, nor any fear of incurring reproach and mistrust as innovators, to deter us from that necessary and loyal return to the reality of the Person in whom our creed centres and on whom it rests. To find Jesus anew, to see Him again, as if for the first time, in the wondrous glory of His humility, is the secret of the revival of Christianity in every age. This is not innovation; it is renovation.

Human theories not to be insisted upon.

On the other hand, we have no right and we ought to have no inclination to insist exclusively upon any particular theory as the only possible explanation of the facts of the Incarnation. Every earnest and thoughtful man must feel that these facts are so deep and mysterious that the plummet of human reason cannot sound their ultimate recesses. With all our thinking upon this subject, there must ever mingle a consciousness of insufficiency and a confession of ignorance. But with this confession of ignorance there must go also a clear recognition of those portions of the truth which are unques tionably revealed in the New Testament. Three things are there made plain to faith.

Three vital points.

1. God is not such a being, absolute, immutable, and impassible, that the Divine Logos cannot descend by a free act of self-determining love into the lower estate of human existence, and humble Himself to the conditions of manhood without losing His personal identity.[1]

2. The essence of the Gospel is its declaration of the fact that this act of condescension, of self-humiliation, actually has been performed, and that Jesus Christ is the eternal Son of God who has taken upon Him the existence-form of a servant, and lived a truly human life, and been obedient even unto death, in order to reveal to the world the saving love of God.

[1] See Appendix, note 37.

3. The distinctive attributes of personality in Christ (self-consciousness and self-determination) are not dual, as of two persons, the one divine and the other human, co-existing side by side in a double life, but individual, and manifested as the life of one person. That person is the Son of God, who laid aside the glory which He had with the Father, and emptied Himself, and so became the Son of man; and on account of this humiliation God hath highly exalted Him and crowned Him with glory and honour as the God-man forever.

These points must be defended.

These are the points which are vital to the reality of the Gospel of the Incarnation. All theories which make these points clear, safeguard the truth in its integrity and in its reconciling power. The question of the method of the divine humiliation and the human exaltation of Christ, lies beyond these points. It is not necessary to insist upon any particular form of its solution. Indeed, it may well be that the profundity of the question, the inherent mystery of the facts of life and personality with which it deals, and the limitations of human thought and language, preclude the possibility of a complete and final answer at present. It must be frankly acknowledged that none of the solutions which have been propounded hitherto are free from serious perplexities. But it must be recognized with equal frankness that the theories which have been put forward in modern times, with new earnestness and power, by men of unquestionable loyalty to the Christianity of the New Testament, who have sought to find a clear and positive meaning for the great word *Kenosis*, which St. Paul uses to describe the self-emptying of Christ in the Incarnation, — theories which have been stigmatized as *kenotic*, as if the name were enough to mark them as unorthodox, — are so far from being heretical that they have the rare merit of conserving and emphasizing a truth of surpassing value, undoubtedly taught in the Bible, and too much neglected, if not practically denied, during many centuries of theological speculation. It may be, as Julius Müller held, that the distinctive attributes of personality are, abstractly considered, identical in God and man, so that, by the divine self-limitation in the Incarnation, they are actually unified, like two circles which have a common centre.[1] It may be, as Dr. Fairbairn holds that the Son of God, being the eternal repre-

Various methods of safe-guarding them.

[1] For this statement of Müller's view, which he gave in his lectures, I am indebted to Dr. George P. Fisher, who was one of his hearers.

sentative of the filial relationship within the Godhead, the symbol of the created within the uncreated, needed but to surrender the form and status of the uncreated Son in order to assume, by the same act, the form and status which man as the created Son was intended to realize.[1] It may be, as Godet holds, that the Incarnation was by deprivation, and that the Eternal Word renounced His divine mode of being, and entered into life, without omnisci ence, omnipresence, or omnipotence, as an un conscious babe.[2] It matters little in what form of words we try to express the transcendent truth. But it matters much, it is supremely important for the integrity of our Gospel and for its influence upon the heart of this doubting age, that we should hold fast to the fact that the life of Jesus of Nazareth is the human life of God.

The new study of Christ.

The time is at hand when this simple and profound view of Christ, which beholds in Him the God-man in whom Deity is self-limited and humbled in order that humanity may be divinely exalted and perfected, must break through the clouds which have obscured it, and become the leading light of religion and theol-

[1] *The Place of Christ in Modern Theology*, p. 476.
[2] Godet, *Commentary on John* i. 14.

ogy. The life of Christ needs to be restudied and rewritten under this luminous guidance, in absolute and unhesitating loyalty to the facts as they lie before our eyes in the Gospels.[1] The doctrine of Christ's person needs to be reconstructed and restated in this light. It must include, as the creed of Chalcedon included, not only the truth of a Homoöusia — a sameness of nature and experience — with God, which the past has vindicated; but also the equal truth of a Homoöusia with man, which the future is to unfold as the universality of Christ's manhood is exhibited through His progressive triumphs among all the races of men and all the modes of human life. The humanity of the incarnate Christ must stand out as clear, as pos-

[1] "No *action* of our Saviour's earthly life, from Bethlehem to Calvary, exhibits divinity. He appears first as a helpless babe in the manger. He is subject to His parents. As the child grows, He waxes strong in spirit and increases in wisdom. Such an increase in wisdom implies increase in knowledge, and less knowledge or greater ignorance to-day than to-morrow. Omniscience could not have been exercised by the Jesus who was growing in wisdom. If any say here, as we usually do, that the humanity grew but the divinity was omniscient, let us ask if there were two persons in Jesus. This Nestorianism is practically the creed of the present day with the Reformed Churches. They have gone over to a virtual duplication of the person of Christ." — Howard Crosby, *The True Humanity of Christ* (New York, Randolph, 1880).

itive, as indubitable, as His Deity. Nay, more, it must stand where the New Testament puts it, in the foreground of faith. For it is only in this humanity that we can truly find the Son of God who loved us and gave Himself for us.

The old definitions inadequate.

How urgent and pressing are the needs of our own age which call us to this work! How far behind us, how effete and inadequate, are the terms and illustrations which were used in former ages to express the results of human thought in regard to the person of Christ! Recall, for instance, that fine similitude of the heated sword which the Lutheran theologians borrowed from the Fathers to explain the union of the divine with the human in Christ! To them it was satisfactory because they regarded heat as one substance and iron as another substance. In their view the divine nature penetrated and pervaded the human nature as the caloric fluid was supposed to permeate a mass of metal. But in our world the caloric fluid does not exist. Heat is not a substance, but a mode of motion in substances. In the light of modern science the old similitude fades into a meaningless comparison of things which cannot be compared.

We cannot accept the scholastic terminology of "natures" and "subsistences" in the final and absolute sense in which it was once employed. The philosophy of realism, which ascribed an objective existence to universals apart from individuals, is not the philosophy of to-day. Its language is not only foreign, but dead. The philosophy of being and not-being has opened to receive the philosophy of becoming; and, in so doing, it has been utterly transformed.

Life is the regnant idea.

Life is now the regnant idea; personality its utmost expression. It is in the facts of life, its secret potencies, its mysterious limitations in germ and seed, its magnificent unfoldings in the process of development that we must seek our comparisons for the Incarnation. And the very search will bring us face to face with the conviction that life in all its manifestations transcends analysis without ceasing to be the object of knowledge.

We know life but cannot define it.

In the living world the boundaries of imagination are not coterminous with the limits of apprehension. We know many facts and forms of life whose modes of becoming we cannot imagine. It is just as impossible for us to conceive how the life of the oak, root and trunk and branch and leaf, form and colour and massive strength, is all folded in the tiny, colourless, unshaped seed, as it is to conceive how the life of God is embodied in the man Christ Jesus. But the difficulty of conceiving the manner of this infolding, this embodiment, does not destroy for us the reality of the life. Indeed, if we could explain it entirely, if we could trace it perfectly as in a diagram, if we could observe it completely, as in one of those beautiful models of flowers which a skilful artist[1] has recently made to illustrate his lectures on botany, we should know that it was not life, but only a picture of it. The picture is useful, but it is not vital. The metaphor has its value, but it falls far short of the truth. *Self-beggary* and *self-emptying* are but "words thrown out towards" an unimaginable but not unreasonable manifestation of the Divine Love as life. The reality to which they point us is the Son of God descending to live under all the conditions and limitations of energy and consciousness which are proper to the Son of man: the Word made flesh and dwelling among us.

IV

The importance of this view for the present age.

It would be hard to overestimate the significance of this view for the present age, and the importance of setting it forth as a living truth

[1] William Hamilton Gibson.

in the language of to-day. It is the only view which gives us any ground of reality for our faith in the kinship of man with God. If the Son of God, who is the image of the Father, by laying aside the outward prerogatives of His divine mode of existence, actually becomes human, then, and only then, the divine image in which man was created is no mere figure of speech, but a substantial likeness of spiritual being.[1] There is a true fellowship between our souls and our Father in heaven. Virtue is not a vain dream, but a definite striving towards His perfection. Revelation is not a deception, but a message from Him who knows all to those who know only a part. Prayer is not an empty form, but a real communion.

> "Speak to Him, thou, for He hears, and Spirit with Spirit can meet:
> Closer is He than breathing, and nearer than hands and feet."[2]

The kinship of man to God.

This view of the spiritual relation of man to God cannot possibly have any foundation in fact, deep enough and strong enough to withstand the sweeping floods of scepticism, unless it builds upon the rock of a veritable Incarnation. The discoveries of modern science, enlarging enormously our conceptions of the

[1] See Appendix, note 38. [2] Tennyson, *The Higher Pantheism.*

physical universe, have not only put man (as we said in the first lecture) in a position to receive a larger and loftier vision of the glory of God, but they have made such a vision indispensable. And they have emphasized, with overwhelming force, the form in which that vision must come in order to meet our needs and strengthen faith for its immense task. If we are not to be utterly belittled and crushed by the contemplation of the vast mass of matter and the tremendous play of force by which we are surrounded; if we are still to hold that the vital is greater than the mechanical, the moral than the material, the spiritual than the physical; if we are to maintain the old position of all noble and self-revering thought, that "man is greater than the universe,"—there is nothing that can so profoundly confirm and establish us, there is nothing that can so surely protect and save us from "the distorting influences of our own discoveries," as the revelation of the Supreme Being in an unmistakably vital, moral, spiritual, and human form.

The true view of God. Such a revelation at once rectifies, purifies, and elevates our view of God Himself. For if the Son of God can surrender omnipresence, omniscience, and omnipotence without destroying His personal identity, then the central essence of the Deity is neither infinite wisdom nor infinite power, but perfect holiness and perfect goodness. And so from the very lowest valley of humiliation we catch clear sight of the very loftiest summit of theology, the serene and shining truth that God is Love.

The supreme pattern of love.

In the light of this truth we behold also the highest perfection of man and the path which leads to it. Love is the fulfilling of the law, and the supreme pattern of love is the example of Christ. And whether we look at it from the divine side as the supreme self-sacrifice of God, or from the human side as the complete obedience of man, everything depends upon the genuineness and sincerity of this example. Unless the Son of God truly became man, the Incarnation cannot be, as Bishop Westcott calls it, "a revelation of human duties." What strength could we draw from His victory over temptation if He was not exposed as we are to the assaults of evil?[1] What consolation could we draw from His patience if He was not a man of sorrows and acquainted with grief? "Jesus Christ," says one of the greatest of French theologians, "is not the Son of God hidden in the Son of man retaining all the attributes of Divinity in a latent state. This

[1] See Appendix, note 39.

would be to admit an irreducible duality which would make the unity of His person vanish and withdraw Him from the normal conditions of human life. His obedience would become illusory, and His example would be without application to our race. No, when the Word became flesh, He humbled Himself, He put off His glory, being rich He made Himself poor, and became as one of us, only without sin, that He might pass through the moral conflict with all the risks of freedom."[1] When we see Him thus, we know what it means to follow Him and to be like Him.

The value of the atonement.

Finally, the whole value of the Atonement, in its reconciling influence on the heart of man, in its exhibition of the heart of God, depends upon the actuality of the Incarnation. If He who died on Calvary was a mere theophany, like the angel of Jehovah who appeared to Abraham, then His death was merely a dramatic spectacle. The body of Jesus was broken, but God was not touched. But if the Father truly spared not His own Son, but delivered Him up for us all, then the Father also suffered by sympathy, making an invisible sacrifice, an infinite surrender of love for our sakes.

God suffers with and for us.

[1] De Pressensé, *Jésus-Christ* (Paris, 1865), Book I., chap. v., p. 254.

Then the Son also suffered, making a visible sacrifice, and pouring out His soul unto death to redeem us from the fear of death and the power of sin. And this becomes real to our faith and potent upon our souls only when we see the human life of God, agonizing in the garden, tortured in the judgment-hall, and expiring upon the cross. Then we can say

> "Oh Love Divine! that stooped to share
> Our sharpest pang, our bitterest tear."

Doubts dissolve in the thought of God's sympathy.

Then we can look up to a God who is not impassible, as the speculations of men have falsely represented Him, but passible, and therefore full of infinite capacities of pure sorrow and saving sympathy.[1] Then the dumb and sullen resentment which rises in noble minds at the thought of a Universe in which there is so much helpless pain and hopeless grief, created by an immovable Being who has never felt and can never feel either pain or grief, — that sense of moral repulsion from the idea of an unsuffering and unsympathetic Creator which is, and always has been, the deepest, darkest spring of doubt, fades away, and we behold a God who became human in order that He might bear, though innocent and undeserving, all our pains and all our griefs.

[1] See Appendix, note 40.

The finding of the human Christ.

Thus we stand before our doubting age, as David stood before the disillusioned, downcast, despondent Hebrew king, in Robert Browning's splendid poem of "Saul." The word, sought in vain among the glories of nature, among the joys of human intercourse, the word of faith and hope and love and life, comes to us, leaps upon us, flashes through us.

"See the King — I would help him, but cannot, the wishes fall through.
Could I wrestle to raise him from sorrow, grow poor to enrich,
To fill up his life, starve my own out, I would — knowing which,
I know that my service is perfect. Oh, speak through me now!
Would I suffer for him that I love? So wouldst Thou — so wilt Thou!
So shall crown Thee the topmost, ineffablest, uttermost crown —
And Thy love fill infinitude wholly, nor leave up nor down
One spot for the creature to stand in! It is by no breath,
Turn of eye, wave of hand, that salvation joins issue with death!
As Thy Love is discovered almighty, almighty be proved
Thy power, that exists with and for it, of being beloved!
He who did most, shall bear most; the strongest shall stand the most weak.

'Tis the weakness in strength, that I cry for! my flesh, that I seek
In the Godhead! I seek and I find it. O Saul, it shall be
A Face like my face that receives thee; a Man like to me,
Thou shalt love and be loved by, forever; a Hand like this hand
Shall throw open the gates of new life to thee! See the Christ stand!"

V

THE SOURCE OF AUTHORITY IN THE KINGDOM OF HEAVEN

"But Thee, but Thee, O sovereign Seer of time,
But Thee, O poets' Poet, Wisdom's Tongue,
But Thee, O man's best Man, O love's best Love,
O perfect life in perfect labour writ,
O all men's Comrade, Servant, King, or Priest, —
What *if* or *yet*, what mole, what flaw, what lapse,
What least defect or shadow of defect,
What rumour, tattled by an enemy,
Of inference loose, what lack of grace
Even in torture's grasp, or sleep's, or death's,
Oh, what amiss may I forgive in Thee,
Jesus, good Paragon, thou Crystal Christ?"

— SIDNEY LANIER, *The Crystal*.

V

THE SOURCE OF AUTHORITY IN THE KINGDOM OF HEAVEN

The new commandment.

PREACH CHRIST, is the apostolic watchword that rings to-day, with all the force and charm of a new commandment, through the heart of a Church, which has felt, more deeply than it has yet confessed, the age-pervading chill of a winter of doubt and discontent. The very entrance of that mystic and reviving word has already brought a glow of enthusiasm into the Christian life, and caused new blossoms of hope and love, manifold and beautiful activities of help and healing, to appear in the earth. It seems as if some fresh and secret tide of vitality were flowing through the veins of Christendom, and breaking everywhere towards the light in deeds of charity and enterprises of mercy. Hospitals, asylums, red cross societies, rescue missions, salvation armies, spring into existence as if by magic. Never has there been a time when Christian men have tried to

The new har ty.

do so much for their fellow-men in the name and for the sake of Christ. Never has there been a time when they have recognized so clearly and fully that there was so much yet to be done. It is an age of secular doubt, as many other ages have been. But it is also an age of Christian beneficence, as hardly any other age has been. And this beneficence is not self-satisfied and complacent. It is self-reproachful, and, in its best expressions, nobly discontented with all that has been accomplished hitherto. It seeks, not always wisely, but with splendid eagerness, for plans which shall lead beyond the relief, to the prevention of human suffering. It aims to bring about not only the immediate mitigation, but also the ultimate abolition, of war. It demands that charity shall be translated into the terms of national, as well as of individual life. It will not be satisfied until in some real and palpable sense the kingdom of this world is become the kingdom of our Lord and of His Christ.[1]

Christ is the ountain.

Now this renewal, this splendid expansion of Christian activities, evident by many signs to all thoughtful observers, depends for its power and permanence upon the setting forth of Christ, vividly, personally, practically, as the

[1] Rev. xi. 15.

pattern of all virtue and the Prince of Peace among men. The sense of absolute confidence in Him as the perfect example of goodness, and of thorough loyalty to Him as the Master of noble life, is the hidden reservoir of moral force. The organized charities of Christendom are the distributing system. Not more instant and more complete would be the water-famine on Manhattan Island if the great dam among the Croton hills were broken and all the lakes and streams dried up, than the drought that would fall upon the beneficence of the world if there were a sudden break in the reservoir of love and loyalty in Christian hearts to their moral Master, or a stoppage of the myriad and multiform feeders which keep it full by preaching Christ.

The peril of practical Christianity

But in all this renewal and expansion of what is well and proudly called practical Christianity, there is, if I mistake not, a danger, or at least a serious possibility, of loss. The life of man is not only practical, it is also intellectual. His relations to his fellow-men are important, but his relation to truth is no less important. He cannot help acting; neither can he help thinking. When his thinking is divorced from his acting, when he has one standard for truth and a different standard for conduct, he is like a house divided against itself. If the Christianity of to-day, by dwelling exclusively or too much on the ethical side of the Gospel as a beautiful and beneficent rule of conduct illustrated by a perfect Example, tends to ignore the intellectual necessities of man and fails to realize that it has a message to deliver in the realm of truth as well as in the realm of righteousness, it will not and it cannot meet the deepest wants of the present age. Indeed, it may even aggravate those wants and make them more painful. It may seem to give assent, by silence, to the desperate assumption of scepticism that the unseen world is unknown and unknowable, even to the most perfect of men. It may foster the sad feeling that the reality of religion is beyond our reach and that we must content ourselves with the convenient dreams of virtue. It may preach, in effect, a Christ whose character and conduct are to be accepted as infallible, but whose thoughts and convictions in regard to God and the soul and the future life are mere fallacies and illusions.

What does it mean to preach Christ?

Preach Christ, if it is to be a true watchword for our ministry to the present age, must be cleared and vivified and expanded in our consciousness. We must know what we mean by it, and we must try to know what we ought to mean. We must ask ourselves again and again whether the thing that we do mean is always quite, or even approximately, the thing that we ought to mean when we use this precious and powerful phrase. It was commonly employed, say fifty years ago, to describe by way of distinction a presentation of Jesus which dwelt chiefly or entirely upon His death as the vicarious sacrifice for sin. It is frequently employed now as if it meant little or nothing more than the graphic description of Christ's life and actions as the supreme type of virtue and love. But surely to preach Christ exclusively in either of these ways is to divide Him. It is not enough to have a Christocentric theology. It is not enough to have a Christocentric morality. We must not only put Him at the centre; but we must also draw the circumference so that it shall embrace the whole of human life.

A gospel for the whole circle of human life.

If Christ is the Lamb of God that taketh away the sin of the world,[1] He is also the true Light which lighteth every man that cometh into the world.[2] If He is the fulfilment of all dim prophecies of good, He is also the head and source of a new unfolding of spiritual vision. If He is the way and the life, He is also the truth.[3] If He is immortal love, regenerating

[1] St. John i. 29. [2] St. John i. 9. [3] St. John xiv. 6.

the affections, He is also immortal wisdom reorganizing the thoughts, and immortal power strengthening the wills, of men. If His heart is to be the norm of our feeling, His mind is to be the norm of our thinking. If He is the herald and founder of a new and celestial dominion upon earth, He is also the source of authority in the kingdom of heaven.

I

The kingdom of heaven the keynote of Christ's teaching.

The idea of the kingdom of heaven, as an actual reign of God over living men, in which all ancient anticipations of good are accomplished and a new state of virtue and blessedness is established on earth, was foremost and dominant in the teaching of Jesus.[1] It was the keynote of His ministry. Everything that He said, everything that He did, was in harmony with this master thought.

It is passing strange to see how often and how utterly this keynote has been changed in the variations which men have woven about the

[1] The word "kingdom" is used in the Gospels more than a hundred times to express the new condition of human life which Christ came to announce and establish. In St. Matthew's Gospel the favourite phrase is "the kingdom of heaven." St. Mark and St. Luke use "the kingdom of God."

False interpretations.

original theme of Christianity; and how far we are, even yet, from hearing it clearly, and sounding it with dominant fulness, in the music of religion. At times the kingdom of heaven has been identified with the visible church as an outward embodiment of power in the world. And surely this interpretation is far enough away from the thought of Christ, who taught expressly that the kingdom was invisible and inward. At other times men have removed their conception from the present to the future, and looked for its realization in the life of the redeemed after death, or in the second coming of Christ to reign in millennial glory. And surely this interpretation is equally remote from Christ's teaching, at the very outset of His ministry and all through its course, that the kingdom of heaven was at hand, that it had already come near to man, and was lying all around them, close to them, pressing upon them from every side so that many were already entering into it and dwelling within it.[1]

The idea almost lost.

The unreality and incompleteness of these two opposite interpretations of the kingdom produced their natural results. The idea fell out of its true place in Christian thought. It became obscure, subordinate, and was finally

[1] See Appendix, note 41.

almost obliterated. No further illustration of this statement is necessary than that which may be obtained by consulting one of the most popular aids to the study of the Bible: Talbot's *Analysis*, revised by the Rev. Nathaniel West, and again revised by the Rev. Dr. Roswell D. Hitchcock, and set forth under the title of *A Complete Analysis of the Holy Bible; or, the Whole Bible arranged in Subjects.*[1] In the index to this work there is but one solitary reference to the kingdom of God. When we turn to look at it, we find eleven verses, under the heading of "The Millennium; the Growth of the Kingdom of God." The kingdom of heaven is dismissed with a general reference to the Parables. To any one who is really familiar with his New Testament, the insufficiency of such a treatment of one of its controlling ideas must appear evident and surprising.

The idea begins to be restored.

But it may be said that in very recent times there has been an intense revival of interest in this idea and an immense amount of good work done in the study and explication of it. This is true and it should be gratefully recognized. Such books as those which Dr. James S. Candlish and Professor A. B. Bruce have written

[1] Wilmore's *New Analytical Reference Bible* (New York, 1891).

upon "The Kingdom of God," are most valuable gifts to Christian literature.[1] And yet I will frankly confess that these books, and others like them, seem to me rather to point the way than to reach the goal. The fulness of the conception of the kingdom of heaven is not yet restored in current theology. Its regnancy in all spheres of human life is not yet completely rounded. There is still a great deal of work to be done in this direction by the Christian thinker and the Christian preacher. The vision of the kingdom is obscured, the proclamation of the kingdom is weakened, because it is still presented too exclusively as a kingdom of grace, and not with equal emphasis as a kingdom of truth: it is set up too partially as a standard for the character and conduct of men, and not with equal clearness as a standard for their thoughts and convictions.

It must be studied in all four Gospels.

One reason of this one-sidedness, it seems to me, lies in the fact that we have hitherto been looking almost entirely to the first three Gospels as the source of our knowledge of the true

[1] *The Kingdom of God, Biblically and Historically Considered*, James S. Candlish (Edinburgh, Clarks, 1884). *The Kingdom of God, or Christ's Teaching according to the Synoptical Gospels*, Alexander Balmain Bruce (New York, Scribners, 1889).

N

meaning of the kingdom of heaven. But the Fourth Gospel, if indeed it be, as the best modern scholars say it is, "the most faithful image and memorial of Jesus that any man could produce," must be no less important, no less significant in the light which it throws upon this controlling idea of His mind. And when we turn to study it with this aim in view, we find at once that it gives us what we need. It completes and rounds out the record of the three other Gospels. It answers the questions which they suggest. It keeps the promises which they seem to make to our faith. And it is only when we take the fourfold narrative in its entirety that we begin to catch sight of the satisfying and convincing fulness of the idea of the kingdom of heaven.

The kingdom in St. John.

This idea underlies the whole Gospel according to St. John. It is no less fundamental, no less necessary here than it is in the Synoptic Gospels. It is presented in different forms, because the type of the writer's mind and the purpose of his book are different. But it is the same idea. And this presentation of it is essential to its completeness.

In the Synoptics we have the conditions of entrance into the kingdom, a child-like spirit,[1]

[1] St. Matt. xviii. 3.

Compared with the Synoptics.

faith,[1] repentance,[2] and obedience.[3] In St. John we have the spiritual birth by which alone those conditions are made possible.[4] In the Synoptics we have the laws of the kingdom.[5] In St. John we have the new life in which alone those laws can be fulfilled.[6] In the Synoptics we have the parables and pictures of the kingdom.[7] In St. John we have the inmost sense of those parables, spoken directly to the soul, in words of which Christ Himself says "they are spirit, and they are life"[8] In the Synoptics we have the new order of human society in the imitation by the disciples of Christ's obedience to the will of God.[9] In St. John we have the organizing principle of that new order in Christ's revelation of Himself to the disciples as the way, the truth, and the life.[10] In the Synoptics we have the supremacy of Christ's example over men's hearts. In St. John we have the supremacy of Christ's teachings over men's minds.

Of course, I do not mean to say that either

1 St. Matt. ix. 22; St. Mark x. 52.

2 St. Luke xiii. 3.

3 St. Matt. v. 20.

4 St. John iii. 5.

5 The Sermon on the Mount.

6 St. John vi. 22–65.

7 St. Matt. xiii., xxi., xxv.; St. Luke xiii., xvii., xix., etc.

8 St. John vi. 63; viii. 12–51.

9 St. Matt. xii. 50.

10 St. John xiv. 6.

Both views necessary.

of these aspects of the kingdom is confined exclusively to the source in which it is most fully and clearly exhibited.[1] But this is what I mean. The Synoptics give us the first and simplest description of the nature of the kingdom. St. John gives us the fullest and clearest revelation of the mind of the King. We cannot understand the former without the latter. We cannot enter into the full meaning of the initial proclamation of Jesus, when He walked beside the Sea of Galilee crying "The kingdom of heaven has come near,"[2] unless we go on with Him to the judgment-hall, and hear Him give His final answer to Pilate: "Thou sayest that I am a King; to this end have I been born, and to this end am I come into the world, that I should bear witness unto the truth; every one that is of the truth heareth my voice."[3]

When we stand at this point, when we accept this declaration as the key to unlock and open the inmost meaning of the manifestation of the Father in the human life of the Son, we

[1] See Bruce, *The Kingdom of God*, p. 185, on the personal claim of Christ in the Synoptics. See R. F. Horton, *The Teaching of Jesus* (New York, 1896), pp. 219–233, on relation between Synoptic doctrine of the kingdom and Johannine doctrine of eternal life.

[2] St. Matt. iv. 17.

[3] St. John xviii. 37.

begin to apprehend the inexhaustible scope and significance of our call to preach Christ to an age of doubt. It is a gospel not only for the affections, but also for the intellect. It takes up His words as well as His works and makes them vital in the lives of men. It conceives and proclaims the kingdom of heaven as something more than "the reign of divine love exercised by God in His grace over human hearts believing in His love and constrained thereby to yield Him grateful affection and devoted service"[1] It is also the reign of divine truth exercised through a faithful witness over the minds of men who submit to His guidance and are led by Him into inward peace and unity of thought.[2] And the source of authority in this kingdom of heaven, which is equally a realm of truth and a realm of grace, is Jesus the Christ, whose doctrine, as well as His example, is ultimate and supreme.

The kingdom of trutl as well as o grace.

II

Let us observe in passing that we have precisely the same basis to rest upon in our preaching of the doctrine of Jesus as in our preaching of His character and life. If historical criticism

The King as a teacher.

[1] Bruce, *The Kingdom of God,* p. 46.

[2] See Appendix, note 42.

gives us good reason to believe, as all candid inquirers now admit, that the four Gospels contain a veritable picture of an actual personage who once lived on earth, there is equally good reason to believe that they have preserved for us a trustworthy account of His teaching in its substance and spirit. If we can justly claim that His character is so perfect and transcendent that no man of that age, however gifted or learned, and least of all such men as the writers of the New Testament, could possibly have invented it; we can make the same claim, with equal justice, for the body of doctrine which is attributed to Christ. In its coherence, its clarity, its sublimity, and its universality it altogether surpasses the mental abilities and the religious insight of the writers of the four Gospels. Indeed, it is frankly confessed that the disciples of Jesus were so far from being able to invent His doctrine, that they actually misunderstood and misinterpreted many of its truths when they first heard them. It was contrary to their prejudices and expectations. They did not put it into His mouth. He revealed it to their minds. Their faith in it rested upon His personal authority. And it was only as they kept company with Him and followed Him, receiving His word into

The doctrine of Christ.

their souls and translating it into their lives, that it became to them luminous and satisfying and convincing.

An objective reality.

We are entitled, or rather we are compelled, to regard the teaching of Jesus as an objective fact just as much as His life and character.[1] The record of it bears on its face the overwhelming evidence of verity. All the results of literary criticism are squarely against the supposition that such a doctrine as that which is presented to us under His name in the four Gospels, could ever have been pieced together out of the thoughts and imaginations of widely separated and divergent minds, and attributed to an unknown and perhaps mythical Master. It is not a mosaic; it is a living unity. It is not a creation of faith; it is the creator of faith. The hypothesis that four men agreed, or happened, to gather together out of the Hebrew prophets, and the heathen philosophers, and the mysterious and inexplicable inner consciousness of the new-born Christian churches, certain beautiful ideas in regard to God and the soul and the future life, and ascribe them to Jesus, utterly breaks down at the touch of reality. The central, unifying, formative quality of the teaching of Christ is the one thing that

[1] See Appendix, note 43.

is most evident in the record. It is emphasized by all the phenomena of growth, of vital development, of deepening power, which may be traced from the sermon in the synagogue at Nazareth to the discourse in the upper room at Jerusalem. It shines out unmistakably through all the living variety of impressions which it made upon various minds, and through all the consequent many-sidedness of the report which is given of it. Not more certainly did the character of Christ inspire and unite the lives of His followers than His doctrine illuminated and controlled their beliefs. The only view which meets the facts is that Jesus really lived, and really taught, thus and so, as He is presented to us in the Gospels.

The form of 'he record.

This brings us at once to the most important feature in the record of His teaching. It is not given to us in the form of an abstract system, a treatise on theology, or a summary of doctrine, written down by the hand of Jesus. He Himself made no record of His words. Only once do we see Him writing, —in the beautiful episode which a later tradition has added to the eighth chapter of St. John's Gospel. Historical or not, the incident is profoundly suggestive. For Jesus wrote not with a pen upon enduring parchment, nor with a stylus upon imperishable brass·

> "He stooped
> And wrote upon *the unrecording ground.*"[1]

He would not leave even a single line of manuscript where His followers could preserve it with literal reverence and worship it as a sacred relic. He chose to inscribe His teaching upon no other leaves than those which are folded within the human soul. He chose to trust His words to the faithful keeping of memory and love; and He said of them, with sublime confidence, that they should never pass away.[2] He chose that the truth which He declared and the life which He lived should never be divided, but that they should go down together through the ages.[3]

Inseparable from His character.

And this is precisely what has come to pass. The Church in past ages has often been inclined to abstract the doctrines of Christianity concerning the person and work of Christ from their union with His human life, and to condense them into a purely formal system of dogma for the intellect. The Church in the present age shows at least a tendency to separate the image

[1] Katrina Trask, "A Night and Morning in Jerusalem" (*Harper's Magazine*, April, 1896).

[2] St. Mark xiii. 31. [2] See Appendix, note 44.

of Jesus from the truths which He taught, and hold Him up to men merely as an ideal of holiness and goodness. But the one barrier that stands firm against both these false tendencies is the marvellous narrative of the Gospels, in which the life and the doctrine of Christ are woven together, one and inseparable, now and forever.

Words and life interpret each other.

How can we understand His grace, unless we accept His truth? How can we appreciate His truth, unless we receive His grace? At every step, His action is interpreted and explained by His words.[1] He trusts in Providence, and He commands His disciples to trust, not merely because submissive confidence is a beautiful and happy thing, but because He knows and declares that God is really a Father, worthy to be trusted.[2] He prays, secretly and openly; secretly because He is sure that God hears Him always, and openly because He would fain give this assurance to others.[3] He seeks the sinful and the lost, not merely because such a ministry is lovely and gracious, but because He knows and declares that it is the will of God, and that there is more joy in heaven over one sinner that repenteth than over ninety-and-nine just

[1] See Appendix, note 45.

[2] St. Matt. vi. 25–30.

[3] St. John xi. 41, 42.

men that need no repentance.[1] He cares for the bodies of men and He relieves their wants, but He cares infinitely more for their souls and He teaches them to care more, because He knows and declares that the soul is immortal and more precious than all that this world can give.[2] He moves willingly and obediently to the cross, not because it is inevitable, not because resignation is the crown of virtue, but because He knows and declares that this is the sacrifice appointed for Him as the Christ, the laying down of His life as a ransom for many, the lifting up by which He is to draw all men unto Himself.[3] He goes down into death with unshaken courage, not because it is a fine thing to be brave, but because He knows and declares that He is returning to the Father and that He will bring those who love Him to be with Him where He is forever.[4]

The doctrine of Christ the basis of His conduct.

Now these are declarations of great truths. If we deny them, if we make them uncertain, the life which was built upon them has no meaning, no substance, no power in it. It becomes a splendid illusion, a heroic mistake.

[1] St. Luke xv. 7.
[2] St. John vi. 27; St. Mark viii. 36, 37.
[3] St. Mark ix 12; St. Matt. xx. 28; St. John xii. 32.
[4] St. John xiv. 1–3.

But if we accept them, then, and only then, that life becomes the rock of our confidence, the substance of things hoped for and the evidence of things not seen.[1] For it was on the knowledge of these things that Jesus actually founded His own character and His conduct. It was by believing thus and so, and by living up to His belief, that He was made perfect. And it was by teaching His disciples to believe thus and so that He would bind them to follow His example and inspire them to share His life. "Whosoever heareth these sayings of mine and doeth them, I will liken him unto a wise man which built his house upon a rock."[2] "Now ye are clean through the word which I have spoken unto you." "If ye abide in me, and my words abide in you, ye shall ask what ye will and it shall be done unto you."[3]

[1] "Nicht das Leben Jesu an sich in seinem geschichtlichen Verlaufe, sondern die Auffassung der religiosen Bedeutung desselben, auf welche die älteste N. T. liche Verkundigung ruht, bildet den Ausgangspunkt fur die biblische Theologie. Diese Auffassung war aber zunächst bedingt durch die Lehre Jesu, sofern dieselbe die authentische Erlauterung über die Bedeutung seiner Person und seiner Erscheinung gab, und daher muss eine Darstellung dieser Lehre den grundlegenden Abschnitt der biblischen Theologie bilden." — BERNHARD WEISS, *Lehrbuch der Biblischen Theologie des Neuen Testaments* (2te Auflage, Berlin, 1873), p. 31.

[2] St. Matt. vii. 24. [3] St. John xv. 3, 7.

III

The authority of Christ's teaching.

The importance which Christ ascribed to His words as the authoritative revelation of unseen verities to the confused and darkened minds of men, cannot be denied or overlooked by any one who reads the Gospels candidly and intelligently. It is true, indeed, that He expressly disclaimed the idea that His doctrine was created, or invented, or even discovered by Himself. He said, "My doctrine is not mine but His that sent me,"[1] "All things that I have heard of my Father I have made known unto you."[2] But it is equally true that He claimed an absolute infallibility for the message which was revealed in Him, committed unto Him, and delivered by Him. This claim is made with equal force in the Synoptics and in St. John. "No one knoweth who the Son is, save the Father; and who the Father is, save the Son, and he to whomsoever the Son willeth to reveal Him."[3] "We speak that we do know, and bear witness of that we have seen."[4] This is not the language that an honest and conscientious teacher would use to describe his religious opinions or his spiritual

[1] St. John vii. 16.
[2] St. John xv. 15.
[3] St. Luke x. 22.
[4] St. John iii. 11.

hopes. The wisest and the best of men have always hesitated to assume this tone of certainty in regard to their deepest reflections upon the mysteries of being. But from first to last this tone marks the teaching of Jesus. "They were astonished at His teaching; for He taught them as having authority, and not as the scribes."[1]

It is original.

It is evident that He intended to speak thus. For nothing is more striking in the manner of His teaching than the absence of all reliance upon corroborative testimony or traditional support.[2] He did not seek to defend His positions with a formidable array of great names. He did not make a long catena of quotations from learned sources. He gave out His doctrine from the depth of His own consciousness as a flower breathes perfume, fresh, pure, original, and convincing. He certainly felt a Divine inspiration in the ancient Hebrew Scriptures. The law and the prophets conveyed to Him the

[1] St. Mark i. 22.

[2] "Avec une certitude sereine, qui ne semble pas terrestre, il disait ces choses. Il chantait, comme aucun prophète n'avait su le faire, le chant des revoirs éternels qui a bercé pendant des siècles les souffrances et les agonies. Et ce chant-là, voici que de nos jours, au triste déclin des temps, les hommes se meurent de ne plus l'entendre." — PIERRE LOTI, *La Galilée* (Paris, 1896), p. 94.

word of God. He used them on certain occasions to repel the assaults of evil, as in the temptation in the wilderness. He used them on other occasions to convince and convict the Scribes and Pharisees out of their own Scriptures. But He never rested upon them as the sole and sufficient basis of His doctrine. He was not a commentator on truths already revealed. He was a revealer of new truth. His teaching was not the exposition; it was the text. And this higher revelation not only fulfilled, but also surpassed, the old; replacing the temporal by the eternal, the figurative by the factual, the literal by the spiritual, the imperfect by the perfect. How often Jesus quoted from the Old Testament in order to show that it was already old and insufficient; that its forms of speech and rules of conduct were like the husk of the seed which must be shattered by the emergence of the living germ. His doctrine was in fact a moral and intellectual daybreak for the world. He did far more than supply a novel system of conduction for an ancient light. He sent forth from Himself a new illumination, transcending all that had gone before, as the sunrise overfloods the pale glimmering of the morning star set like a beacon of promise upon the coast of dawn.

A new revelation.

It is self evidencing.

He did not rely upon reasoning for the proof of His doctrine. He put no trust in the compulsion of logic, in the keenness of dialectics. We look in vain among His words for an exhibition of the "evidences of Christianity." He did not endeavour to demonstrate the existence of God or the immortality of the soul. What He said was meant to be its own evidence. His method was not apologetic; it was declaratory.

"He argued not, but preached, and conscience did the rest."

The result of this is marvellous and magnificent. His teaching is cleared and disentangled from all that is temporary and transient in human thought. If He had reasoned with men, it must have been done upon the premisses and in the forms of philosophy current in that age. Otherwise He could not have reached their intelligence, His reasoning would have been of none effect. But because He passed by all these processes and left them on one side while His doctrine moved simply, directly, and majestically to the heart of the truth, it comes to us to-day free and unencumbered by any of those theories of physical science, of psychology, of political economy, which the growth of knowledge has changed, discredited, or discarded. His teaching is neither ancient nor modern, neither deductive nor inductive, neither Jewish nor Greek. It is universal, enduring, valid for all minds and for all times. There are no more difficulties in the way of accepting it now than there were when it was first delivered. It fits the spiritual needs of the nineteenth, as closely as it fitted the spiritual needs of the first, century. It carries the same attractions, the same credentials in the Western Hemisphere as it carried in the Eastern. It stands out as clearly from all the later, as it did from all the earlier, philosophies. It finds the soul as inevitably to-day as it did at first. And the men of this age who hear Christ can only say, as His disciples said long ago, "Lord, to whom shall we go? Thou hast the words of eternal life."[1]

It is universal.

And yet how few are those words, compared with the utterances of other teachers. How small in compass is the doctrine of Jesus as it has come down to us. Eighty pages of a duodecimo book will hold all of His recorded discourses and the story of His life. Other words He must have spoken while He was on earth, but I doubt not that they moved within the same circle. For even in the present record

It is small in compass.

[1] St. John vi. 68.

we find the same truths recurring again and again, expressed in different language, arranged in different sequence, as the evangelists retrace, each from his own point of view, the memory of the things which Jesus taught to the multitudes and to His disciples. The literature of the world holds no other doctrine so limited in bulk, so limitless in meaning.

'ts fontal quality.

The teaching of Christ differs from that of all other masters in its fontal quality. It is comprised in a little space, but it has an infinite fulness. Its utterance is closely bounded, but its significance is inexhaustible. The sacred books of other religions, the commentaries and expositions on the Christian religion, spread before us a vast and intricate expanse, like lakes of truth mixed with error, stretching away into the distance, arm after arm, bay after bay, until we despair of being able even to explore their coasts and trace their windings. When we come back to Christ, we find, not an inland sea of doctrine, but a clear fountain of living water, springing up into everlasting life.

An unfailng source.

Calm, pure, unfathomable, it is never clouded and it never fails. The inspiration of other teachers rises and falls like an intermittent spring. To-day it is brimming full; to-morrow it is empty and dry. But the truth that flows from Jesus is constant and unvarying. The Spirit always rests upon Him. The Father is always with Him. Out of the deep serenity of His soul, as from some secret vale of peace high among the eternal hills, the vital spring of truth wells up forever, and forever the crystal stream runs down to refresh and revive the souls of men.

Always renewed.

New meanings come out of the teaching of Jesus in every land and in every age. New stars are mirrored in its depths. New flowers blossom on its banks. New fields of love are fertilized by its waters. It is not that each succeeding century and race adds something of its own to the doctrine of Christ. It is that each finds in that source something which was meant to become its own, and so to satisfy its deepest needs. The old questions are repeated in new words, and the new answer comes in the old words.[1] The truth as it is in Jesus does not have to be changed and adapted to fit it for a world-wide missionary enterprise. It needs only to be purified from the things that men

[1] "Socrates asked questions which his disciples tried to answer; Jesus provoked His disciples to ask questions which He answered."—JAMES STALKER, *Imago Christi* (New York, Armstrongs, 1889), p. 270.

have mingled with it, restored to the simplicity that is in Christ, and it proves itself as fresh, as satisfying, as life-bestowing to the thirsty soul in America or in the islands of the sea, as it did in Galilee or on the hillsides of Judea.

The simplicity that is in Christ.

When we ask ourselves why it is that the doctrine of the Master has this enduring, self-renewing, fontal character, I think we must find the answer in the fact that it simply bears witness, with a directness and inevitableness altogether unparalleled, to the actual existence of a spiritual world corresponding to the spiritual faculties and aspirations of men. It does not turn aside to discuss metaphysical problems or theological subtleties. The distinction between the natural and the supernatural does not even appear in the teaching of Jesus. There may, or there may not, be such a distinction. If there is, He at least does not think it important enough to speak of it. The one thing of which He wishes to make men sure is that the same God who sends His sunshine and His rain upon the evil and upon the good, the same God whose bounty feeds the birds of the air and clothes the lilies of the field with beauty, hears in secret the prayers of the penitent and believing and rewards them openly. The question of the how and the where of the life after death is not even touched in the teaching of Jesus. It matters little. The one thing that He declares with unfaltering certainty is the reality of that life. The one thing that He presses home upon the minds of men with calm intensity is the danger of losing it through sin and unbelief. The one thing that He tenderly and urgently pleads with them to do, is to make sure of its immortal blessedness through faith and love and obedience to Him. And so, at every point, He passes by the non-essential to touch the essential, He disregards the passing curiosity to satisfy the real anxiety, He neglects the shadows to reveal the substance of the unseen world.

Words of eternal life.

Teaching like this is the only kind of teaching that will always renew itself, always have something more to bestow upon us. It cannot grow obsolete. It cannot be drained of its significance. It is like life. Nay, it is life, and it gives life.

IV

Loyalty to Christ's teaching.

Let us understand, then, that if our Christianity is to satisfy our whole nature, if it is to have its real and full meaning, and power to bring in the kingdom of heaven, it must include this element. We must be as loyal to the teaching of Jesus as we are to His example. We must count no pains too great to spend upon the study of that teaching as it lies in the records, and no effort too severe to make in order that it may be restored in its integrity and entirety, rounded and harmonized, within the very centre of our minds. And then we must preach it, simply, sincerely, certainly, as the only doctrine which can lead men out of the intellectual anarchy of doubt into the peaceful realm of truth.

The age demands authority.

This is what the age is looking and longing for. It can find no joy in the kingdom of heaven unless it finds there a source of authority for the mind as well as for the heart. Authority is what the sociologist demands, in order that he may have a sure basis for the precepts of altruism. Authority is what the philosopher seeks, in order that he may have a fixed point of departure and certain limits of speculation. Authority is what the poet craves, as he clings to

> "The truths that never can be *proved*,
> Until we close with all we loved
> And all we flow from, soul in soul."[1]

Men are crying lo here! and lo there! We must find the source of authority in an in-

[1] Tennyson, *In Memoriam*.

errant Book, or in an enlightened reason, or in an infallible Church, or perhaps in all three; as if there could be three sources of one authority, or as if a channel could ever be rightly called a source. Let us not hesitate to pass through this confusion of tongues and of ideas, serene and untroubled, with the message of a more excellent way.

Christ is th supreme authority.

Christ is the Light of all Scripture. Christ is the Master of holy reason. Christ is the sole Lord and Life of the true Church. By His word we test all doctrines, conclusions, and commands. On His word we build all faith. This is the source of authority in the kingdom of heaven. Let us neither forget nor hesitate to appeal to it always with untrembling certainty and positive conviction. If Christ did not know and preach the truth, then there is no truth that can be known or preached. Unless we are sure of this, we would better go out of business entirely. It is inconceivable that the loftiest character in history should be the most mistaken man that ever thought about the real basis and meaning of life. It is incredible that the noblest life in the world should be founded upon a faith that was vain. It is impossible that a supreme devotion and a real likeness to Christ should have been produced and perpetuated in the world without a veritable apprehension of that which He knew and taught concerning God and man.

Our great task, to learn His creed.

To have this apprehension clearly formed within us must be our ardent and joyful intellectual endeavour. We are not to rest content with the study of single words and separate phrases. The limitations of language, the conditions of transmission, will always expose us to error if we follow that course. The truth as it is in Jesus does not lie in fragments, but in the rounded whole.[1] We must get back to the unity and integrity of the thoughts of Jesus, the creed of Christ. The broad outline of His vision of things human and divine, the central verities which appear firm and unchangeable in all the reports of His teaching, the point of view from which He discerned and interpreted the mystery of life, — that is what we must seek. And when we find it we must take our stand there as men who feel the solid ground beneath their feet. Illustrations and confirmations we may gather from science and history and philosophy. But the rock of certainty is the mind of Jesus, expressed in His living words and in His speak-

[1] See Appendix, note 45.

ing life. Beyond this we need not and we cannot go. Here is the ultimatum. This is the truth, we say to men, because Jesus knew it, and said it, and lived it.

We must live in Him to know His doctrine.

But one thing we may not, we dare not, forget. The condition of apprehending, and how much more of preaching, the truth revealed by Christ is that we abide in Him. The word of Jesus in the mind of one who does not do the will of Jesus, lies like seed-corn in a mummy's hand. It is only by dwelling with Him and receiving His character, His personality so profoundly, so vitally that it shall be with us as if, in His own words, we had partaken of His flesh and His blood, as if His sacred humanity had been interwoven with the very fibres of our heart and pulsed with secret power in all our veins, — it is thus only that we can be enabled to see His teaching as it is, and set it forth with luminous conviction to the souls of men.

Return to Jesus.

And if ever we ourselves become afraid of our own task, and shrink from it; if the scepticism of our age appalls us and chills us to the very marrow; if we question whether a gospel so simple, so absolute, as that which is committed to us can find acceptance in such a world, at such a time as this, — be sure it is because we have gotten out of fellowship with Him who is our Peace and our Hope, our Light and our Strength. A Christless man can never preach Christ. We have been anxious and troubled about many things, and have forgotten the one thing needful. Peace we must have before we can have power. Let us straightway return, in prayer, in meditation, in trust, in faithful simple-hearted obedience, to Him who is the only centre of Peace because He is the only source of authority.

"I have a life in Christ to live,
But ere I live it must I wait
Till learning can clear answer give
Of this and that book's date?
I have a life in Christ to live,
I have a death in Christ to die;—
And must I wait till science give
All doubts a full reply?

Nay, rather, while the sea of doubt
Is raging wildly round about,
Questioning of life and death and sin,
Let me but creep within
Thy fold, O Christ, and at Thy feet
Take but the lowest seat,
And hear Thine awful voice repeat
In gentlest accents, heavenly sweet,
Come unto Me and rest;
Believe Me, and be blest."[1]

[1] John Campbell Shairp.

VI

LIBERTY

"But, perfect in every part,
  Has the potter's moulded shape
Leap of man's quickened heart,
  Throe of his thought's escape,
Stings of his soul which dart

"Through the barrier of flesh, till keen
  She climbs from the calm and clear
Through turbidity all between
  From the known to the unknown here,
Heaven's 'Shall be,' from Earth's 'Has been'?

"Then life is — to wake and not sleep,
  Rise and not rest, but press
From earth's level where blindly creep
  Things perfected, more or less,
To the heaven's height, far and steep,

"Where, amid what strifes and storms
  May wait the adventurous quest,
Power is Love — transports, transforms
  Who aspired from worst to best,
Sought the soul's world, spurned the worms.'"

— Robert Browning, *Reverie.*

LIBERTY

Three great problems.

There are three points at which the teaching of Jesus comes into closest contact with the needs of the present age. Three problems of profound difficulty are pressing to-day upon all thoughtful men: the psychological problem of the freedom of the will; the theological problem of the actual relation of God to the universe; and the moral problem of man's duty to his fellow-men in a world of inequality. Out of the depths of these problems dark and multitudinous doubts are forever rising, like the clouds of smoke and steam which issue from the labouring bosom of Vesuvius, while subterranean thunder is muttering and rolling underneath. Most of the intellectual perplexities and practical perils of our times come directly from these questions, to which modern scepticism gives an answer of despair, or at best only a dubious and uncertain reply.

But the gospel of Christ, rightly apprehended and interpreted, offers us a solution

Three great truths — liberty, sovereignty, and service.

of these problems which is full of light and hope and moral certainty. There is a breath of the Spirit in His teaching, pure and strong, pouring like a clean wind out of heaven, to scoff away the obscuring vapours, and reveal the changeless verities and glories of the spiritual landscape. Three truths emerge in His doctrine, and stand out clear and sharp as mountain peaks against the blue: the truth of human liberty, the truth of Divine sovereignty, and the truth of universal service. Of these three truths we must never lose sight, if our thinking is to be in accordance with the mind of Jesus. To these three truths we must bear witness, unhesitatingly, faithfully, and joyfully, if our preaching is to be a gospel for this age of doubt.

I

Modern fatalism.

No one who has looked steadily upon the face of modern life as it is reflected in popular literature can doubt that it is "sicklied o'er" with the dark shadow of fatalism. It is evident in the writings of the learned and in the seribblings of the ignorant. Everywhere there is a tendency to explain the whole life of man as the product of heredity and environment. The student of physiology, tracing the strange and subtle correspondence between the processes of consciousness and the changes and movements of the nervous system, makes the enormous assumption that the correspondence amounts to identity. All the hopes and fears, all the affections and aspirations, which glorify this mortal life, are in their last analysis the result of certain puckerings and tintinnabulations of the gray matter of the nerves. The actions which flow from them are as necessary as the fall of an apple when the stem is broken. The caress which a mother gives to her child, and the blow with which a murderer strikes his victim dead, are equally automatic and inevitable. They are the motions of delicately constructed puppets, and the triumph of modern investigation is the discovery of the string which moves them and the forces which pull it.

Materialism disavowed but taught.

It is true that many of the teachers who steer us, more or less openly, towards this conclusion are careful to disavow the idea that they are teaching materialism. The name is highly unpopular at the present moment, and there is hardly one of the men of science of to-day who has not protested with indignation that no one should dare to call him a materialist. They have devised subtle theories of something called "mind-stuff" which they hold, with W. K. Clifford, "is the reality which we perceive as matter." They distinguish, with Huxley, between matter and force, and a third thing which they call consciousness and which they admit cannot conceivably be a modification of either of the first two things; but they go on to say that "what we call the operations of the mind are functions of the brain, and the materials of consciousness are products of cerebral activity."[1] In short, they give a materialistic explanation of the origin and processes of thought, and then protect themselves against the imputation of being materialists, by solemnly averring that they have not the slightest idea of what matter really is, nor the slightest intention of suggesting that it has any resemblance to the so-called mental operations which are probably produced by one of its own forms of activity.

Responsibility crowded out. A scheme like this certainly has no room for free-will or personal responsibility. It makes a man's character and action entirely dependent upon the amount and quality of nervous energy that has been transmitted to him by his ancestors and developed by the circumstances of his life. He lives, as Professor Tyndall

[1] T. H. Huxley, in *The Fortnightly Review*, vol. xi., 793.

says, in a realm of "physical and moral necessity," — though why he should be at pains to say "moral," I can hardly conceive. One adjective would serve as well as two, when they both mean the same thing. It requires but a little exercise of this nervous energy on our part, in the form of imagination, to trace it back to its previous form of heat stored up in certain hundredweights of food and appropriated by digestion. From this point our cerebral activity skips lightly and altogether without volition along the various lines of animal and vegetable life, of chemical and physical transformations of energy, until we arrive at the idea of the sun. From this idea a certain uncontrollable change in the gray substance of our brain produces the further notion that the arrangement of certain quantities of matter and force which took place in some inexplicable way long before the birth of the solar system was really the thing that settled the question whether you and I should prefer telling the truth to lying, — if we do. Indeed, there never has been any question at all about it; it was fixed from the beginning. We have no more responsibility for it than we have for the colour of our eyes or the shape of our noses.

"Thoughts of an Automaton."

I have found a brief and explicit statement of the position to which this method of thinking forces those who follow it, in an article ironically entitled "Thoughts of a Human Automaton" in a recent English periodical.[1]

"I am an automaton — a puppet dangling on my distinctive wire, which Fate holds with an unrelaxing grip. I am not different, nor do I feel differently, from my fellow-men, but my eyes refuse to blink away the truth, which is, that I am an automatic machine, a piece of clockwork wound up to go for an allotted time, smoothly or otherwise, as the efficiency of the machinery may determine. Free-will is a myth invented by man to satisfy his emotions, not his reason. I feel as if I were free, as if I were responsible for my thoughts and actions, just as a person under the influence of hypnotism believes he is free to do as he pleases. But he is not; nor am I. If it were once possible for a rational being to question this fact, the discoveries of Darwin must have set his doubts at rest. . . .

"What is crime? A crime is an action threatened by the law with punishment, says Kant; and freedom of action or free-will

[1] Henry Beauchamp, in *The Fortnightly Review*, English edition, March, 1892.

is a legally necessary condition of crime. But the law of heredity conclusively demonstrates that free-will and freedom of action stand in the category of lively imaginings. Therefore crime, as the law understands it, is non-existent, since no imputability can be recognized when a man is not responsible for his actions. Therefore the law is not justified in inflicting punishment. . . .

"Briefly to conclude. Religion can no more mix with science than oil with water. Science acknowledges no necessity for the existence of religion, and finally severs the bonds between morality and religion. Morality, altogether independent of religion, is entirely based upon self-interest. The supposed connection between religion and morality is an illusion most pernicious to the general welfare and advance of mankind. Religion, as a superfluity, should be excluded from all educational institutions. Its place will be supplied by the creed of scientific philosophy — Determinism. The primary principle of Determinism, namely, that a human being is an automaton, and therefore not responsible for his thoughts or his acts, taken together with its corollaries, more than suffices for every intellectual need hitherto provided for by religion. For the two great factors in the value of religion are its ethics and its sedative properties, and in both these uses Determinism displays overwhelming intellectual superiority. Its ethics are more universal and its consolation more assured; for they both rest on irrefragable scientific truth. The Determinist is consequently never harassed by doubts — the Rock of Ages is fragile compared with the adamantine foundation of his creed."

The creed of necessity.

This curious claim of an automaton to have a "creed" would be deliciously humorous, if it were not so unutterably sad, and so detestably dangerous. For though, as a matter of fact, there are few men who will make, even under an assumed name, such a candid confession of faith in their own moral non-entity as that which we have just read, there are many men who are, consciously or unconsciously, preaching the same black creed of Necessity in the subtle forms of literary art, and multitudes who are silently accepting it as gospel truth. Fatalism broods over modern fiction and the modern drama like a huge, shapeless spectre; and its influence is felt in all the judgments and conceptions and unspoken but clearly revealed sentiments of a society which finds its chief intellectual pabulum in novels and plays.

Here is the famous French realist, Zola, of whose books it is said that enough have been sold to build a pile as high as the Eiffel tower. He writes a novel called *La Bête Humaine*, in which he shows how unswervingly the lines of evil run through the plan of life. He describes seven inevitable murders, occurring within eighteen months in close connection with a certain fated house, and closes his book with the description of a railway train, crowded with soldiers, dragged by an engine whose driver has been killed, dashing at headlong speed into the midnight. The train is the world; we are the freight; fate is the track; death is the darkness; God is the engineer, — who is dead.[1]

"The Human Beast."

Here is the leader of the Dutch Sensitivists, Louis Couperus, who writes a romance called *Noodlot*, "*Destiny*," in which four human lives are tangled together in an inextricable and horrible coil. One of his characters pauses for an instant in the shameful career to which he is impelled. "He threw himself back in his chair, still feebly wringing his hands, and the tears trickled again and again down his cheeks. He saw his own cowardice take shape before him. He stared into its frightened eyes, and he did not condemn it. For he was as fate had made

"Footsteps of Fate."

[1] See Appendix, note 46.

him. He was a craven, and he could not help it. Men called such an one as he a coward; it was but a word. Why coward, or simple and brave, or good and noble? It was all a matter of convention, of accepted meaning; the whole world was mere convention, a concept, an illusion of the brain. There was nothing real at all — nothing!"[1]

'Ghosts."

Here is the Norse dramatist, Ibsen, — the new Shakespeare by the grace of heredity. He writes a drama of life which he calls *Ghosts*, and shows how every player is haunted by dead ancestors who look through his eyes, speak in his words, and act in his deeds. Echoes of spent passion, shreds and patches of worn-out sin, rags and tatters of the past, — that is the stuff of which life is fabricated, like a piece of shoddy cloth, in the great mill of circumstance which stands on the banks of the river of time and turns out the shabby lives of men and women.[2]

The small fatalists.

Nor is this view of life confined to the great foreign masters of realism. It pervades almost all the minor schools of fiction; it diffuses itself insensibly through the work of the feeble and fatuous imitators. A keen and wholesome

[1] Louis Couperus, *The Footsteps of Fate* (New York, Appletons), p. 65. [2] See Appendix, note 47.

critic of our own literature, Mr. Charles Dudley Warner, put his finger upon the fact when he wrote: "It has come about that the novels and stories which are to fill our leisure hours and cheer us in this vale of tears have become what we call tragic. It is not easy to define what tragedy is, but the term is applied in modern fiction to scenes and characters that come to ruin from no particular fault of their own,—not even when the characters break most of the ten commandments,—but by an unappeasable fate that dogs and thwarts them. This is the romance of fatality, and if it is tragedy, it is the tragedy of fatalism." [1]

Melancholy marionettes.

It is not possible that such a theory of existence should prevail without bringing sadness and heaviness into the hearts of men. The modern melancholy of which we spoke in the first lecture is largely the result of this general sense of a godless predestination. It is Calvinism with the bottom knocked out. It robs life of all interest, of all joy, of all enthusiasm. Was it morphine that drove Guy de Maupassant, the most brilliant of the younger French novelists, to insanity? Or was it his philosophy that drove him to morphine as a refuge from the despair and ugliness of exist-

[1] See Appendix, note 48.

ence? Pessimism exudes from fatalism like sepia from the cuttlefish.[1] What could be more dispiriting than to doubt the reality of all effort, to deny the possibility of self-conquest and triumph over circumstances, to find heroism an illusion and virtue a dream? What could break the spring of life more completely than to feel that our feet are tangled in a net whose meshes were woven for us by our ancestors, and for them by tailless apes, and for them by gilled amphibians, and for them by gliding worms, and for them by ciliated larvæ, and for them by amœbæ, and for them by God does not know what?[2] It does not help the case in the least to do as some theologians have tried to do and bring back into the theory by the aid of certain misconstrued and very much overworked passages of Scripture, the idea of a supreme Deity who has constructed the loom and devised the pattern of the net and decreed the weaving of every loop. The chain of Fate is not made less heavy by fastening the end of it to the distant throne of an omnipotent and impassive Creator. If our false sense of freedom comes from such a Being, who is Himself free, it is all the more a cruel and bitter enigma. If moral responsi-

[1] See Appendix, note 49. [2] See Appendix, note 50.

bility has been imposed upon us by the same hand which has bound us to an inalterable destiny, it is all the more a crushing and miserable fraud. To baptize fatalism with a Christian name does not change its nature. To hold fast to the metaphysical conception of God while accepting Heredity and Environment as His only and infallible prophets is simply to add a new ethical horror to the dismal delusion of life, and to revolt to the pessimism of Omar Khayyám.

Baptized fatalism.

"We are no other than a moving row
Of Magic Shadow-shapes, that come and go
Round with this Sun-illumined Lantern, held
In Midnight by the Master of the Show;

"Impotent Pieces of the Game He plays
Upon this Checker-board of Nights and Days;
Hither and thither moves, and checks, and slays,
And one by one back in the Closet lays.

"The Moving Finger writes; and, having writ,
Moves on; nor all your Piety nor wit
Shall lure it back to cancel half a Line,
Nor all your tears wash out a Word of it.

"And that inverted Bowl they call the Sky,
Whereunder crawling coop'd we live and die,
Lift not your hands to It for help—for it
As impotently rolls as you or I."[1]

[1] *Rubáiyát of Omar Khayyám.* Rendered into English verse by Edward Fitzgerald, with an accompaniment of drawings by Elihu Vedder (Boston, 1884), stanzas 72, 73, 75, 76.

II

Is determinism proved?

This is the solution which modern positivism, christened or unchristened, offers for the problem of the freedom of the will. Before we turn to consider the very different answer which Christ gives to the same question, let us stay for a moment to ask whether this current and popular solution is of the nature of a demonstration, or of the nature of a doubt. Is it so clearly proven that science forces us to accept determinism? Or is it an unverifiable assumption, which is made under the influence of a general scepticism in regard to spiritual realities, and which leaves out of view quite as many and quite as important facts as those which it professes to explain? Are we compelled to admit it; or is it only one of two alternatives, neither of which is scientifically demonstrable, so that the choice between them must rest upon other considerations?

I do not hesitate to say that the whole weight of sober and sane criticism inclines to the latter conclusion. Determinism has not yet been established either by physiological, psychological, or metaphysical argument.

Philosophy says no.

The common assumption that the abstract reasoning of Jonathan Edwards against the liberty of the will has never been and cannot be refuted, is based upon ignorance of the facts. An American philosopher, Mr. Rowland Hazard, has answered it with great clearness and force. Professor George P. Fisher says: "The fundamental point of Mr. Hazard's criticism of Edwards is fully established. It must be allowed that his confutation of that conception of the will which underlies the reasoning of the great theologian is sound and conclusive."[1]

Science say no.

The support which modern science is supposed to give to the theory of determinism turns out, upon closer examination, to be alto gether illusory. The soundest and most careful investigators utterly decline to commit themselves to that metaphysical dogma, or to bind out science as a maid-of-all-work in the service of fatalistic theology.

Free-will a daily miracle.

The most distinguished of living English scientists recently said: "The influence of animal or vegetable life on matter is infinitely beyond the range of any scientific inquiry hitherto entered on. Its power of directing the motions of moving particles, *in the demonstrated daily miracle of our human free-will*, and

[1] Rowland Hazard, *Freedom of Mind in Willing* (Boston, Houghton, Mifflin & Co., 1889). Introduction by George P. Fisher, p. xxxi.

in the growth of generation after generation of plants from a single seed, are infinitely different from any possible result of the fortuitous concourse of atoms. The real phenomena of life infinitely transcend human science."[1] The theory that consciousness is a function of the brain breaks down completely when it attempts to explain the phenomena of sleep. Why should all the other functions of the body be carried on without fatigue and without interruption while this alone demands rest and admits of intervals of cessation? If consciousness is a function of nerve-matter, sleep abolishes it. How does it come back again without losing the sense of personal identity?

Thought is not a secretion.

Is it conceivable that the highest character, the loftiest genius, is purely an intermittent secretion of certain nerve-cells, and that during the hours of sleep, embracing one-third of its entire history, it is absolutely non-existent? "Function," says an eminent neurologist, "is a physiological term, and it is, I submit, improper to speak of states of consciousness as being functions of the brain. . . . It is not the mind, but the physical basis of mind, which is a product of physical evolution. It is the

[1] Lord Kelvin (Sir William Thomson), in *The Fortnightly Review*, March, 1892.

organ of mind, not the mind of itself, which being an evolution out of the rest of the body is representative of it."[1]

The brain the organ of the mind.

The fact that the brain is a double organ, — that there are really two brains, only one of which is used, — cannot be explained on the theory that consciousness is merely the result of the vibration of nerve filaments, as the music of the Æolian harp is the result of the passage of the wind over its strings. A distinguished physiologist has cleverly shown that if this were the case a double brain would mean a double amount of thought, just as twice the number of strings would mean twice the quantity of music.[2] But the fact that this is not so, points clearly to the hypothesis that the brain is not an Æolian harp helplessly vibrating under external impulses, but a double organ with two sets of keys, and the mind is like the player who can use either one of them to make the music. And this corresponds closely with our own sense of the process. For we are conscious not only of passive thoughts and

[1] Dr. J. Hughlings Jackson, "Lecture on the Comparative Study of Diseases of the Nervous System" (*British Medical Journal*, August 17, 1889).

[2] Dr. William H. Thomson, *Materialism and Modern Physiology of the Nervous System* (New York, Putnams, 1892), pp. 83 ff.

feelings, evoked within us by external causes, but also of thoughts and feelings voluntarily directed and combined, woven together in creative harmonies, and moving under the guidance of chosen ideals towards a symphonic completeness. Even the sense of discord and conflict which often rises within us is an evidence that there is a player as well as an instrument. For it is inconceivable that an Æolian harp, ill-strung, should dislike its own bad music, and endeavour, or think that it could endeavour, to make a better, sweeter sound.

Heredity not final.

Heredity is undoubtedly a real and powerful force. It supplies the outfit of life. But does it determine the use which we shall make of it? The very extension of the doctrine by the investigations of science dissolves this narrow and absolute conclusion. We inherit from thousands, from hundreds of thousands, of ancestors. The blood of many families and tribes and races is mingled in our veins. What is it that decides which of these many lines we shall follow? It must be either blind chance or free choice. All the phenomena of society, all the facts of consciousness, are in favour of the latter supposition. We see men whose heritage is of the lowest and the worst, working their way up, by sheer strength of moral choice and effort, to a higher plane.[1] We see men whose heritage is of the loftiest and the best, declining

> "thro' acted crime,
> Or seeming-genial venial fault,
> Recurring and suggesting still,"[2]

to the very depths of infamy. It is true that a man cannot bring out of himself anything that is not already there. But it is true also, by virtue of heredity, that there are many potential men in every man, and which of them is to emerge, he chooses for himself by a thousand silent moral preferences; by yielding or by resisting; by the cowardice and corruption, or by the courage and purification of his own free-will.

Moral judgments assume liberty.

Even those who write of human life from a professedly naturalistic standpoint cannot get rid of this conviction. Take Zola, for example. If he were consistent, he would speak with equal and impassive coldness of all his characters, tangled together in the inextricable toils of heredity. But he cannot help letting his hatred and contempt for the selfish, the luxurious, the vicious, express itself in the very accent with which he describes them. He cannot help showing his admiration and affec-

[1] See Appendix, note 51. [2] Tennyson, [*Will.*]

tion for those who, like ***Denise*** and ***Doctor Pascal***, and ***Clotilde***, rise out of the infamy which envelops the family ***Rougon-Macquart***. Virtue and vice may be scientifically treated as if they were merely natural products like sugar and vitriol; but when we come to talk of them from a human and humane standpoint, there is something within us which demands that we shall recognize a merit in being virtuous, and a shame in being vicious,—qualities which can never belong to mere secretions, whether of plants or of nerves,—qualities which have no possible meaning unless there is a free-will in man, capable of choosing between the evil and the good.

The testimony of modern psychology.

Now that a free-will is possible, modern psychology assures us, as the result of its latest researches. It does not attempt to demonstrate the existence of such a power by physiological investigation. It confesses that this demonstration is impossible with our present knowledge. But it declares with equal candour that the contrary attempt to show that the sense of freedom is a delusion, is inconclusive. "The last word of psychology here," says Professor William James, "is ignorance, for the forces engaged are too delicate and numerous to be followed in detail." He points out the extremely reckless and inconsequent nature of the reasoning by which the determinists seek to make mere analogies drawn from the course of rivers, and reflex actions, and other material phenomena, serve as proofs that the will is a mechanical effect. He exposes the bold assumption by which they ignore the testimony of consciousness in the presence of feeling and effort. He shows that the utmost which any argument for determinism can do is to present a possible hypothesis, which a man who has already determined to hold fast to the idea that the whole universe is one chain of inevitable causation may accept if he likes. But meanwhile the other alternative stands equally open. The moral arguments all point in that direction. The only course, in such a situation, is voluntary choice. "For scepticism itself, if systematic, is also voluntary choice. If, meanwhile, the will be indetermined, it would seem only fitting that the belief in its indetermination should be voluntarily chosen from amongst other possible beliefs. Freedom's first deed should be to affirm itself.

Free-will is possible.

Thus not only our morality but our religion, so far as the latter is deliberate, depends on the effort which we can make. '*Will you or won't you have it so?*' is the most probing question we are ever asked: we are asked it every hour of the day, and about the largest as well as the smallest, the most theoretical as well as the most practical, things. We answer *by consents or non-consents*, and not by words. What wonder if these dumb responses should seem our deepest organs of communication with the nature of things! What wonder if the effort demanded by them should be the measure of our worth as men! What wonder if the amount which we accord of it be the one strictly underived and original contribution which we make to the world!"[1]

III

Christ says liberty is real.

Here, then, modern science, careful, exact, reverent, as distinguished from modern scepticism, leaves us before the two doors. And here Christ comes to us, calling us to enter through the door of liberty into the pathway of eternal life. "Ask, and it shall be given you; seek and ye shall find; knock and it shall be opened unto you."[2] "If any man willeth to do His will, he shall know of the teaching."[3]

[1] William James, *Psychology*, vol. ii., p. 579. See Appendix, note 52.

[2] St. Matt. vii. 7. [3] St. John vii. 17.

The life of Jesus, a revelation of free-will.

The whole life and ministry of Jesus is a revelation of moral freedom.[1] His entrance into the world was voluntary. His continuance in human life was voluntary. His death was voluntary. At the first crisis of His life He chose to go about His Father's business. In the temptation He chose to resist the allurements of the Evil One. On the way to the cross He chose not to call on God for the deliverance which He knew would come in answer to His call. He was, indeed, fulfilling an appointed task, treading the path which had been marked out for the feet of the Christ; but He was fulfilling the task freely; He was walking in liberty because He loved to do the will of God. The triumph of His virtue lay in the freedom of His choice.

The preaching of Jesus a gospel of liberty.

There was a singular propriety in the text of His first public discourse. It was a declaration of liberty, as well as of grace. It was an emancipation proclamation as well as a gospel of comfort and help. "The spirit of the Lord is upon me, because He anointed me to preach good tidings to the poor; He hath sent me to proclaim release to the captives, and recovering of sight to the blind, to set at liberty them that are crushed, to proclaim the acceptable year of

[1] See Appendix, note 53.

the Lord "[1] And what was the oppressive bondage from which He proclaimed release? Was it not the tyranny of a false doctrine of necessity over the minds of men, as well as the enslaving influence of sin over their inert and hopeless wills?

The Pharisees taught Fate.

Here were the scribes and Pharisees teaching that the whole world was divided into two classes,—the chosen and the not-chosen, the righteous for whom salvation was secure whatever they might do, and the sinners for whom salvation was impossible whatever they might do. Here were the outcast, the lost, the neglected, shut out, by no choice of their own, but by their birth, by the occupations in which they were engaged, by their ignorance, by the very conditions of their life, from all part in the kingdom of heaven as the scribes and Pharisees conceived it; not only the harlots and the publicans, but also *Am Haarez*, "the people of the land," with whom it was not fitting that a righteous person should have any dealings;[2] miserable souls, bound by inheritance to a desperate and unhallowed fate. Here came Jesus, taking His way directly to these lost ones, these outsiders, and telling them that all this doctrine of inevitable doom was a chain

[1] St. Luke iv. 18. [2] Bruce, *Kingdom of God*, 145.

Jesus taught Freedom.

of lies, breaking the imaginary fetters from their souls and assuring them by His first word that they were free, even though they were ignorant of it. "Repent," He cried, "for the kingdom of heaven has approached unto you."[1] "Except ye be converted and become as little children, ye shall not enter into the kingdom of heaven."[2] And what is the significance of these words, "repentance" and "conversion," — their real significance, I mean, not that which has been read into them by centuries of false and formal theology? They are not passive and involuntary words; they do not rest upon the idea of qualifications which may or may not be in the possession of those to whom Christ speaks. They are active words, — words of inward movement and exertion. "Repent" means change your mind; make that simple effort of the soul for internal change which is the ultimate act of the free will;[3] put forth

[1] St. Matt. iv. 17.

[2] St. Matt. xviii. 3.

[3] "Every intelligent being, capable of conceiving of higher ethical conditions than he has yet attained, has in his own moral nature for the exercise of his creative powers an infinite sphere, within which . . . he is the supreme disposer. . . . A man who does not want to be pure and noble, may yet begin one step lower in the scale of moral advancement, with the wish to want to be pure and noble; and, here commencing the cultivation of his moral nature, ascend from this lower

that power of fixed attention to the new motive which is the central essence of liberty and the creative force of the soul.[1] "Be converted," as Christ spoke the word, is not passive; it expresses an action exercised by the soul within itself; it means simply "turn around"; set yourself in a new relation to God, to truth, to virtue. The name of this relation is faith. "Believe" is Christ's great word. It is the "*open sesame*" of the kingdom. "Believe in God, believe also in Me."[2] "He that believeth hath everlasting life"[3] "All things are possible to him that believeth."[4] But it is never spoken of as a mere intellectual opinion, or emotional experience, an irresistible conviction wrought by external evidence in the mind, or bestowed without effort upon the soul. The Bible never says that faith is a gift. There is a voluntary element in it. It is something to be done by the exercise of an inward power. It is a coming of the soul to Christ; it is a following of the

Faith is free.

point, through the want to be pure and noble, to the free effort to gratify this want." — Rowland Hazard, *Freedom of Mind in Willing*, "Of Effort for Internal Change" (Boston, Houghton, Mifflin & Co., 1889), chap. xiv.

[1] "The essential achievement of the will when it is most 'voluntary,' is to *attend* to a difficult object and hold it fast before the mind." — James, *Psychology*, vol. ii., p. 561.

[2] St. John xiv. 1. [3] St. John vi. 47. [4] St. Mark ix. 23.

soul after Him; it is the first step in a long course of spiritual activity. It is a deed. The disciples said unto Christ, "What must we do that we may work the works of God?" Jesus answered, "This is the work of God, that ye believe on Him whom He hath sent."[1]

All may believe.

Now there is not a hint in all the teaching of Jesus that this first act of freedom is impossible for any soul to whom He speaks. He has no idea of an eternal predestination binding some to belief and others to unbelief, a secret decree including certain men in the kingdom and excluding others from all possibility of entering into it. It is true that He says, "No man can come unto Me except the Father draw him";[2] but what He means by this drawing He tells us in the parable of the Lost Son, where it is the simple knowledge of the Father's abundant love that draws the prodigal back from the far country of sin;[3] and in the parable of the Publican in the Temple,[4] when it is the sense of the Divine mercy and forgiveness that makes the outcast man cry, "God, be merciful to me a sinner." There is prevenient grace in the doctrine of Jesus. But the grace is there. It has already come. All that man has to do is to meet it, to

[1] St. John vi. 28, 29.
[2] St. John vi. 44.
[3] St. Luke xv.
[4] St. Luke xviii. 10-14.

put himself into the upward swing of it, that it may lift and help him heavenward.

Christ is God's call to faith.

A calling and a choosing by God are necessary before any man can be saved. But Jesus does not speak of this choosing and calling as eternal. Christ Himself is the call, and all who answer it are chosen. "If any man thirst, let him come unto Me and drink."[1] "Him that cometh unto Me I will in no wise cast out."[2] The heavenly invitation is set forth in all its generosity and sincerity in the story of the Marriage Feast.[3] The bidding went out into the highways and hedges, to the bad and to the good; and all who heard and accepted it were welcome. And if a single guest was turned away, it was only because his own conduct showed that he had not really taken the invitation honestly and accepted willingly all that was provided for him.

No predestination to death.

There is not a single word in all that Jesus said to suggest any other reason than this for the exclusion of a single person from the blessings of the kingdom. "*Ye will not* come unto Me that ye might have life."[4] "How often would I have gathered thy children together even as a hen gathereth her chickens under

[1] St. John vii. 37.
[2] St. John vi. 37.
[3] St. Matt. xxii. 1–14.
[4] St. John v. 40.

her wings, *and ye would not.*"[1] There is not one statement that anything else but mercy and grace has been eternally prepared by God for any human soul. In that awful parable of judgment which discloses the convincing picture of the final separation of the evil from the good, Christ says distinctly that the joy of the blessed has been prepared for them from the foundation of the world, but of the punishment of the cursed, He says with equal distinctness that it was not prepared for them, but for the devil and his angels.[2] No one is ever lost because he cannot do good, but only because he will not do what he can.

Christ on heredity.

As for the doctrine of heredity, while Christ recognizes the truth that it contains, it seems as if He purposely set Himself to expose, and to ridicule with a Divine scorn, the falsehood of its fatal extremes. He said to those who were relying upon heredity to save them: "Think not to say within yourselves, We have Abraham to our father; for I say unto you that God is able of these stones to raise up children unto Abraham."[3] He said to His disciples when they foolishly, taking up the cant of the day about inherited sin and inevitable

[1] St. Matt. xxiii. 37 [2] St. Matt. xxv. 34–41.
[3] St. Matt. iii. 9.

punishment, asked whether the blind man or his parents had sinned that he was born blind, "Neither hath this man sinned, nor his parents, but that the works of God should be made manifest in him."[1] The true inheritance, the deepest inheritance which Jesus recognizes in the human race, is an inheritance from God; a nature made in the Divine image, spiritual, free, responsible, and capable, though so sadly marred, though so far astray, of returning to communion with the Heavenly Father.[2]

The weakness of man.

Undoubtedly Christ perceived and taught the immense difficulty of being good; the infirmity which long centuries of sin has wrought into the very fibres of the soul; the awful and almost inaccessible height of true holiness; the enormous obstacles which lie in the way of attaining it. The gate is strait, and we must agonize to enter in by it. The road is steep, and we must toil to climb it. "How hardly shall they that have riches enter into the kingdom of God."[3] And yet "the kingdom of heaven suffered violence, and men of violence take it by force"[4] There is an effort which succeeds even in this greatest of all endeavours, not in its own strength,

[1] St. John ix. 3.
[2] See Appendix, note 54.
[3] St. Mark x. 23.
[4] St. Matt. xi. 12.

but because it is sure of a Divine assistance. "With man it is impossible, but not with God."[1] To the human will, enfeebled and corrupted, so that it is like a sick man, barely able to turn himself upon his couch, and look and long and cry for help, three great sources of strength are always open and accessible.

The grace of God.

The first is prayer. "Men ought always to pray, and not to faint."[2] How sweet and serene is the voice that rings through the vain disputations and doubtful wranglings of the scribes and Pharisees, and calls every sinful soul to pray! Pray! you may not be able to realize your own ideal, but you can ask God to help you hold fast to it and struggle towards it. Pray!

Prayer.

> "More things are wrought by prayer
> Than this world dreams of."[3]

Pray! For God is not deaf, nor sleeping, nor gone upon a journey; He has not bound you to an inexorable fate and bound Himself not to interfere with it. Pray! The liberty of your own soul, and the liberty of God Himself, dwells in that word; for when you stretch your feeble hand to Him, a Divine hand will meet it, and

[1] St. Mark x. 27. [2] St. Luke xviii. 1.
[3] Tennyson, *The Passing of Arthur*.

break your fetters, and lift you out of darkness and death into life and light.

The Holy Spirit.

The second source of strength is the Holy Spirit. It is inconceivable, morally impossible, that there should be such a Spirit, and yet that His influence should be withheld from those who need and implore it. "If ye then, being evil, know how to give good gifts unto your children, how much more shall your heavenly Father give the Holy Spirit unto them that ask Him."[1]

Christ our Helper.

The third source of strength is Christ Himself. Does the sense of past guilt stand in the way of future effort? He says, "I have power on earth to forgive sins."[2] Does the soul feel dead and hopeless under the burden of evil habits? He says, "I came that they may have life, and may have it abundantly."[3] Do the works of a true and vital righteousness seem far beyond our power? He says, "Without Me ye can do nothing;"[4] but, "Lo, I am with you alway, even unto the end of the world."[5] "He that believeth on Me, the works that I do shall he do also, and greater works than these shall he do, because I go unto the Father."[6] The whole

[1] St. Luke xi. 13.
[2] St. Mark ii. 10.
[3] St. John x. 10.
[4] St. John xv. 5.
[5] St. Matt. xxviii. 20.
[6] St. John xiv. 12.

life of Christ is summed up in the words, "But as many as received Him, to them *gave He power* to become the sons of God."[1]

The way of deliverance.

But this receiving, we need to remember and assert again and again, is not a passive thing. It is an action of the soul, the opening of a door within the heart, the welcoming of a heavenly master. God does not save men as a watchmaker who repairs and sets a watch, but as a King who recalls his servants to their duty, as a Father who makes new revelations of His love to draw His lost children back to Himself. The dogmas of the schools in regard to the working out of what they call the scheme of redemption sound like the creak and rattle of some vast machine. The doctrine of Christ is like the soft breath of spring, evoking the songs of birds and the unfolding of new life. No fiery chariot of grace swoops down to snatch men to glory. But a living Messenger comes forth from God to ask men to turn and walk back with Him to their soul's home. The invitation itself is a guarantee of the power to accept it. With authority Christ commanded the winds and the sea and they obeyed Him. But with gracious pleading He invited the hearts of men, and those that were willing gladly heard and followed Him.

[1] St. John i. 12.

God helps those who help themselves.

"If any man *wills* to come after Me,"[1] — that is the prelude of His message. He offers a leadership to men who can follow, a mastership to men who can obey. Out of this first movement He promises to guide and direct the whole development of the new life, — not a passive life of retirement, of ascetic meditation, of reflection upon secret truth, — but an active life of service, of warfare against evil in the world, a life which translates truth into conduct.

Christus Liberator.

Contrast the religion of Jesus in this respect with the Oriental religions, and with those forms of Christianity which have borrowed the garments of Buddha and speak with the accent of Mahomet. They despise and slight personality. Christ respects and emphasizes it. They aim to reduce and evaporate responsibility. Christ aims to deepen and increase it. They point forward to a blank Nirvana in which the individual is lost and absorbed, or a Paradise in which he is forever lapped in sensual ease and pleasure. Christ speaks of the perfecting of the individual through the Divine communion and service on earth, and his entrance in heaven upon a new stage of the same communion, the same service, — "not in a blessed idleness, but in an exalted

[1] St. Matt. xvi. 24.

kingly work and activity." And the entrance to this kingdom on earth, the continuance in its realm of liberty, the attainment of its final glory, are all through an act of the will. The freedom which originated in God is only to be preserved by returning to God and abiding in Him.

> "Our wills are ours, we know not how;
> Our wills are ours, to make them Thine."[1]

That is the teaching of Jesus. That is the truth which, when it comes to men, makes them and keeps them free.

IV

The age needs this message.

It is impossible that we should be faithful preachers of Christ to the present age, unless we preach this truth. There may have been ages in which it was important to dwell upon other sides and aspects of the manifold reality of the spiritual world. But to-day this is the important side; this is the aspect which demands a clear recognition and an unfaltering proclamation by those who mean to be true to Christ and loyal to the needs of humanity. I do not believe that there is a single passage in the Old Testament which contradicts Christ's

[1] Tennyson, *In Memoriam*, Proem.

doctrine of the real liberty of the soul. But if there were such a passage, I would leave it forever alone, as belonging to that knowledge which was in part, and which was done away when that which was perfect had come. I do not believe that there is a single word in the writings of St. Paul which stands against this doctrine of the real liberty of the soul. I cut loose from the false interpretations which men have read into his words. I take the light of Christ's teaching in my hand, and I go back to interpret by that light the teachings of the great Epistle to the Romans with its glorious revelation of "the mystery which hath been kept in silence through times eternal, but now is manifested, and by the Scriptures of the prophets, according to the commandment of the eternal God, is made known unto all the nations *unto obedience of faith.*"[1] I hear again the cry of the struggling, labouring, conquering apostle: "*To will is present with me*, but to do that which is good is not. . . . O wretched man that I am, who shall deliver me out of the body of this death? I thank God *through Christ Jesus our Lord;*"[2] and I know that St. Paul also was a believer in the freedom of the will, and that he received this

St. Paul on Freedom.

[1] Rom. xvi. 26. [2] Rom. vii. 18, 24, 25.

gospel and the power to fulfil it, through the proclamation of liberty in Jesus Christ.

Free-will the pressing question.

"This matter of free-will," wrote one of the most orthodox of theologians, but a few years before his death, "underlies everything. If you bring it to question, it is infinitely more than Calvinism. . . . I believe in Calvinism, and I say that free-will stands before Calvinism. Everything is gone if free-will is gone; the moral system is gone, if free-will is gone; you cannot escape except by Materialism on the one hand or by Pantheism on the other. Hold hard therefore to the doctrine of free-will."[1]

Yes, and we may say more than this. Not only is the moral system gone, but the great attraction of Christ is gone, the power of His gospel to liberate men is gone, if free-will is gone.

The age has hypnotized itself.

The age has hypnotized itself. It is drifting steadily towards fatalism. It denies freedom, and therefore it is not free. It is in bondage to its own doubt. It is enslaved by its own denial. If there is such a thing as liberty, it can only be developed, as everything else has been developed, by action, by exercise.

[1] A. A. Hodge, *Popular Lectures on Theological Themes* (Philadelphia, 1887), p. 184.

Life is self-change to meet environment. Liberty is self-exertion to unfold the soul. The law of natural selection is that those who use a faculty shall expand it, but those who use it not shall lose it. Religion is life, and it must grow under the laws of life. Faith is simply the assertion of spiritual freedom ; it is the first adventure of the soul. Make that adventure towards God, make that adventure towards Christ, and the soul will know that it is alive. So it enters upon that upward course which leads through the liberty of the sons of God to the height of heaven,

> " Where love is an unerring light
> And joy its own security."[1]

We must proclaim liberty in Christ.

This is the truth with which we are to go out a-gospelling in this age of doubt. We are to tell men that though much has been determined for them by causes beyond their control — their circumstances, their talents, their facul ties, — one thing has not been determined, and that is what they will do with them. Much has been ordained before their birth, — their nationality, their family, their station in life, — but one thing has not been ordained, and that is whether they are to move from this starting-

[1] Wordsworth, *Ode to Duty.*

point towards life or towards death. They may be like men sunken in a nightmare dream of helplessness, muttering in their sleep, "If I am to be saved, I shall be saved; if I am to be lost, I shall be lost," — but we must cry to them with the voice of the Spirit· "Awake, thou that sleepest, and arise from the dead, and Christ shall give thee light."

VII

SOVEREIGNTY

"I say to thee, do thou repeat
To the first man thou mayest meet
In lane, highway, or open street

"That he and we and all men move
Under a canopy of love,
As broad as the blue sky above;

"That doubt and trouble, fear and pain
And anguish, all are shadows vain,
That death itself shall not remain;

"That weary deserts we may tread,
A dreary labyrinth may thread
Through dark ways underground be led;

"Yet if we will one Guide obey,
The dreariest path, the darkest way,
Shall issue out in heavenly day;

"And we, on divers shores now cast,
Shall meet, our perilous voyage past,
All in our Father's house at last."

Richard Chenevix Trench
The Kingdom of God.

VII

SOVEREIGNTY

The boundaries of science.

THE questions about the world which science considers and answers, all have to do with secondary causes. Beyond that sphere she does not need to go, and within that sphere her wisdom is sufficient. We come to her like curious children. We "want to see the wheels go round." We want to know what the wheels are made of. She tells us, and there she stops. All that we have a right to ask of her is that she shall be true to facts, and that she shall confine herself to them. When the astronomer Laplace was reproached for not mentioning God in his treatise on the dynamics of the solar system, he answered, "I had no need of that hypothesis." And this reply was just, as Mr John Fiske has pointed out, because "in order to give a specific explanation of any single group of phenomena, it would not do to appeal to divine action, which is equally the source of all phenomena." [1]

[1] *Christian Literature*, January, 1896, "The Everlasting Reality of Religion," p. 306.

The great questions lie beyond them.

But the moment we take this reasonable and modest position (and it is a great pity that theology has not been more ready to take it), we perceive that curiosity in regard to single groups of phenomena by no means satisfies or exhausts the activity of the questioning spirit in man. There is a deeper curiosity in regard to the relation of these single groups of phenomena to each other, and to ourselves, and to the possibility of a meaning, a purpose, an end, underlying all things and all their workings. Out of this deeper curiosity rise the questions which are most urgent and vital, — questions which, when we consider them abstractly, are philosophical, and condition the unity of our intellectual life; but when we consider them personally, they are religious, and upon their answer our spiritual peace and moral action absolutely depend. How are we to think about the things that we know? What are we to believe in regard to the things that science tells us we cannot know, but which we still feel are necessary conditions of all intelligent and right conduct? Is there an invisible unity beneath all the visible diversity of phenomena? What is the nature of that unity, personal or impersonal, conscious or unconscious? Is there anything behind the mechanical working of the world, now so wonderfully explained, which corresponds to what there is in us when we make and use a machine or an instrument, when we plant and cultivate a garden, or when we select and train a noble race of animals? Is there a final cause towards which things work together, and a supreme power which guides them to that end?

The question of sovereignty.

This is the question of sovereignty. We can no more help asking it than we can help thinking.

We are in the world like voyagers on a ship. We inquire what the ship is made of; and science tells us, — iron and wood. And what makes it float? The buoyancy of the air which it contains. And what makes it go? Steam. And what makes the steam? The heat of the furnace. Then, if we are sufficiently interested, science takes us down into the engine-room, and shows us all the condensers and pistons and cranks and wheels, more fully than they have ever been shown before; and we are amazed and profoundly grateful. We come up again into the light of day. We look into the overarching heaven, the home of sunshine and storm, the deep mother of light and darkness. We look out upon the great and wide sea, full of mystery and terror. New questionings

Ias the 𝑤orld a aptain?

spring to our lips. Where is the ship going? Is there a captain on board? Does he know, does he care, what is to become of it? Is he wise, is he faithful, is he a good captain? Can he direct the vessel through tempests and dangers? Can he tell us how to work with him, how to act in times of peril and perplexity? Can we be sure of him, can we trust him?

Doubt answers, No.

Now to this questioning, scepticism gives a reply of desperate uncertainty; and positivism answers with a stern and sullen, No! The world is a derelict vessel, and we are masterless and lost mariners. This answer has been expressed by a French poet in powerful and pathetic verse.

> "Jouet de l'ouragan, qui l'emporte et le mène,
> Encombré de tresors et d'agrès submergés,
> Ce navire perdu, mais c'est le nef humaine,
> Et nous sommes les naufragés.
>
> "L'equipage affolé manœuvre en vain dans l'ombre;
> L'Épouvante est à bord, le Désespoir, le Deuil;
> Assise au gouvernail, la Fatalité sombre
> Le dirige vers un écueil."[1]

But Christ gives a very different answer. It seems as if His very words were chosen to contradict this view of life as a helpless, hope-

[1] L. Ackerman, *Ma Vie, Poesies*, etc. (Paris, 1885), "Le Cri," p. 180.

Christ answers, Yes.

less voyage, and humanity as a shipwrecked race. For what is it that He says to His disciples as they look out upon the mystery of existence?

"Seek not what ye shall eat, and what ye shall drink, *neither be ye as a ship that is tossed on the waves of a tempestuous sea* (μὴ μετεωρίζεσθε), for your Father knoweth that ye have need of these things."[1]

The vessel is not driving masterless over the ocean. The Captain is on board. He is God. He is also our Father. For all who trust and serve Him, it is a sure voyage, a certain port, a safe harbour.

The sovereignty of God.

The doctrine of the presence and sovereignty of God in His world, in one form or another, is essential to the validity of any reasoning which attempts to go beyond the mere appearance of things. Without it we find ourselves, as one has well said, "put to permanent intellectual confusion." Without it the world lies before us, as Pope wrote in the first draft of his *Essay on Man*,—

"A mighty maze, and all without a plan."

[1] St. Luke xii. 29.

And if we follow the poet in that cold philosophical deism which led him to revise his famous line so that it now reads

"A mighty maze, but not without a plan,"[1]

we are still in the dark, still confused and hopeless, unless we go further and learn enough of Him who made the plan, to trust Him even when we cannot perfectly understand His working, and to confide absolutely in "His most holy, wise, and powerful preserving and governing all His creatures and all their actions."[2]

Christ's view of it.

This is what Christ gives us: a view of God in His world which requires faith to accept it, but which when it is accepted, satisfies the reason and the heart better than any other view, clears away many of the intellectual and moral difficulties which beset us, and becomes the inward source not of doubt and distress, but of certainty and peace.

Contrasted with other views.

This is not true, we must admit, of some of the forms in which the doctrine of divine sovereignty has been preached in Christ's name. They have often disregarded the facts of nature. They have often outraged the moral instincts of humanity. They have created new obstacles to faith. They have driven men

[1] Pope's *Essay on Man*, part i., line 6.
[2] *The Shorter Catechism*, question xi.

back in dumb resentment to believe in the positivist's "sombre Fatality," rather than in an absentee God who has foreordained, by one and the same decree, all the evil and all the good, all the sorrow and shame and suffering that are in the world.

Not so with Christ's teaching. It is sane and sweet. It allays resentment and begets serenity. It gives a reconciling, harmonizing, atoning view of God's sovereignty. And if we can see it clearly and preach it faithfully, it will be to-day, as it was in His day, one of the great attractions of the gospel for an age of doubt.

II

Christ's doctrine old and new.

Christ's doctrine of the divine sovereignty was both old and new. It was old because it recognized the truth, uttered so magnificently by prophets and psalmists, of God's right and power to rule the universe which He has made. "Thy throne, O God, is for ever and ever."[1] "The Lord hath prepared His throne in the heavens and His kingdom ruleth over all."[2] "He doeth according to His will in the army of heaven, and among the inhabitants of the earth: and none can stay His hand, or say unto Him, What doest Thou?"[3]

[1] Psalm xlv. 6. [2] Psalm ciii. 19. [3] Daniel iv. 35.

A simpler revelation.

But Christ's doctrine was new because it revealed the presence of the sovereign God in the physical universe more simply, more naturally, more intimately, than it had ever been revealed before. How gentle, how plain, how mildly luminous, is the language in which Jesus expresses this truth, compared with the flashing, rolling speech of the prophets! He uses the words of common life, transfigured with emotion, — the language of lyric, rather than of epic, poetry.

God in His world.

The manifestations of divine power in the Old Testament appear chiefly as mighty works, exceptional forthputtings of supernal force. It seems sometimes as if they came from a distance; as if God had withdrawn from the world and had been called back to it by the peril and the cry of His people. But Christ would teach us to feel that He has never gone away for an instant. He is always here. Nothing that happens is hidden from Him. Nor does He hide Himself from any who would behold Him. We may see Him every day, in the feeding of the birds, in the blossoming of the flowers,

"And every wayside bush aflame with God."

In all the processes of nature He is present and sovereign.

The divine immanence

This view of the relation of God to the material world is not external and mechanical. It is inward and vital. God has not made the world and wound it up and left it to run by itself. He is in it, as really as a man is in the house that he inhabits, and all the potencies that move and animate it flow directly from Him. The Jews thought that God had fabricated the universe in six days and sat down to rest on the seventh, laying aside His work as a clock-maker would put down a finished clock. But Christ said, "My Father worketh until now, and I work"[1] Creation is not ended, it is going on all the time. Yesterday was a creative day; and so is to-day; and so to-morrow will be. The divine thought is still weaving its beautiful garment on the roaring loom of Time.

The divine orderliness.

But God's activity in the world is not capricious or disorderly. No one was more sensitive than Jesus to "the rhythmic element in nature, — the flow of rivers, the procession of stars, the antiphony of day and night, the silent but inviolate order of the seasons."[2] It was He who expressed the law of growth ·

[1] St. John v. 17.

[2] H. W. Mabie, *Essays on Nature and Culture* (New York, 1896), p. 295.

"first the blade, then the ear, and after that the full corn in the ear."[1] It was He who suggested the analogy of natural law in the spiritual world, applying the figure of germination to His own death and resurrection: "Except a corn of wheat fall into the ground and die, it abideth alone; but if it die, it bringeth forth much fruit."[2] The parables which He used to describe the kingdom of heaven were drawn from nature and based on law. It was like "leaven which a woman took and hid in three measures of meal until the whole was leavened," or "like a grain of mustard seed, which a man took and sowed in his field; which indeed is the least of all seeds, but when it is grown it is the greatest among herbs."[3] He taught His disciples to look upon the regular and steadfast ordinances of nature as the proof that their Heavenly Father was mindful of them and would take care of them. You will not find any such superfluous phrase as "special Providence" in the teaching of Jesus. His thought was of a general and universal Providence, wide enough and deep enough to embrace the wants of all creatures and provide for them. God's chil-

[1] St. Mark iv. 28. [2] St. John xii. 24.
[3] St. Matt. xiii. 32, 33.

dren were not to trust in miracles and marvels for their daily bread; they were not to be always looking and calling for the extraordinary, — manna from the sky, water from the riven rock. They were to rest rather upon the course of nature in quiet confidence, and work with it in cheerful joy, knowing that He who clothes the grass of the field will much more clothe them,[1] — and by the same power working in the same way.

Miracles not against nature.

Yet Jesus did not think of God as having exhausted all possible modes of His activity in those which are familiar to us.[2] His presence in the world is of such a personal kind that it necessarily brings with it the power of direct, personal, infinitely varied action. Out of this power spring those strange signs and wondrous works which we call miracles. Jesus never said that they were against nature. He never even said that they were supernatural. He claimed only that they were proofs of a divine mission, because they were such works as could only come from God. They were signs, just as all uncommon and extraordinary acts are signs. But signs of what? Of personality, of that power of choice in modes of

Signs of personality.

[1] St. Matt. vi. 30.

[2] See Appendix, note 55.

action which is the essential attribute of a free spirit. They were wrought in order that men might believe, not in order that they might be astonished; and just as truly in order that they might believe in the order of nature as in the Person who upholds it by His presence.

The reign of God through law.

"An energy," says Mr. Ruskin, "may be natural without being normal, and divine without being constant." Jesus did not teach the reign of law. He taught the reign of God through law. And in order that men might be sure that the law did not bind God like a chain, but freely expressed His sovereign will, it was given unto Jesus to show men those rare works, unique and transcendent, like strokes of genius, which reveal, as if by flashes of light, the true relation between the sovereign God and the universe which He is making and ruling.[1]

The secret of Jesus.

It is always to this personal God that Jesus would direct the thoughts and confident affections of men. How is it possible for any one to miss His meaning, and translate it into something entirely different, as Matthew Arnold does in his misinterpretation of what he calls "the secret of Jesus"? It is not merely the joy

[1] See Appendix, note 56.

and peace of self-renunciation that Jesus sets forth to His disciples. It is the inward quietude and rest of self-surrender to a loving Father who is also the Mighty God. And it is not from the sense of His resistless power, but from the consciousness of His love, of His Fatherhood, that peace comes. "Yea, Father, for so it was well-pleasing in Thy sight."[1] "Father, all things are possible unto Thee; remove this cup from Me: howbeit not what I will, but what Thou wilt."[2] "Father, into Thy hands I commit My spirit."[3] This is the secret of Jesus. He does not teach bare sovereignty to which we must yield because it is irresistible. He teaches sovereignty of a certain kind, — the sovereignty of a Father, who is as much better, as He is more powerful, than all earthly parents or rulers, and who will never forsake His world, nor suffer His children to slip from His mighty hand.

Trust in a sovereign Father.

III

But sovereignty of this kind necessarily implies distinctions in the manner of its exercise. It cannot possibly be conceived of in terms of

[1] St. Matt. xi. 26. [2] St. Mark xiv. 36. [3] St. Luke xxiii. 46.

The highest kind of sovereignty discriminates.

any single force or confined to any one mode of operation. It must be flexible and discriminating. It must include within itself as many forms of rule as there are forms of being under its dominion. What, for example, should we say of a king who had but one way of dealing with all his subjects, young and old, wise and ignorant, loyal and disloyal, and who treated his servants under precisely the same conditions as his horses and his chariots? Or what should we say of a father who attempted to regulate and rule his children without reference to their character, and who made no distinction between them and the furniture of his house? Yet this, in effect, is the theory of the divine sovereignty which has frequently been set forth by theologians as if it were the only one which did justice to the glory of God.

A lower kind of sovereignty mechanical.

"The will of God," according to this theory, "is the irresistible force. It is the source of all things, all persons, all events. From it they all proceed, under it they all act, by an invariable necessity. This will has already determined from all eternity everything that comes to pass. Every character in the world, like every rock and every plant, is just what God willed it to be. Everything that happens, happens because He willed it and precisely as He willed it. The life of mankind is far from being in any sense a voyage, an adventure, a probation. It is simply the process of printing a history which has already been written and set in type down to the last letter. The great press is in motion. Our souls are the blank pages. On one is printed a foreordained prayer. On another a foreordained blasphemy. Death is the folding knife. Judgment is the act of binding, in which the fair pages will be preserved and the foul pages rejected and burned. The sovereignty of God is exercised in seeing that the book goes through the press exactly as it was written, without the addition or subtraction of a single syllable of the foreordained text."

The lower kind less glorious.

But surely, even if this theory were true and could be proved, it is not of a nature to give aid and comfort to those who are zealous for the glory of God. It does not really exalt and magnify the divine sovereignty, but narrows and degrades it. It does not call for the perfect wisdom and unlimited resources of a potent Ruler able to meet emergencies, to overcome oppositions, to guide and direct intelligent and free subjects like Himself, and to conduct a high enterprise, through all the difficulties that may arise, to a successful end. It calls for qualities of a lower kind and a strictly limited scope; the exact knowledge and the applied strength of a skilful machinist; not the broad intelligence, the swift genius, the inexhaustible patience, and the triumphant personal influ ence of a great Captain, a Master and Lord of men.

Which kind has God chosen?

It is conceivable, of course, that God might have chosen to create a universe in which His sovereignty should be exercised in this one unvarying line of foreordained necessity. Being supreme, He has both the right and the power to make such a sphere, or spheres, for the revelation of His attributes as may please Him. But it is not humanly conceivable that He should have made this particular choice which is ascribed to Him for His own glory. If He had chosen this kind of a universe, so far as we can see, it must have lowered and hidden His glory. It must have left Him with a field in which the highest qualities of personality could not possibly be exercised. It must have made all subsequent choice, and all approval or disapproval, and all truly moral government impossible. The existence of rewards and punishments, the sense of merit or demerit among the creatures of such a world, would be inexplicable. Nay more, it would be a cruel delusion, which, since it must come like everything else, according to this theory, from the will of the Maker, would reflect a dark shadow of discredit upon His moral character. To claim that this sense of responsibility, like all other parts of the system, may be a necessity, a legal fiction which is essential to the working of a scheme far above our comprehension and therefore above our judgment, makes it more awful, but not more admirable. If there is any validity whatever in our moral instincts, we need not hesitate to say, that from our present point of view, which is for us the only one attainable, this theory of the absolute and unconditional sovereignty of God, exercised by one law of necessity over all creatures, is so far from being for God's glory that it is apparently for His shame and dishonour.

The difficulties of absolutism.

As a matter of fact, it has been, and still is, the most fertile mother of doubts. "A universe in which all the power was on the side of the creator, and all the morality on the side of creation, would be one compared with which the universe of naturalism would shine out as a paradise indeed."[1] The idea of an irresponsible God ruling by an eternal and inflexible *fiat* over responsible men, is a moral nightmare,

[1] *Foundations of Belief*, p. 326.

under which humanity groans, and from which it struggles to awake, even though it should have to open its eyes upon the blank darkness of an unsearchable night. Between the unknowable God of agnosticism and the unlovable God of absolutism, there is indeed little to choose. But the choice, such as it is, lies on the side of agnosticism. It is unspeakably better to doubt God's personality, His supremacy, His very being, than it is to doubt His eternal goodness and His moral integrity.

Jesus delivers us from them.

But the teaching of Jesus is designed and fitted to deliver us, if we will accept it, from both of these doubts. He reveals a God who is not only Lord of all, but who exercises His sovereignty in discretion, in justice, and in love. He does not look upon all His creatures with the same eyes. He discriminates, He distinguishes, He has regard to their differences of nature and character. The human soul is of more value to Him than many sparrows.[1] How much is a man better than a sheep?[2] By so much as he is more like God, spiritual, free, responsible, immortal. These qualities, which God Himself has created, God Himself respects. Every word of Jesus takes it

[1] St. Matt. x. 31. [2] St. Matt. xii. 12.

God is a fair master.

for granted that God is not an infinite Autocrat, a hard master, reaping where He has not sown, and gathering where He has not strewed, but a fair and equitable Lord, who takes into consideration all the conditions of His subjects and renders unto all their dues. The forces of nature obey His will inevitably, and for them there is neither praise nor blame. The souls of men are invited to love Him, and commanded to serve Him, but they are left free to choose whether they will obey or disobey, and upon their choice the approval and blessing of God depend.

The divine omnipotence self-limited in action.

Who can question for a moment that this is the view of the divine sovereignty which underlies all the parables of Christ? The omnipotence which He teaches is not sheer, absolute, unconditioned. It is a self-restrained power. It is able to limit itself, to act in such a way and under such conditions as God chooses to create. If He could not do this, He would not be truly omnipotent. If there were but one method in which He could manifest His will, and that the method of necessity, He would be forever shut out from personal relations, which can only exist where there are different wills, capable of agreement or disagreement, of co-operation or conflict, of harmony or discord.

Jesus believed and taught that God has actually chosen to limit the autocratic exercises of His sovereignty by creating beings who have the power of yielding to His will or of resisting it.[1]

The origin of evil not in God.

And from this resistance flow all the evil, all the sorrow, all the misery of the world. God does not ordain sin. God does not even permit sin, in the sense that He allows it to exist without opposition and condemnation on His part. It may be a necessary feature of a world of free choice and moral probation. Jesus seems to imply as much when He says "It must needs be that offences come." But He adds at once, "Woe unto that man by whom the offence cometh."[2] That man is not doing the will of God. He is a rebel, a traitor, an apostate. Sin is a perversion of the heart from its true purpose just as blindness is a perversion of the eye from its true function.[3] When the tares appear in the field, Christ does not leave us to suppose for a moment that they were planted by the same hand that sowed the good seed. He says, "An enemy hath done this."[4] Satan, who is the embodiment of evil and the leader of all who are opposed to God,

[1] See Appendix, note 57.
[2] St. Matt. xviii. 7.
[3] St. Luke xi. 34–36.
[4] St. Matt. xiii. 28.

is the great enemy, the adversary not only of souls, but also of the Divine will.

Sin is the work of an enemy.

Turn for a moment to the narrative of the temptation of Christ.[1] He was led up by the Spirit into the wilderness to be tempted of the devil. But did the same Spirit lead the devil? Was Satan acting under the divine sovereignty in the same sense, in the same way, that Jesus was? Set aside, if you will, the question of the personality of the evil one. There was a suggestion of evil before the mind of Jesus. Did that suggestion come from the same source as the holy strength that resisted it, — the all-creating, all-controlling will of God? Can the same fountain send forth sweet and bitter waters? Why then should the one be called cursed and the other blessed? Such a view simply obliterates all moral distinctions. It completely undermines and ruins the significance of Christ's life as a free obedience to the will of God, and it utterly paralyzes His gospel as a divine call to men to enter freely into the same obedience.

Two spheres of God's sovereignty.

Jesus teaches very distinctly that there are two spheres in which the sovereignty of God is exercised, — in heaven and on earth.[2] These

[1] St. Matt. iv. 1–11.

[2] Beyschlag, *New Testament Theology*, vol. i., pp. 84, 85.

two spheres are not conceived locally but spiritually. They are realms in which the power of God is working under different conditions. In heaven the Divine will is unopposed, and therefore the empire of heaven is peace and holiness and unbroken love. On earth the Divine will is opposed and resisted, and therefore earth is a scene of conflict and sin and discord. For this reason the kingdom of heaven must *come* to earth, it must win its way, it must strive with the kingdom of darkness and overcome it. God's sovereignty in heaven is triumphant. God's sovereignty on earth is militant, in order that it may triumph, — and triumph not in universal destruction, but in the salvation of all who will submit to it and embrace it and work with it, — triumph not by bare force, as gravitation triumphs over stones, but by holy love, as fatherly wisdom and affection triumph over the reluctance and rebellion of wayward children.

Triumphant in heaven.

Militant on earth.

Divine omniscience.

It must be admitted frankly that this view of Divine sovereignty does not seem to be consistent with the theory of absolute divine foreknowledge of all volitions and all events.[1] This has been urged as a fatal objection against it. But the objection cannot be pressed because

[1] See Appendix, note 58.

it lies in a region where our ignorance is so great that dogmatism is, to say the least, unbecoming. There may be some way of reconciling the self-limitation of God's omnipotence with the certainty of His foreknowledge, which is beyond the reach of our logic. But whether there be any such reconciliation or not, one thing is clear: we have not the right to make a logical statement of our ignorance of one divine attribute a reason for refusing to accept, frankly and sincerely, Christ's revelation of the mode in which another divine attribute is exercised.

Foreknowledge corresponds with the facts.

God knows everything. But when we say that, we mean simply that He knows everything which can be the object of knowledge. He knows all things as they are. He does not know them as they are not. The very perfection of His knowledge consists in its exact correspondence with the nature of its object. If an event is certain, fixed, and foreordained, then God knows it as certain, fixed, and foreordained. If it is contingent upon the free, self-determining, preferential action of a human will, then God knows that it is contingent, for He Himself has foreordained that it should be so.

God waits.

God waits to hear whether His children will call upon Him in their distress; and if they call, He hears and helps them. If Jesus teaches anything, He teaches that prayer really influences the purpose and action of God.[1]

The probation of men.

God waits to see whether His husbandmen will return to Him the fruits of His vineyard; whether they will receive and honour the messengers whom He sends unto them; and if they are rejected, He sends other messengers; and last of all He sends His Son, saying, "It may be they will reverence him"[2] But when this last *maybe* does not come to pass, then judgment falls upon the wicked husbandmen, not because they have fulfilled the secret will of the King, but because they have rebelled against Him.

The Lord of Hosts.

This conception of God in His world, not as the mere spectator of the fulfilment of His own immutable decrees, but as the Lord of Hosts, presiding over the great scene of conflict between good and evil in the souls of men who can only attain to real holiness through real liberty, and warring mightily on the side of good in order that it may win the victory, infinitely exalts and glorifies Him. We see Him in the teaching of Jesus, as the High Captain of the armies of love, working salvation in the midst of the earth, pleading with men to accept His mercy, warning them

[1] See Appendix, note 59. [2] St. Luke xx. 13.

to escape from His judgments, sustaining the good in their goodness, overthrowing the wicked in their wickedness, bringing light out of darkness and triumph out of defeat, amid all strifes and storms maintaining His kingdom of righteousness and peace and joy in the Holy Ghost. His sovereignty embraces human liberty as the ocean surrounds an island. His sovereignty upholds human liberty as the air upholds a flying bird. His sovereignty defends human liberty as the authority of a true king defends the liberty of his subjects, — nay, rather, as the authority of a father tenderly and patiently respects and protects the spiritual freedom of his children in order that they may learn to love and obey him gladly and of their own accord. For this is the end of God's sovereignty: that His kingdom may come; that His will may be done on earth, — not as it is done in the circling of the stars or in the blossoming of flowers, — but as it is done in heaven, where created spirits freely strike the notes that blend in perfect harmony with the music of the Divine Spirit, where

Sovereignty embraces liberty.

> "Thousands at his bidding speed
> And post o'er land and ocean without rest;
> They also serve who only stand and wait."

IV

Does this reate uncertainty?

But does not the acknowledgment that God has thus limited the operation of His sovereignty on earth by conditioning His actions upon the character and conduct of other beings than Himself, throw us back into confusion and uncertainty? Does it not make the course of the world insecure and the end of all things doubtful?

The reserve of power.

It would do so if it were not for the other truth which Jesus reveals with equal clearness, that God is in the world guiding, ruling, and directing it, and that He has kept the supremacy in His own hands. His presence is the talisman of creation. He is the master of the ship; His hand is on the helm; and whether the sailors obey or mutiny, He will guide the vessel to her appointed haven.

Evil transient, good eternal.

The power of evil is a finite, transient, self-destroying power. It disintegrates, it dies, it passes away with the enfeeblement and destruction of the soul that yields to it. But the power of goodness is eternal and incorruptible, because it is of God. Satan is the prince of this world, but his might is limited to the perverted and enslaved wills that submit to him. He is not the ruler of nature.

God is the master of winds and waves and earth and stars. The great battalions are on His side and under His control. If for one instant the cause of Christ were in real danger, He could summon celestial hosts without number to His assistance.[1] But because He knew this, He knew also that His cause was never in danger. He knew that His kingdom was an everlasting kingdom. He knew that He had already overcome the world.

God the rock of our trust.

How serene and splendid are the words with which He reassures His disciples, again and again! "*Fear not! Care not! Be not anxious! O thou of little faith, wherefore didst thou doubt? Have faith in God! Upon this rock will I build my church and the gates of hell shall not prevail against it! Fear not, little flock, for it is your Father's good pleasure to give you the kingdom!*" How glorious is the vision of that kingdom which Jesus unfolds as He looks forward to the new birth of earth and heaven in the perfect fulfilment of the purpose of God! How absolute is the confidence with which He rests upon God's power to work out all that may be needed to bring about that blessed consummation. The unwavering faith of Jesus in the permanence and world-wide diffusion and

[1] St. Matt. xxvi. 53.

ultimate triumph of His kingdom of truth and holiness and love, is not the least — sometimes I think it is the greatest — evidence of His divinity and charm of His gospel.

The inspiration of heroism.

Communicated by His divine influence to the hearts of His disciples, this faith has been a force of incalculable potency and inspiration in the lives of men. The noblest deeds of heroism and self-sacrifice and liberation have been wrought in the strength of it. The greatest conquests over self and sin, the supreme victories of righteousness and love and peace in human hearts, have been won through this faith. *Deus vult* — God wills it! — is the war-cry that rouses the human will to its highest endeavour.

The secret of courage.

Here is a man struggling against evil, longing and striving to rise to high and holy life. And if he is alone in the struggle, what assurance has he, what promise or hope of success? He may fail, he may perish. But when the great truth flashes into his heart that God is with him in the fight, that God is "not willing that any should perish but that all should come to repentance,"[1] that God is the captain of his salvation and the leader of his soul, — then he is emancipated, then he triumphs, then he is joined to the Invincible. He cries

[1] 2 Pet. iii. 9.

sovereignty by preserving and rescuing and delivering His people from overwhelming perils! Even when it has seemed to be otherwise, even when the Church has appeared forsaken and helpless, when the billows of persecution have rolled fathom-deep above her head, when avalanches of falsehood have buried the truth out of sight, it has only been for a time, and the end has been the victory of the defeated. The blood of the martyrs has been the seed of the Church. The boastful shouts of error have been the advertisement of the silent truth. Error has had kings and generals, philosophers and orators, empires and armies; truth has had God. Error has had swords and spears, ships and cannons, fortresses and dungeons, racks and fires; truth has had God. God and one make a majority. Unless the Church doubts, she cannot fear. Unless the Church denies, she cannot despair. In the darkest days, when the confusion seems greatest, the conflict most unequal, she can look out on the great battle-field and cry

Truth and God.

"History's pages but record
One death-grapple in the darkness 'twixt old systems and the Word;
Truth forever on the scaffold, Wrong forever on the throne,—

Yet that scaffold sways the future, and behind the dim unknown
Standeth God within the shadow, keeping watch above His own."[1]

The victory is sure.

But is it for the Church alone, is it not for the whole world that this truth of God's sovereignty shines? To our eyes the conflict of life and death, of good and evil, seems to be undecided, and we think it may be perpetual. The dust blinds us; the uproar bewilders us; as far as our sight can pierce we see nothing but the rolling strife, — sin always in arms against holiness, the created will always resisting and defying the creator. But Christ sees that the conflict is decided, though it is still in progress. Christ sees that the victory is won, though it is not yet manifest. On the hill of the cross the captain of salvation met the captain of sin and conquered him. Calvary is victory. Through death Christ hath overcome him that had the power of death, that is the devil.[2] Satan has received his mortal wound; and if he still fights more fiercely, it is because he knoweth that he hath but a short time.[3] The

The final consummation.

day is coming when he must perish; the day is coming when sin and strife shall be no more;

[1] James Russell Lowell, *The Present Crisis.*
[2] Heb. ii. 14. [3] Rev. xii. 12.

the day is coming when Christ shall put all enemies under His feet[1] and shout above the grave of death, "O thou enemy, destructions are come to a perpetual end"; the day is coming when the great ship of the world, guided by the hand of the Son of God, shall float out of the clouds and storms, out of the shadows and conflicts, into the perfect light of love, and God shall be all in all. The tide that bears the world to that glorious end is the sovereignty of God.

O mighty river, strong, eternal Will,
In which the streams of human good and ill
Are onward swept, conflicting, to the sea,
The world is safe because it floats in Thee.

[1] 1 Cor. xv. 25–28.

VIII

SERVICE

"Thyself and thy belongings
Are not thine own so proper as to waste
Thyself upon thy virtues, they on thee.
Heaven doth with us as we with torches do
Not light them for themselves; for if our virtues
Did not go forth of us, 't were all alike
As if we had them not. Spirits are not finely touched
But to fine issues; nor Nature never lends
The smallest scruple of her excellence,
But, like a thrifty goddess, she determines
Herself the glory of a creditor —
Both thanks and use."

— *Measure for Measure.*

VIII

SERVICE

This uneven world.

THAT strange and searching genius, Nathaniel Hawthorne, in one of his spiritual phantasies has imagined a new Adam and Eve coming to the earth after a Day of Doom has swept away the whole of mankind, leaving their works and abodes and inventions, — all that bears witness to the present condition of humanity, — untouched and silently eloquent. The representatives of a new race enter with wonder and dismay the forsaken heritage of the old. They pass through the streets of a depopulated city. The sharp contrast between the splendour of one habitation and the squalor of another, fills them with distressed astonishment. They are painfully amazed at the unmistakable signs of inequality in the conditions of men. They are troubled and overwhelmed by the evidence of the great and miserable fact that one portion of earth's lost inhabitants was rich and comfortable and full of ease, while the multitude was poor and weary and heavy-laden with toil.[1]

The sense of distress at life's inequality. This feeling of sorrowful perplexity over the unevenness and apparent injustice of human life, which the prose poet puts into the heart of his new Adam and Eve, is really but a reflection from the tender and pitiful depths of his own. Who is there that has not sometimes felt it rising within his own breast, — this profound sentiment of inward trouble and grief, this feeling of spiritual discord and wondering repugnance at the sight of a world in which the good things of life are so unequally distributed, in which at the very outset of existence, before the factor of personal merit or demerit, the element of work and wages, enters into the problem at all, so much is given to one man and so little to another man that they seem to be forever separated and set at enmity with each other by the unfairness with which they are treated?

The sympathy of the age. This sentiment has been strangely deepened and intensified in the nineteenth century by innumerable causes, until it has become one of the most marked characteristics of the present age. Never before have men felt the sorrows

[1] Hawthorne's Works, Riverside Edition, 1884; *Mosses from an Old Manse*, p. 297.

and hardships of their fellow-men so widely, so keenly, so constantly as to-day. In one sense this is the honour and glory of our age. It is an evidence of quickened moral sensibility, a revival or renewal of the noblest capacities of our human nature.

A noble sentiment driven to madness.

But in another sense it is the greatest peril of our age. For it has been seized by the spirit of scepticism and transformed into an ally of annihilating doubt. It has been used as an argument against the possibility of discovering a moral order in such a "hungry, ill-conditioned world" as this. Man's inhumanity to man has been employed to prove God's indifference or injustice to man. The feeling of sorrow and perplexity has been aggravated by wild and whirling words into a passion of resentment against the present conditions of life. Rash and sweeping schemes for their total destruction have been proclaimed as a new gospel. Christianity has been first claimed as a supporter of these schemes, and then denounced and repudiated as the chief obstacle to their success. The cry goes up that the whole world is out of joint. "Everything is wrong and crooked and unfair: the race of man has been deceived and maltreated and oppressed by the creation of such an order of life as the present. If God created it, so much the worse for God. But it is almost certain that He did not create it, almost certain that there is no God. The world of inequality is man's mistake. There is but one thing to do, and that is to break it all up, at once and utterly, and begin anew. Create a new world if possible. If not, then let the old wreck sink and be blotted out, for it is worse, infinitely worse, than the blank desolation of an unconscious chaos."

What shall we do?

This cry of anger and despair rings to-day in the ears of all earnest and thoughtful men and women. The element of sincerity, of truth, of justice, that thrills unmistakably through its strange, fierce music, stirs our hearts to the core. We are filled with perturbation and distress and deep anxiety to know the right and to do it, to understand the meaning of this exceeding great and bitter cry, and the duty to which it calls us. Is it indeed the utterance of true equity and wisdom? Is it the voice of a new Adam, appearing after so many ages of delusion, with open eyes to condemn the old world, and with ruthless hand to break it in pieces? Must we welcome him and hearken to him and believe in him, as the true judge and regenerator and leader of mankind?

Christ's answer and example.

The very form of the question points the way to the only Master who can answer it. Hawthorne's picture of the second Adam was a poetic dream. But the Apostle Paul uses the same figure to reveal a historic truth. "The first man Adam became a living soul. The last Adam became a life-giving spirit. Howbeit that is not first which is spiritual, but that which is natural; then that which is spiritual. The first man is of the earth, earthy; the second man is of heaven."[1] The new Adam has already come upon the earth, eighteen centuries ago. He was called Jesus. With pure and perfect heart He entered into the world, not desolate and depopulate, but thronged with the myriads of toiling, suffering men. With clear eyes He looked upon their different conditions, their manifold inequalities, their outward and inward joys and sorrows. With steadfast heart He set Himself to the divine task of beginning a new humanity and inaugurating the kingdom of heaven on earth.

His calmness and sanity.

He did not strive nor cry, neither was His voice heard in the streets.[2] He did not protest against the moral government of the universe, because one man was rich and another poor, one strong and another weak, one happy and

[1] 1 Cor. xv. 45–47. [2] St. Matt. xii. 19.

another wretched, one good and another evil. He did not say that God must be unjust because He has given, in things spiritual as well as in things temporal, much to one and little to another. He did not teach His followers that the only way to help the world was to rebel against this order, and refuse to submit to it, and denounce it, and fight against it. He did not even proclaim a social and political revolution. He was the most peaceful, orderly, obedient, loyal citizen of all that subject land of Palestine; rendering unto Cæsar the things that were Cæsar's, discharging every duty of His lowly lot with cheerful fidelity, and labouring patiently for His daily bread.

He knows the secret.

He was not blind, nor dull of heart to feel the troubles of life. The problem of inequality lay wide open before Him. But it did not agitate nor distract Him. He neither raved nor despaired. He was serene and sane.

"He saw life clearly and He saw it whole."

He looked through the problem to its true solution. He knew the secret which justifies the ways of God to man. He knew the secret by which an eternal harmony is to be brought into the apparent discords of life. He knew the secret by which men living in an unequal world, and accepting its inequality as the condition of their present existence, can still become partakers of a perfect, peaceful equity, and citizens of an invisible, imperishable city of God. That secret was none other than the highest, holiest doctrine of Jesus, the divine truth of election to service.

I

Christ's gospel for the present world.

Before we set our hearts to take in the meaning and the fulness of this truth let us try to get them in tune for it by listening to some of the other teachings of Jesus which are meant to quiet and steady us in the contemplation of the unevenness of human existence.

And first of all He reminds us that our real happiness in this world does not depend upon our outward condition, but upon our inward state. "The life is more than meat and the body than raiment."[1] "A man's life consisteth not in the abundance of the things which he possesseth."[2] The land of wealth is not the empire of peace. Joy is not bounded on the north by poverty, on the east by obscurity, on the west by simplicity, and on the south by servitude. It runs far over these borders on

[1] St. Matt. vi. 25. [2] St. Luke xii. 15.

every side. The lowliest, plainest, narrowest life may be the sweetest. Most of the disciples of Jesus were peasants, but they were as happy, as contented, even in this world, as if they had been princes. There was more gladness and singleness of heart in that frugal breakfast of broiled fish and bread beside the boats on the shore of the sea of Tiberias,[1] than in the splendid feast in the house of Simon the Pharisee. Life has its compensations and its comforts for all estates. Work means health. Obscurity means freedom. The best pleasures are those that are most widely diffused.

The secret of happiness.

I do not mean to say that Jesus overlooked the bitter hardships of toil under bad masters, under false and cruel and oppressive laws. I do not mean to say that He would not have been full of pity and indignation at the sight of the crushed and crippled state of great multitudes of human beings in our modern cities. But I am sure that He teaches us to believe that the real source of human misery is not in poverty, but in a bad heart; that envy is not a virtue, but a vice; that life is a great gift to all who will receive it cheerfully and contentedly, even in a world where its material things are unevenly distributed; and that the true beati-

[1] St. John xxi. 1-13.

tudes are not monopolies reserved for the few, but blessings within the reach of all, and gloriously independent of all outward contrasts in the lives of men. Indeed it seems as if He would go even beyond this, and remind us that some of these blessings could not be ours except in a world of contrast and temporal inequality. Of the eight beatitudes which Jesus Himself pronounced, four at least, — the blessing of the mourners, and of the meek, and of the merciful, and of the peace-makers, — imply the existence of differences and degrees among men; and one — the blessing of those who are persecuted for righteousness' sake — is only possible in a world where evil is sometimes actually more powerful and prosperous than good.

The compensations of life.

I have not been able to find a single word of Christ that looks forward to a time in which there shall be no more inequalities on earth, no more rich and poor, no more masters and servants, no more wise men, and no more babes. But there are many words of His that pierce with mild and gracious light through all these outward distinctions to reveal the truth that this kind of inequality is superficial and illusory, that the babes rejoice in beholding those mysteries which are hidden from the wise and prudent, that servants are often nobler and more free than their masters, that the poor may have treasures laid up in heaven which are beyond all earthly reckoning, and that this is the true wealth which brings contentment and peace.

Peace on earth. It is a great mistake to suppose that Jesus preached a gospel which was melancholy and depressing for those who received it in this world. It is a great mistake to suppose that He taught men that they must resign themselves to earthly misery and make the journey of life as a weary and mournful pilgrimage. He came to cheer and brighten the hearts of all who would accept His guidance and tread the path of virtue with courage and fidelity and hope. He came to give us rest in the midst of toil, and that refreshment which only comes from weariness in a good cause. He came to tell us not to despair of happiness, but to remember that the only way to reach it on earth is to seek first usefulness, first the kingdom of God, and then the other things shall be added. He that loseth his life for Christ's sake shall not lose it but find it,[1]—find it in deep inward contentment,

"And vital feelings of delight,"

[1] St. Matt. x. 39.

which make up the true and incomparable joy of living.

The secret of felicity.

Jesus does not differ from other masters in that He teaches us to scorn earthly felicity. The divine difference is that He teaches us how to attain earthly felicity, under all circumstances, in prosperity and in adversity, in sickness and in health, in solitude and in society, by taking His yoke upon us, and doing the will of God, and so finding rest unto our souls. That is the debt which every child of God owes not only to God, but also to his own soul, — to find the real joy of living.

Joy is a duty.

"Joy is a duty," — so with golden lore
The Hebrew rabbis taught in days of yore.
And happy human hearts heard in their speech
Almost the highest wisdom man can reach.

But one bright peak still rises far above,
And there the Master stands whose name is Love,
Saying to those whom heavy tasks employ
"Life is divine when duty is a joy."

The world that is to come.

The second point in the teaching of Jesus which is meant to rectify our views of the unevenness of the world, is His doctrine of a future life, — not a different life, but the same life moving on under new conditions and to new issues. This world is not all. There is another world, a better age, a more perfect state of being, in which the sorrows and losses of those who now suffer unjustly will be compensated, and in which—let us not hesitate to say it as calmly and as firmly as Jesus said it—those who have unjustly and selfishly enjoyed their good things in this world will suffer in their turn. It is the fashion nowadays to sneer at such teaching as this; to call it "other-worldliness"; to declare that it has no real power to strengthen or uplift the hearts of men. Jesus did not think so. Jesus made much of it. Jesus pressed home upon the hearts of men the consolations and warnings of immortality. He showed the miserable failure of the man who filled his barns and lost his empty soul.[1] He bade His disciples, when they suffered and were persecuted for righteousness' sake, "rejoice and be exceeding glad, for great is your reward in heaven."[2]

The errors of time call for the balance of eternity.

Let us not impoverish our gospel by flinging away, in our fancied superiority, this precious truth. It is impossible to justify the present fragmentary existence of man if we look at it and speak of it as the whole of his life. Earth has mysteries which naught but heaven can explain. Earth has sorrows which naught but heaven can heal. Yes, and earth has evils,

[1] St. Luke xii. 16–21. [2] St. Matt. v. 12.

black and secret offences of man against man, false and foul treasons against the love of God, crimes which take a base advantage of His patience and long-suffering and hide themselves like poisonous serpents in the shelter of the very laws which He has made for the good of the world, sins all entangled with the present structure of society and beyond the reach of human law, undiscoverable iniquities, unpardonable and unpunishable cruelties,—which naught but hell can disclose and consume. The errors of time call for the balance of eternity. Patient labour, patient endurance, patient resignation in this present life shall be greatly rewarded in the life to come. Now is the day of toil and trial; but the pay-day will surely dawn. Much of the best that is done in this world receives no earthly wages. Those to whom it is done,—the poor, the maimed, the lame, the blind,—"they cannot recompense thee; but thou shalt be recompensed at the resurrection of the just."[1]

This unequal life our education for the future.

Thus Jesus teaches; and He shows us that the present order of inequality, so far from being an obstacle to this result, is the very means by which it is to be accomplished. The discipline of this uneven life is the education

[1] St. Luke xiv. 14.

by which alone we can be prepared for the heavenly life. Jesus does not present Himself as a rectifier of life's unequal conditions of outward fortune. He distinctly refuses this office. "Man, who made me a judge or a divider over you?"[1] Jesus does not preach an equality which is synonymous with life on a dead level. He does not preach equality at all. He preaches fraternity. And fraternity implies differences, — older and younger, stronger and weaker, higher and lower. The elder brother is the heir; all that the father has is his; but his sin lies in holding fast to his inheritance selfishly, in shutting out his younger brother, in forgetting and denying that he is a brother at all.[2] The distinctions of life are not meant to obscure, but to reveal and to beautify its best virtues. Out of dependence spring the sweet blossoms of gratitude and loyalty. Out of mastership flow the refreshing streams of forbearance and justice and mercy. The apostle tells us that the love of money is a root of all kinds of evil.[3] But Christ shows us the deeper truth that the right use of money is a means of all kinds of good. "It is more blessed to give

Fraternity better than equality.

[1] St. Luke xii. 14. [2] St. Luke xv. 25–32.
[3] 1 Tim. vi. 10.

than to receive."[1] Every gift of Providence to us is an opportunity and therefore a responsibility, and the blessing does not come with the gift until we recognize the responsibility, and use the opportunity. The mammon of unrighteousness can only be destroyed by a process of transformation which transmutes it into the pure gold of the celestial treasury.[2] The name of that process is charity. And the translation of that name is wise and holy love.[3]

Christianity and Communism.

Let us try to think distinctly. It is said nowadays that Christianity means communism, and that it is the duty of all Christians to give away everything that they possess. It is strange that Christ never proclaimed this duty except to one man, and that man was not a Christian.[4] Of course it must be admitted at once that this would be the duty of all Christians if it could be shown that it would be for the real good of their fellow-men. But this never has been shown. On the contrary, communism has always turned out badly. It was tried in Jerusalem, in a limited way, when the early Christians sold all that they had and made a common purse; but it led, in less

[1] Acts xx. 35.
[2] St. Luke xvi. 19.
[3] See Appendix, note 60.
[4] St. Mark x. 21.

than ten years, to confusion and strife, and sank the Jerusalem church into a condition of pauperism and dependence upon the other churches, which had avoided the well-meant but dangerous experiment. It was tried in France, under atheistic auspices, and its fruit was wide-spread misery and injustice. It was tried to some degree in England, under a system of poor laws which were based upon the idea that every man had a right to eat whether he would work or not, and it resulted in such disorder and demoralization that it had to be discarded as a menace to society.

Love thy neighbour as wisely and well as thyself.

There is nothing in the teachings of Christ which would make us blind to these plain lessons of history. On the contrary, He desires and commands us to discover and do that which will really bless and help our fellow-men. "Thou shalt love thy neighbour as thyself,"[1]—the same kind of love, the same inward regard for the higher ends and aims of life, which is the saving grace of the individual soul, is to be the saving grace of society.[2] And what kind of love is that? It is a wise and holy love, a love which puts character first and comfort second, a love which seeks to purify and bless and uplift the whole

[1] St. Matt. xxii. 39. [2] See Appendix, note 61.

man. Such a love may be shown by withholding as truly as by bestowing. False charity pampers self and pauperizes others. True charity educates self by helping others. The so-called Christian who never gives is a false Christian. The Christian who gives carelessly, blindly, indiscriminately, however generously, is a very imperfect Christian. The Christian who gives thoughtfully, seriously, fraternally, bending his best powers to the accomplishment of a real benefaction of his fellow-men, bestowing himself with his gift, is in the true and only way of the following of Jesus.

Every privilege is a call to service.

Preach this truth. Preach it home to the hearts of men, without fear or favour for rich or poor. Preach it home to your own heart so close that it shall save you from the minister's besetting sins of spiritual selfishness and cant. Tell the Lady Bountiful that she is not called to discard her ladyhood, but to give herself with all her refinements, with all her ac complishments, with all that has been given to her of sweetness and light, to the ennobling service of humanity. Tell the Merchant-Prince that he is not called to abandon his place of influence and power, but to fill it in a princely spirit, to be a true friend and father to all who are dependent upon him, to make his prosperity a fountain of blessing to his fellow-men, to be a faithful steward of Almighty God. And then let us tell ourselves, as members of the so-called "educated classes," to whom God has given even greater gifts than those of rank and riches, — privileges of knowledge, opportunities of culture, free access to the stored-up wisdom of the ages, — let us tell ourselves with unflinching fidelity that God will hold us to a strict account for all these things. If our salt loses its savour it shall be trodden under foot of men. If our culture separates us from humanity we shall be cast into the outer darkness. Our light must shine or be shamefully extinguished. Every faculty and every gift we possess must be honestly and entirely consecrated to the service of man, in Christ's name and for Christ's sake.[1] This is the gospel for the present age, and for every age. This is the way in which the kingdom of heaven is to be established on earth. This is the way in which the inequality of this mortal life is to be transfigured and irradiated with a divine equity. "What we look for, work for, pray for, as believers, is a nation where class shall be bound to class by the fullest participation in the treasure of the one life; where the mem-

Social regeneration.

[1] See Appendix, note 62.

bers of each group of workers shall find in their work the development of their character and the consecration of their powers: where the highest ambition of men shall be to be leaders of their own class, so using their special powers without waste and following the common traditions to noble issues: where each citizen shall know, and be strengthened by the knowledge, that he labours not for himself only, nor for his family, nor for his country, but for GOD."[1]

II

Inequality in the spiritual world.

Thus far the teaching of Christ leads us with clear serenity in our understanding of the differences among men in the distribution of the goods of this present world. But the deeper problem still remains untouched. There is an apparent inequality in the bestowal of spiritual blessings. In the life of the soul also, it seems that much is given to one and little to another. Some men are born very close to the kingdom of heaven and powerfully drawn by unseen hands to enter its happy precincts. Other men are born far away from the gates of light, and it looks to us as if all the influences of their life were hindrances rather than helps to holiness.

[1] B. F. Westcott, Bishop of Durham, *The Incarnation and Common Life* (London, Macmillan, 1893), p. 82.

There is an undeniable contrast in the religious world which can only be interpreted as a divine foreordination, — that is to say, an act by which some men are set before others, given the precedence, offered an earlier and apparently an easier opportunity of spiritual life. If God is sovereign, this act, by which the means of grace are unevenly dispensed, must be the result of a divine choice.

The doctrine of election.

The formal recognition of this choice is the doctrine of election. It is an inevitable doctrine. It is founded upon facts which admit of no denial. And it brings every thoughtful and earnest soul face to face with the question of questions, upon the answer to which the nature and reality of religion depend.

The searching question.

Is God arbitrary, is God partial, is God unjust? Does He bless some of His children and leave the rest under an irremediable curse without a single reason which can be exhibited to human faith and justified in perfect love? In the last and highest realm of life, the realm of the spirit, does He make it more blessed to receive than to give, and exercise His sovereignty in favouritism, and establish heaven as a kingdom of infinite and eternal and inexplicable inequality?

False answers.

It is an idle thing to answer this question by an appeal to God's absolute right to dispose of all His creatures as He will. For the very essence of true religion is the faith that He is such a God that He wills to dispose of all His creatures wisely and fairly and in perfect love. And the very essence of a true revelation, as the message which calls religion into being, is that it makes God's wisdom and fairness and love manifest, and so helps us to understand and adore and trust Him, not only for ourselves but for the whole world.

An arbitrary God.

It is an idle thing to answer this question by saying that God is under no obligation to be good to everybody, and therefore that He may be good to whomsoever He pleases. The idea of an irresponsible God is a moral mockery. Poisonous doubt exhales from it as malaria from a swamp. To teach that all men are God's debtors, and that therefore it is right for Him to remit the debt of one man, and to exact the penalty from another to the last farthing, is to teach what is logically true and morally false. Our hearts recoil from such a doctrine. If God has made us, and made us spiritual paupers, utterly incapable of anything good, we are not His debtors. Jesus teaches us that God asks of us only to give as freely as we have received.[1] He demands only that which He

An irresponsible God.

[1] St. Matt. x. 8.

Himself has made us able to pay. And He forgives like the good master in the parable, with a free pardon which needs but the confession of helplessness and poverty to call it forth.[1]

A God whose glory is not goodness.

It is an idle thing to answer this question by an appeal to ignorance, and to say that God elects some men to be saved and leaves the rest of mankind to be lost simply for His own unsearchable and inexplicable glory! For God's glory, as revealed by religion, is identical with His goodness. Faith, true and joyful and uplifting faith, answers only to a gospel which makes that identity more clear and luminous, and shows that the divine election in the realm of grace is perfectly consistent with that wide and deep love wherewith God so loved the whole world that He sent His only begotten Son that whosoever believeth in Him should not perish but have everlasting life.[2]

Election perverted in human theology.

Now it is because men have forgotten this that they have found no answer, or a false and misleading answer, to the problem of inequality in the spiritual world. It is because they have torn the doctrine of election from its roots in the divine love, and petrified it with unholy logic, that it has lost its beauty, its perfume,

[1] St. Matt. xviii. 27. [2] See Appendix, note 63.

its power of fruitfulness to everlasting life. We must go back from the dead skeleton as it is preserved in the museum of theology to the living plant as it blossoms in the field of the Bible. We must go back of Jonathan Edwards, and back of John Calvin, and back of Augustine, to St. Paul, and see how, under his hand, all the mysterious facts of election as they are unfolded in human history, break into flower at last in the splendid faith that "God hath shut up all unto disobedience that He might have mercy upon all."[1] We must go still farther back, to Christ, and learn from Him that election is simply the way in which God uses His chosen ones to bless the world,— the divine process by which the good seed is sown and scattered far and wide and the heavenly harvest multiplied a thousand-fold. "I elected you," He says to His disciples and to us, "I elected you, and appointed you, that ye should go and bear fruit, and that your fruit should abide."[2]

Christ's doctrine of election to service.

Christ's doctrine of election is a living, fragrant, fruitful doctrine. It is the most beautiful thing in Christianity. It is the very core and substance of the gospel, translated

[1] Romans xi. 32; see Appendix, note 64.
[2] St. John xv. 16.

from the heart of God into the life of man. It is the divine law of service in spiritual things. It is the supreme truth in the revelation of an all-glorious love; the truth that God chooses men not to be saved alone, but to be saved by saving others, and that the greatest in the kingdom of heaven is he who is most truly the servant of all.[1]

Christ as the elect servant.

Is not this true of Christ Himself? He is the great example of what it means to be elect. He is the beloved Son in whom the Father is well pleased. And He says "Behold, I am in the midst of you as he that serveth."[2] Service was the joy and crown of His life. Service was the refreshment and the strength of His soul, the angel's food, the "meat to eat" of which His disciples did not know.[3]

The disciple must be as his Lord.

Was not this the lesson that He was always teaching them by practice and by precept, that they must be like Him if they would belong to Him, that they must share His service if they would share His election! "I have appeared unto thee for this purpose," He said to Saul, "to make thee a servant (ὑπηρέτην, *a rower in the ship*), and a witness both of those things which thou hast seen and of the things

[1] See Appendix, note 65. [2] St. Luke xxii. 27.
[3] St. John iv. 32.

in the which I will appear unto thee."[1] The vision of Christ is the call to service. And if Paul had not been obedient to the heavenly vision could Saul have made his calling and election sure? But he answered it with a noble faith. "It pleased God to reveal His son in me *in order that I might preach him among the nations.*"[2] Henceforward, wherever he might be, among his friends in Cilicia, in the dungeon at Philippi, on the doomed vessel drifting across the storm-tossed Adriatic, in the loneliness of his Roman prison, this was the one object of his life, to be a faithful servant of Christ, and therefore, as Christ was, a faithful servant of mankind.[3]

Parables of privilege and service.

How can we interpret Christ's parables, without this truth? The parables of the Pounds and the Talents are both pictures of election to service. They both exhibit the sovereignty of God in distributing His gifts; they both turn upon the idea of man's accountability for receiving and using them; and they both declare that the reward will be proportioned to fidel ity in serving. The nature and meaning of this is explained by Christ in His great descrip tion of the judgment, which immediately follows the parable of the Talents in St. Matthew's

[1] Acts xxvi. 16. [2] Gal. i. 16. [3] 2 Cor. iv. 5.

Gospel.[1] Many of those who have known Him will be rejected at last because they have not served their fellow-men. Many of those who have not known Him will be accepted because they have ministered lovingly, though ignorantly, to the wants and sorrows of the world.

Service, the key-note of the kingdom.

Service is the key-note of the heavenly kingdom, and he who will not strike that note shall have no part in the music. The King in the parable of the Wedding Feast[2] chose and called his servants, not to sit down at ease in the palace, but to go out into the highways and bid every one that they met, to come to the marriage. And if one of those servants had refused or betrayed his mission, if he had neglected his Master's business, and sat down on the steps of the palace or walked pleasantly in the garden until the supper was ready, do you suppose that he would have found a place or a welcome at the feast? His soul would have stood naked and ashamed without the wedding-garment of love. For this is the nature of God's kingdom, that a selfish religion absolutely unfits a man from entering or enjoying it. Its gate is so strangely strait that a man cannot pass through it if he desires and tries

[1] St. Matt. xxv. 31–46.
[2] St. Matt. xxii. 1–13.

to come alone; but if he will bring others with him, it is wide enough and to spare.

Who seeks for heaven alone to save his soul,
May keep the path, but will not reach the goal;
While he who walks in love may wander far,
Yet God will bring him where the blessed are.

The prayer of intercession.

How wonderfully all this comes out in the great intercessory prayer of Christ at the last supper.[1] That prayer is the last and highest utterance of the love wherewith Christ, having loved His own which were in the world, loved them unto the end. He prays for His chosen ones: "I pray for them: I pray not for the world but for those whom Thou hast given Me." "Holy Father, keep them in Thy name which Thou hast given Me, that they may be one even as We are. For their sakes I consecrate Myself, that they themselves also may be consecrated in truth. Neither for these only do I pray, but for them also that believe on Me through their word; that they may all be one, even as Thou, Father, art in Me, and I in Thee, that they also may be in Us; that the world may believe that Thou didst send Me." How the prayer rises, like some celestial music, through all the interwoven notes of different fellowships, the fellowship of the Father with the Son, the fellowship

[1] St. John xvii.

of the Master with the disciples, the fellowship of the disciples with each other, until at last it strikes the grand chord of universal love. Not for the world Christ prays, but for the disciples in the world, in order that they may pray for the world, and serve the world, and draw the world to faith in Him. And so, in truth, while He prays thus for His disciples, He does pray for the whole world. Circle beyond circle, orb beyond orb, like waves upon water, like light from the sun, the prayer, the faith, the consecrating power spread from that upper room until they embrace all mankind in the sweep of the divine intercession. The special, personal, elective love of Christ for His own is not exclusive; it is magnificently and illimitably inclusive. He loved His disciples into loving their fellow-men. He lifted them into union with God; but He did not lift them out of union with the world; and every tie that bound them to humanity, every friendship, every fellowship, every link of human inter course, was to be a channel for the grace of God that bringeth salvation, that it might appear to all men.[1]

Christ's Ideal. This is Christ's ideal: a radiating gospel: a kingdom of overflowing, conquering love; a

[1] Titus ii. 11.

church that is elected to be a means of blessing to the human race.[1] This ideal is the very nerve of Christian missions, at home and abroad, the effort to preach the gospel to every creature, not merely because the world needs to receive it, but because the Church will be rejected and lost unless she gives it. 'Tis not so much a question for us whether any of our fellow-men can be saved without Christianity. The question is whether we can be saved if we are willing to keep our Christianity to ourselves. And the answer is, No! The only religion that can really do anything for me, is the religion that makes me want to do something for you. The missionary enterprise is not the Church's afterthought. It is Christ's forethought. It is not secondary and optional. It is primary and vital. Christ has put it into the very heart of His gospel. We cannot really see Him, or know Him, or love Him, unless we see and know and love His ideal for us, the ideal which is embodied in the law of election to service.

Missions essential to Christianity.

For this reason the spirit of missions has always been the saving and purifying power of the Christian brotherhood. Whenever and wherever this ideal has shined clear and strong,

[1] See Appendix, note 66.

it has revealed the figure of the Christ more simply and more brightly to His disciples, and guided their feet more closely in the way of peace and joy and love.

Missions emancipated the early hur h.

In the first century it was the spirit of foreign missions that saved the Church from the bondage of Jewish formalism. Paul and his companions could not live without telling the world that Christ Jesus came to seek and save the lost — lost nations as well as lost souls. The heat of that desire burned up the fetters of bigotry like ropes of straw. The gospel could not be preached to all men as a form of Judaism. But the gospel must be preached to all men. Therefore it could not be a form of Judaism. The argument was irresistible. It was the missionary spirit that made the Emancipation Proclamation of Christianity.

Missions keep the gospel pure.

In the dark ages the heart of religion was kept beating by the missionary zeal and efforts of such men as St. Patrick, and St. Augustine, and Columba and Aiden, and Boniface, and Anskar, who brought the gospel to our own fierce ancestors in the northern parts of Europe and wild islands of the sea. In the middle ages it was the men who founded the great missionary orders, St. Francis and St. Dominic, who did most to revive the faith and purify the life of the Church. And when the Reformation had lost its first high impulse, and sunken into the slough of dogmatism; when the Protestant churches had become entangled in political rivalries and theological controversies, while the hosts of philosophic infidelity and practical godlessness were sweeping in apparent triumph over Europe and America, it was the spirit of foreign missions that sounded the *reveillé* · to the Christian world, and lit the signal fire of a new era — an era of simpler creed, more militant hope, and broader love — an era of the Christianity of Christ. The desire of preaching the gospel to every creature has drawn the Church back from her bewilderments and sophistications closer to the simplicity that is in Christ, and so closer to that divine ideal of Christian unity in which all believers shall be one in Him. You cannot preach a complicated gospel, an abstract gospel, to every creature. You cannot preach a gospel that is cast in an inflexible mould of thought, like Calvinism, or Arminianism, or Lutheranism, to every creature. It will not fit. But *the* gospel, the only gospel which is divine, must be preached to every creature. Therefore, these moulds and forms cannot be an essential part of it. And so we work our way back out of the tangle of human speculations toward that pure, clear, living message which Paul carried over from Asia to Europe, the good news that God is in Christ, reconciling the world to Himself.

One message and many ways of preaching it.

This is the gospel for an age of doubt, and for all ages wherein men sin and suffer, question and despair, thirst after righteousness and long for heaven. There are a thousand ways of preaching it, with lips and lives, in words and deeds; and all of them are good, provided only the preacher sets his whole manhood earnestly and loyally to his great task of bringing home the truth as it is in Jesus to the needs of his brother-men. The forms of Christian preaching are manifold. The spirit is one and the same. New illustrations and arguments and applications must be found for every age and every race. But the truth to be illuminated and applied is as changeless as Jesus Christ Himself, in whose words it is uttered and in whose life it is incarnate, once and forever. The types of pulpit eloquence are as different as the characters and languages of men. But all of them are vain and worthless as sounding brass and tinkling cymbals, unless they speak directly and personally and joyfully of that divine love which is revealed in

Christ in order that all who will believe in it may be saved from doubt and sin and selfishness in the everlasting kingdom of the loving God.

The only gospel.

This is the gospel which began to shine through the shadows of this earth at Bethlehem, where the Son of God became the child of Mary, and was manifested in perfect splendour on Calvary, where the Good Shepherd laid down His life for the sheep. For eighteen centuries this simple, personal, consistent gospel has been the leading light of the best desires and hopes and efforts of humanity. It is the one bright star that shines, serene and steady, through the confusion of our perplexed, struggling, doubting age. He who sees that star, sees God. He who follows that star, shall never perish. It has dawned upon my heart so clearly and so convincingly that the one thing I have cared and tried to do in these lectures is to make it plain that this is the essence of Christianity, the only gospel that is worth preaching in all ways to all men, that Jesus Christ is God who loves us in order that we may learn to love one another. But if I have failed to make this view of religion clear, if an imperfect utterance has beclouded and obscured the message, at least let this last word be plain, at least let nothing hide from your soul or from mine, this supreme, saving truth of election to service.

The last word.

The vision of God in Christ is the greatest gift in the world. It binds those who receive it to the highest and most consecrated life. To behold that vision is to be one of God's elect. But for our own souls the result of that election depends upon the giving of ourselves to serve the world for Jesus' sake. *Noblesse oblige.*

Believers in Christ, the servants of God's love to the whole world.

Let us not miss the meaning of Christianity as it comes to us and claims us. We are chosen, we are called, not to die and be saved, but to live and save others. The promise of Christ is a task and a reward. For us there is a place in the army of God, a mansion in the heaven of peace, a crown in the hall of victory. But whether we shall fill that place and dwell in that mansion and wear that crown, depends upon our willingness to deny ourselves and take up our cross and follow Jesus. Whatever our birthright and descent, whatever our name and profession, whatever our knowledge of Christian doctrine and our performance of Christian worship may be, — when the great host is gathered in the City of God, with tattered flags and banners glorious in their bloodstained folds, with armour dinted and swords worn in the conflict, with wounds which tell of courage and patient endurance and deathless loyalty, — when the celestial knighthood is assembled at the Round Table of the King, our name will be unspoken, our crown will hang above an empty chair, and our place will be given to another, unless we accept now, with sincere hearts, the only gospel which can deliver us from the inertia of doubt and the selfishness of sin. We must enter into life by giving ourselves to the living Christ who unveils the love of the Father in a Human Life, and calls us with Divine Authority to submit our Liberty to God's Sovereignty in blessed and immortal Service to our fellow-men for Christ's sake.

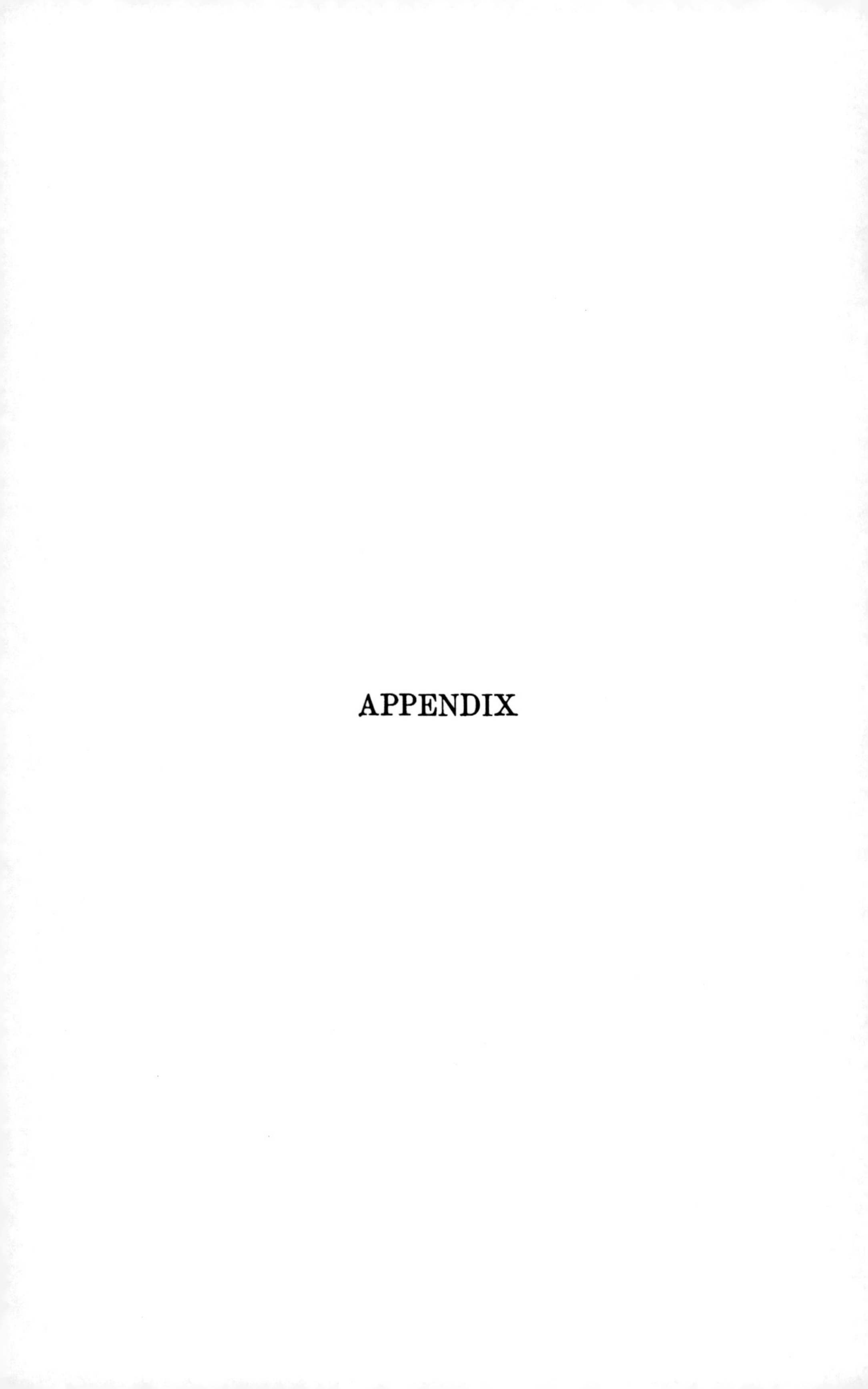

APPENDIX

APPENDIX

FORE-WORD

Note 1. — "Every living preacher must receive his message in a communication direct from God, and the constant purpose of his life must be to receive it uncorrupted, and to deliver it without addition or subtraction.

"It is a truism, but, I think you will all agree, a neglected truism. If in our brief better moments we see it, we constantly are tempted to recede from it. Not without some suspicion of what may be involved in unflinchingly accepting it as true, we are apt to take refuge in modifications, compromises, denials. Flesh shrinks, and the heart cries out. Let some one else go up the rugged steep of the mountain and see Him face to face. Let some one else stand awestruck in the passing of the Almighty. I will do some humbler task. Let me read the lessons, or let me recite the creed, or let me be a priest, clad in the robes of office which are a discharge from personal fitness. On many grounds and in many ways we disclaim our calling. The truth remains as a truism, but we dare not grasp it ourselves. The world notices our disclaimer, and accepts us on the level of our own elected degradation." — ROBERT F. HORTON, *Verbum Dei* (Macmillan, 1893), p. 17.

Note 2. — "So much of the preaching to-day seems to be preaching to yesterday, or preaching about yesterday. It does not touch as it ought the contemporary life, and grapple with its problems, its duties, its difficulties, its dangers. There is, in consequence, a sense of unreality about it, a foreignness, a far-away-ness; and to men who are of necessity preoccupied with the exigencies of contemporary life, it is not helpful preaching. . . . We should try to make them understand that there is a heaven here in this world, and a hell here in this world, and that those who at present are living in this world are in this heaven or in this hell. And Jesus comes as light, we should try to make them understand, to show them how to get out of the hell which is here, or the hell-fire which is here, into the heaven which is here. . . . We should try to teach men and women to-day that the way in which to use the light of another world shining in Jesus Christ, is not to stand gazing up into heaven and acquiring thus a kind of spiritual myopia, or shortsightedness, which prevents them from seeing clearly the forms of duty immediately about them, but to walk on the earth in the light of that other world which in Jesus Christ so brightly and beautifully appears." — DAVID H. GREER, *The Preacher and His Place* (Scribners, 1895), pp. 46, 47.

"Pére Gratry says, 'It is not enough to utter the mysteries of the Spirit, the great mysteries of Christianity, in formulas, true before God, but not understood of the people. The apostle and the prophet are precisely those who have the gift of interpreting these obscure and profound formulas for each man and each age. To translate into the common tongue the mysterious and sacred language . . . to speak the word of God afresh in each age, in accordance with both the novelty of the age and the eternal antiquity of the truth, this is what St. Paul means by interpreting the unknown tongue. But to do this, the first condition is that a man should appreciate the times he lives in. "Hoc autem tempus quare non probatis." ' " — *Lux Mundi* (John Murray, London, 1890), p. viii.

LECTURE I

Note 3. Page 5. — "Je ne crois pas énoncer une vérité bien neuve en affirmant que la Littéra ture · est un de ces éléments, le plus important peut-être, car dans la diminution de plus en plus évidente des influences traditionnelles et locales, le Livre devient le grand initiateur. Il n'est aucun de nous qui, descendu au fond de sa conscience, ne reconnaisse qu'il n'aurait pas été tout à fait le même s'il n'avait pas lu tel ou tel ouvrage; poème ou roman, morceau d'histoire ou de philosophie. À cette minute précise, et tandis que j'écris cette ligne, un adolescent, que je vois, s'est accoudé sur son pupitre d'étudiant par ce beau soir d'un jour de juin. Les fleurs s'ouvrent sous la fenêtre, amoureusement. L'or tendre du soleil couché s'étend sur la ligne de l'horizon avec une délicatesse adorable. Des jeunes filles causent dans le jardin voisin. L'adolescent est penché sur son livre, peut-être un de ceux dont il est parlé dans ces Essais. C'est les Fleurs du Mal de Baudelaire, c'est la Vie de Jésus de M. Renan, c'est la Salammbô de Flaubert, c'est le Thomas Graindorge de M. Taine, c'est le Rouge et le Noir de Beyle. . Qu'il ferait mieux de vivre! disent les sages. . . . Hélas! c'est qu'il vit à cette minute, et d'une vie plus intense que s'il cueillait les fleurs parfumées, que s'il regardait le mélancolique Occident, que s'il serrait les fragiles doigts d'une des jeunes filles. Il passe tout entier dans les phrases de son auteur préféré. Il converse avec lui de cœur à cœur, d'homme à homme. Il l'écoute prononcer sur la maniére de goûter l'amour et de pratiquer la débauche, de chercher le bonheur et de supporter le malheur, d'envisager la mort et l'au delà ténébreux du tombeau, des paroles qui sont des révélations. Ces paroles l'introduisent dans un univers de sentiments jusqu'alors aperçu à peine. De cette premiére révélation à imiter ces sentiments, la distance est faible et l'adolescent ne tarde guére a la franchir. Un grand observateur a dit que beaucoup d'hommes n'auraient jamais été amoureux s'ils n'avaient entendu parler de l'amour." — PAUL BOURGET, *Essais de Psychologie Contemporaine* (Paris, 1895), p. vi.

"It may be alleged that the popular opinion is merely a reflection of the popular literature, and that the truth of the assumption I am calling in question is generally believed by the many who read, simply because it is constantly asserted by the few who write. This no doubt is accurate, and up to a certain point is an explanation. There exists now a kind of literature, already large and of growing importance, produced by experts for the benefit of those who desire to be 'generally informed'; which, unlike most ephemeral literature, leads public opinion rather than follows it. Of course the greater part of this, whether it consists of handbooks or of review articles, has no bearing whatever on the relation which ought to exist between Religion and Science, or with the positive evidence that may exist for either. But just as popular accounts of chemistry, physiology, or history appear in answer to the natural desire of an educated but busy public for as much knowledge as possible, about as many things as possible, with as little trouble as possible; so there are easily found eminent authors anxious to purvey for that apparently increasing class of persons who aspire to be advanced thinkers, but who like to have their advanced thinking done for them." — A. J. BALFOUR, *A Defence of Philosophic Doubt* (Macmillan, 1879), p. 308.

Note 4. Page 7. — "With sorrow and reluctance it must be confessed that the majority of Oxford and Cambridge undergraduates are without, or at least profess to be without, any religious beliefs at all. There are, of course, many exceptions. Exceptions, however, they remain ; certainly the greater number are Gallios so far as the church is concerned." — Article in *The Nineteenth Century,* October, 1895, in "The Religion of the Undergraduate." Things are not quite so bad in the United States, but in France and Germany they are worse.

Note 5. Page 11. — Among these books, which take a distinctly spiritual and religious view of evolution, some of the most interesting have been written in America. *The Idea of God,* and *The Destiny of Man,* by John Fiske; *Agnosticism and Religion,* by President Schurman of Cornell University; *The Evolution of Christianity,* by Dr. Lyman Abbott; and *Moral Evolution,* by Prof. George Harris of Andover, may be named as works of great value to the student who wishes to understand the deeper tendencies of modern thought. One of the first of undoubtedly orthodox theologians to assert that the theory of evolution is not hostile to religion, was President James McCosh of Princeton. The general course of the argument as it is developing in the light of science to-day, may be seen in the following extracts from the writings of Dr. John Fiske.

"The Darwinian theory, properly understood, replaces as much teleology as it destroys. From the first dawning of life we see all things working together toward one mighty goal, the evolution of the most exalted spiritual qualities which characterize Humanity. The body is cast aside and returns to the dust of which it was made. The earth, so marvellously wrought to man's uses, will also be cast aside. The day is to come, no doubt, when the heavens shall vanish as a scroll, and the elements be melted with fervent heat. So small is the value which Nature sets upon the perishable forms of matter! The question, then, is reduced to this: Are Man's highest spiritual qualities, into the production of which all this creative energy has gone, to disappear with the rest? Has all this work been done for nothing? Is it all ephemeral, all a bubble that bursts, a vision that fades? Are we to regard the Creator's work as like that of a child, who builds houses out of blocks, just for the pleasure of knocking them down? For aught that science can tell us, it may be so, but I can see no good reason for believing any such thing. On such a view the riddle of the universe becomes a riddle without a meaning. Why, then, are we any more called upon to throw away our belief in the permanence of the spiritual element in Man than we are called upon to throw away our belief in the constancy of Nature? The more thoroughly we comprehend that process of evolution by which things have come to be what they are, the more we are likely to feel that to deny the everlasting persistence of the spiritual element in Man is to rob the whole process of its meaning. It goes far toward putting us to permanent intellectual confusion, and I do not see that any one has yet alleged, or is likely to allege, a sufficient reason for our accepting so dire an alternative."— John Fiske, *The Destiny of Man* (Houghton, Mifflin, & Co., 1895), pp. 113–116.

"As to the conception of Deity, in the shape impressed upon it by our modern knowledge, I believe I have now said enough to show that it is no empty formula or metaphysical abstraction which we would seek to substitute for the living God. The infinite and eternal Power that is manifested in every pulsation of the universe is none other than the living God. We may exhaust the resources of metaphysics in debating how far his nature may fitly be expressed in terms applicable to the physical nature of Man; such vain attempts will only serve to show how we are dealing with a theme that must ever transcend our finite powers of conception. But of some things we may feel sure. Humanity is not a mere local incident in an endless and aimless series of cosmical changes. The events of the universe are not the work of chance, neither are they the outcome of blind necessity. Practically there is a purpose in the world whereof it is our highest duty to learn the lesson, however well or ill we may fare in rendering a scientific account of it. When from the dawn of life we see all things working together toward the evolution of the highest spiritual attributes of Man, we know, however the words may stumble in which we try to say it, that God is in the deepest sense a moral Being. The everlasting source of phenomena is none other than the infinite Power that makes for righteousness. Thou canst not by searching find Him out; yet put thy trust in Him, and against thee the gates of hell shall not prevail; for there is neither wisdom nor understanding nor counsel against the Eternal." — JOHN FISKE, *The Idea of God* (Houghton, Mifflin & Co., 1886), pp. 166, 167.

"So, as we look back over the marvellous life-history of our planet, even from the time when there was no life more exalted than that of conferva scum on the surface of a pool, through ages innumerable until the present time, when man is beginning to learn how to decipher nature's secrets,— we look back over an infinitely slow series of minute adjustments, gradually and laboriously increasing the points of contact between the inner life and the world environing it. Step by step in the upward advance toward humanity the environment has enlarged, from the world of the fresh-water alga, with its tiny field and its brief term of existence, to the world of civilized men, which comprehends the stellar universe during æons of time. Every such enlargement has had reference to actual existences outside. The eye was developed in response to the outward existence of radiant light, the ear in response to the outward existence of acoustic vibrations. The mother's love came in response to the infant's needs. Fidelity and honour were gradually developed as the nascent social life required them. Everywhere the internal adjustment has been brought about so as to harmonize with some actually existing external fact. Such has been nature's method: such is the deepest law of all life that science has been able to detect.

"Now there was a critical moment in the history of our planet, when love was beginning to play a part hitherto unknown, when the notions of right and wrong were germinating in the nascent human soul, when the family was coming into existence, when social ties were beginning to be knit, when winged words first took their flight through the air. *This is the moment when the process of evolution was being shifted to a higher plane,* when civilization was to be superadded to organic evolution, when the last and highest of creatures was coming upon the scene, when the dramatic purpose of creation was approaching fulfilment. At that critical moment we see the nascent human soul vaguely reaching forth toward something akin to itself, not in the realm of fleeting phenomena, but *in the eternal presence beyond.* An internal adjustment of ideas was achieved in correspondence with an unseen world. That the ideas were very crude and childlike, that they were put together with all manner of grotesqueness, is what might be expected. The cardinal fact is that the crude, childlike mind was groping to put itself into relation with an ethical world not visible to the senses. And one aspect of this fact not to be lightly passed over is the fact that *religion, thus set upon the scene coeval with the birth of human-*

ity, has played such a dominant part in the subsequent evolution of human society that what history would be without it is quite beyond our imagination. As to the dimensions of this cardinal fact, there can thus be no question. None can deny that it is the largest and most ubiquitous fact connected with the existence of mankind upon the earth.

"Now, if the relation thus established, in the morning twilight of man's career, between the human soul and the world invisible and immaterial, is a relation of which only the subjective term is real and the objective term is non-existent, then I say it is something utterly without precedent in the whole history of creation. All the analogies of evolution, so far as men have been able to decipher it, are overwhelmingly against any such supposition. All the analogies of nature fairly shout against the assumption of such a breach of continuity between the evolution of man and all previous evolution. So far as our knowledge of nature goes, the whole momentum of it carries us forward to the conclusion that the unseen world, as the objective term in a relation that has coexisted with the whole career of mankind, has a real existence; and it is but following out the analogy to regard that unseen world as the theatre where the ethical process is destined to reach its full consummation.

"*The lesson of evolution is that through all these weary ages the human soul has not been cherishing in religion a delusive phantom; but, in spite of seemingly endless groping and stumbling, it has been rising to the recognition of its essential kinship with the everliving God. Of all the implications of the doctrine of evolution with regard to man, I believe the very deepest and strongest to be that which asserts the everlasting reality of religion.*" — *Christian Literature.* February, 1896. "The Everlasting Reality of Religion." p. 428.

Note 6. Page 17. — "It has been said that fiction is harmful not so much by what is put in it as by what is left out. A few grains of wit, a leaven of literary skill, and a little of fancy go far to neutralize the septic properties of romance. The most harmful of all are — at least for young and unlearned people — the class usually styled 'harmless,' because the Seventh Commandment is never mentioned in them. These, tossed aside by mature readers, are read by the young in default of better: these ruin mind and weaken imagination, give false and sickly views of life, degrade taste, and enervate both character and feeling." — Article by "Maxwell Grey" in *The Nineteenth Century.* January, 1896. "The Influence of Fiction."

Note 7. Page 24. — "At first sight it might seem that these two kinds of pessimism, the popular and instinctive, and the philosophic and reasoned, have nothing to do with one another, and that no light can be thrown on the latter by the earlier development. It is, no doubt, true that modern German pessimism as a philosophy of existence must be examined and estimated on its own grounds, and be accepted or rejected according as it shows itself to be or not to be a consistent and well-reasoned system of thought. At the same time, the full significance of this speculative doctrine cannot be understood except by a reference to pre-philosophic pessimism. Systems of philosophy do not spring from pure isolated intellect, but are the products of concrete minds made up in part of certain emotional and moral peculiarities which mould and colour in numberless particulars their intellectual workmanship. It is at least *a priori* supposable that the philosophic pessimists partake somewhat of those habits of feeling and thought which underlie the more popular type of pessimism." — JAMES SULLY, *Pessimism* (Appleton, 1891), pp. 2, 3.

Note 8. Page 28. — "Il y a d'abord dans Baudelaire une conception particulière de l'amour. On la caractériserait assez exactement, semble-t-il, par trois épithètes, d'ordre disparate comme notre société. Baudelaire est tout à la fois, dans ses vers d'amour: mystique, libertin, et analyseur. . . . Il est libertin, et des visions dépravées jusqu'au sadisme troublent ce même homme qui vient d'adorer le doigt levé de sa Madone. Les mornes ivresses de la Vénus vulgaire, les capiteuses ardeurs de la Vénus noire, les raffinées délices de la Vénus savante, les criminelles audaces de la Vénus sanguinaire, ont laissé de leur ressouvenir dans les plus spiritualisés de ses poèmes. À travers tant d'égarements, où la soif d'une infinie pureté se mélange à la faim dévorante des joies les plus pimentées de la chair, l'intelligence de l'analyseur reste cruellement maitresse d'elle-même. La mysticité, comme le libertinage, se codifie en formules dans ce cerveau qui décompose ses sensations, avec la précision d'un prisme décomposant la lumière. Le raisonnement n'est jamais entamé par la fièvre qui brûle le sang ou par l'extase qui évoque les chimères. Trois hommes à la fois vivent dans cet homme, unissant leurs sensations pour mieux presser le cœur et en exprimer jusqu'à la dernière goutte la sève rouge et chaude. Ces trois hommes sont bien modernes, et plus moderne aussi est leur réunion. La fin d'une foi religieuse, la vie à Paris, et l'esprit scientifique du temps ont contribué à façonner, puis à fondre ces trois sortes de sensibilités, jadis séparées jusqu'à paraître irreductibles l'une a l'autre, et maintenant liées jusqu'à paraître inséparables, au moins dans cette créature, sans analogue avant le XIXe siècle français, qui fut Baudelaire." — BOURGET, *Psychologie Contemporaine*, pp. 5, 6, 8.

Note 9. Page 29. — "So hat Sudermann vor wenigen Wochen auf dem litterarischen Congress in Dresden unumwunden auf Ibsen, Tolstoi und Zola als die eigentlichen Lehrmeister seiner Generation hingewiesen. Welcher Meinung, über die Wahl dieser Muster man auch sein mag, gewiss ist dass diese strengen und überstrengen Richter ihrer Mitmenschen ihren deutschen Jüngern nicht zu geben vermochten, was ihnen selbst fehlte: innere Harmonie. Ganz im Geiste ihrer Vorbilder gingen unsere Neuerer mit grausamer Freude den Schäden und Schwächen unserer kranken Welt nach. Unbekümmert um die welthistorischen Vorgänge im Zeitalter Bismarcks, fernab von jedem Versuch oder Verdacht einer byzantinischen Litteratur waren und blieben sie das böse Gewissen ihrer Landsleute. Bald gab es kein verborgenes oder offenes Laster der herrschenden Klassen, kein kleines oder grosses Leid unserer Arbeiter und Bauern, das uns nicht auf den Bühnen und in den Büchern deutscher Naturalisten heimgesucht hätte. Drama und Roman spielten sich auf das Wunderwerkzeug hinaus, von dem ein feiner Humorist getraumt und gescherzt hat: *das Misèrophon.* Wie der Apseolonius in Otto Ludwigs 'Zwischen Himmel und Erde' hatten unsere Neusten den Katzenjammer von den Räuschen, die sich Andere antranken."—ANTON BETTELHEIM, *Cosmopolis,* January, 1896, pp. 272, 273.

Note 10. Page 34. — "Karl Peters is undoubtedly right, when he says of the systems both of Frauenstadt and of Hartmann, that they represent the transition to Theism without knowing it. 'I maintain that the Philosophy of the Unconscious represents the transition from Pantheism to Theism. As in Schopenhauer we have the transition from an idealistic to a realistic, so in Hartmann there is executed the transition from a pantheistic to a theistic *Weltanschauung.* The former, indeed, believed himself to stand on quite the other side, and no doubt the latter also thinks that he is planted on the opposite bank. But as Schopenhauer could not prevent the historical development from growing beyond his standpoint, so Hartmann will seek in vain to guard himself against such a breaking up of his system. . . . Ed. v. Hartmann's *Unconscious* is an almighty and all-wise Providence, raised above the world-process, which comprehends and holds within itself the whole world-development.'" — JAMES ORR, D.D., *The Christian View of God and the World* (New York, 1893), p. 457.

LECTURE II

Note 11. Page 46. — "Gradually one phenomenon after another of those discovered and attested by De Puysègur, Esdaile, Elliotson, etc., has been admitted into orthodox science under some slightly altered name. Certain phenomena, rarer and more difficult to examine, but attested by the same men with equal care, are still left in the outer court of the scientific temple. But when one has seen the somnambulic state, the insensibility under operations, etc., which were once scouted as fraudulent nonsense, becoming the commonplaces of the lecture-room, one can await with equanimity the general acceptance of the thought-transference and the clairvoyance which, from De Puységur's day onwards, have repeatedly occurred in the course of those same experiments — experiments which sometimes ruined the careers of those who made them, but which are now recognized as epoch-making in a great department of experimental psychology."

"The time for *a priori* chains of argument, for the subjective pronouncements of leading minds, for amateurish talk and pious opinion, has passed away; the question of the survival of man is a branch of Experimental Psychology. Is there, or is there not, evidence in the actual observed phenomena of automatism, apparitions, and the like, for a transcendental energy in living men, or for an influence emanating from personalities which have over-passed the tomb? This is the definite question which we can at least intelligibly discuss, and which either we or our descendants may some day hope to answer." — F. W. H. MYERS, *Science and a Future Life* (Macmillan, 1893), pp. 34, 44.

Note 12. Page 47. — "Now it *is* surely not unreasonable to surmise that there are limitations in the nature of the universe which must circumscribe the achievements of speculative research. Every astronomer knows that there was only one secret of the universe to be discovered, and that when Newton told it to the world the supreme triumph of astronomy was achieved. Whether Darwin or some one else shall have disclosed the other great mystery of the generation of life, it is none the less certain that all future triumphs will be insignificant by the side of the first luminous hypothesis. Chemistry rests, when all abatements have been made, on the atomic theory, and even if future investigation enables us to forecast with absolute precision what the result of combinations hitherto unattempted will be, so that we can calculate in the study what is now worked out gropingly in the laboratory, that discovery would hardly eclipse the merit of Dalton's contribution to science. So it is in every department of research. Even the greatest men are little more than sagacious interpreters of thought and toil which others have expended obscurely. The discovery of a new metal, a new star, or a new species is now nothing to thrill us with wonder and awe. We know that it has been worked up to by former experiments or is the result of improved instruments, and is no more matter of wonder than that this year's best steamship should make a knot an hour more than was possible five years ago. Then again, not only is science ceasing to be a prophet, but in virtue of her very triumphs, precisely because her thoughts are passing into the life-blood of the world, is she losing visible influence as a liberal educator. It is coming to be matter of history that she has taught us to substitute law for caprice in our conceptions of the Divine will; that she has relegated the belief in secondary causes and the belief in arbitrary interpositions of the First Cause to the lumber-room of fable; that she has given us a broader and intenser view of nature, while she has left us the fairyland of the world's childhood for an appreciable treasure. Other harvests have now been gathered in. The prophet and leader is rapidly becoming a handmaid. Her possibilities can be pretty accurately summed up or forecast in a cyclopædia; and having delivered herself of her one imperishable protest against popular theology, she has no other great moral truth to declare." — CHARLES H. PEARSON, *National Life and Character* (Macmillan, 1893), p. 291.

"But in truth *if* (as is commonly assumed) our discoveries are confined to the physical side of things, there is no ground whatever for this san guine hope. Admitting that the visible universe is, in relation to our present faculties, practically infinite, it by no means follows that our means of scrutinizing it are capable of indefinite improvement. And, in fact, we find the true pioneers of science greatly more cautious in their prognostic. We begin to hear that telescopy and microscopy (which in their brief existence have suggested so many more problems than they have solved) are already approaching ominously near to their theoretic limit. We begin to recognize in the length of the light-wave an irreducible bar to that scrutiny of the 'infinitely little' which we most urgently need. We begin to feel that the sensitiveness of the retina, the percipient power of the brain, however supplemented by sensitive apparatus, must always be inadequate to the more delicate tasks which we would fain assign to them and in short that the human body, developed for quite other purposes, must always be a rude and clumsy instrument for the apprehension of abstract truth. And more than this. Vast as is the visible universe, infinite as may have been the intelligence which went to its evolution, yet while viewed in the external way in which alone we can view *it*, — while seen as a product and not as a plan, — it cannot possibly suggest to us an indefinite number of universal laws. Such cosmic generalizations as gravitation, evolution, correlation of forces, conservation of energy, though assuredly as yet unexhansted, cannot in the nature of things be even approximately inexhaustible." — *Science and a Future Life*, p. 72.

Note 13. Page 48. — "Here terminated the first part of our inquiry. Its general result is to show (1) that from the particular knowledge obtained by observing the phenomena of a world assumed throughout this part of the essay to be persistent, no scientific conclusions could be drawn; and (2) that even if we suppose these phenomena to be part of a world governed by causation, we were not much advanced, and that, therefore, (3) some further principles or modes of inference have need to be discovered before Science is placed on a rational foundation. Of these 'further principles,' since their nature is altogether unknown, no more notice has been taken.

"Assuming then that the arguments attacked are fairly representative of English Philosophy at the present time — as is, I think, the case — and assuming, as I am bound to do, that the answers here given to those arguments are effective, we may say that Science is a system of belief which, for anything we can allege to the contrary, is wholly without proof. The inferences by which it is arrived at are erroneous; the premises on which it rests are unproved. It only remains to show that, considered as a general system of belief, it is incoherent: and this task is undertaken in the two chapters which together form the Third Part.

"The first of these (namely, Chapter XII.) is devoted in the main to showing that there is a discrepancy between the facts which Science asserts to be its (particular) premises and the facts which it puts forward as its ultimate conclusions. But besides this principal contention, it is shown incidentally that the universe, as it is represented to us by Science, is wholly unimaginable, and that our conception of it is what in Theology would be termed purely anthropomorphic.

"The chief argument of Chapter XII. is, however, only indirectly connected with this subject, its principal end being to contrast the world as it appears with the world as Science assures us that it is, and to show that the scientific reasoning which makes our knowledge of the second depend logically upon our knowledge of the first, is inadmissible.

"The fact that the two are in contradiction, is flagrant and undeniable — as any one may see who considers that while perception gives us immediate knowledge of the existence of coloured objects, Science tells us that this appearance is really due either to the vibration of uncoloured particles, or to reflection from uncoloured surfaces. It is also, I imagine, evident that no integral part of a system can contradict the premises of that system without introducing confusion and incoherence *into* the whole; and finally, it must be admitted that since our actual scientific system *does* rest upon the data given in perception, and since its conclusions *are in* contradiction with these data, it must be regarded as incoherent and confused." — ARTHUR JAMES BALFOUR, *A Defence of Philosophic Doubt* (Macmillan, 1879), pp. 284, 285, 287–289.

Note 14. Page 52. — "With the growth of knowledge Theology has enlarged its borders until it has included subjects about which even the most accomplished theologian of past ages did not greatly concern himself. To the Patristic, Dogmatic, and Controversial learning which has always been required, the theologian of to-day must add knowledge at first hand of the complex historical, antiquarian, and critical problems presented by the Old and New Testaments, and of the vast and daily increasing literature which has grown up around them. He must have a sufficient acquaintance with the comparative history of religions; and, in addition to all this, he must be competent to deal with those scientific and philosophical questions which have a more profound and permanent bearing on Theology even than the results of critical and historical scholarship." — ARTHUR JAMES BALFOUR, *The Foundations of Belief* (Longmans, 1895), p. 1.

"What manner of man must he be, who is to give epoch-making expression to the new consciousness of Christ, it is not difficult to imagine. He must know the method of physical science, and be in sympathy with its great generalizations; he must be at home in the kingdom of thought, familiar with the noble and fruitful ideas in philosophy, a companion of the imperial thinkers of the race; he must have at his tongue's end the salient facts of Christian history, and the fundamental conceptions and distinctions of historic theology; he must be a master of the new biblical learning, widely and deeply versed in the classical literatures of the world, and able to work in the consciousness of the true interpretation of the religions of the world; and, in addition to all this, he must have original power. For this apparatus of learning is but the introduction to such work as to-day needs to be done." — GEORGE A. GORDON *The Christ of To-day* (Houghton, Mifflin & Co., 1896), pp. 31, 32.

Note 15. Page 55. — "All human language, all human observation, implies that the mind, the 'I,' is a thing in itself, a fixed point in the midst of a world of change, of which world of change its own organs form a part. It is the same yesterday, to-day, and to-morrow. It was what it is when its organs were of a different shape, and consisted of different matter from their present shape and matter. It will be what it is when they have gone through other changes. I do not say that this proves, but surely it suggests, it renders probable, the belief that this ultimate fact, this starting-point of all knowledge, thought, feeling, and language, this 'final inexplicability' (an emphatic, though a clumsy phrase), is independent of its organs; that it may have existed before they were collected out of the elements, and may continue to exist after they are dissolved into the elements. The belief thus suggested by the most intimate, the most abiding, the most wide-spread of all experiences, not to say by universal experience, as recorded by nearly every word of every language in the world, is what I mean by a belief in a future state, if indeed it should not rather be called a past, present, and future state, all in one, a state which rises above and transcends time and change. I do not say that this is proved, but I do say that it is strongly suggested by the one item of knowledge which rises above logic, argument, language, sensation, and even direct thought, that one clear instance of direct consciousness in virtue of which we say 'I am.' This belief is that there is in man, or rather that man is that which rises above words and above thoughts, which are but unuttered words; that to each one of us, 'I' is the ultimate central fact which renders thought and language possible." — Sir James Fitzjames Stephen, *Liberty, Equality, Fraternity*. Quoted by Hutton, *Contemporary Thought and Thinkers*, I., p. 114.

Note 16. Page 56. — "Now personality is the inevitable and necessary starting-point of all human thought. For we cannot by any conceivable means get out of it, or behind it, or beyond it, or account for it, or imagine the method of its derivation from anything else. For, strictly speaking, we have no knowledge of anything else from which it can have been derived. If we are told that it is the product of pure reason, or unconscious will, or mere matter, or blind force, the answer is obvious — that we know of no such things. For, when spoken of in this way, reason and will and matter and force are only abstractions, and abstractions from my personal experience; that is to say, they are parts of myself, separated from their context and then supposed to exist in the other world; or, to put the same thing in another way, they are phenomena of the outer world, which are supposed to resemble parts of myself taken out of their context. But it is only in their context that these parts of me have any real existence. Will, in the only form in which I know it, is determined by reason and desire. Matter, in the only form in which I know it, — that is, in my own body, — is informed by reason and desire and will. Reason, as I know it, is inseparable from desire and will. And when in my own case I speak of my 'reason' or my 'will' apart, I am making abstraction of a particular aspect of myself, which, as such, has only an ideal or imaginary existence. Consequently, names which are given to phenomena in virtue of their resembling or being supposed to resemble these abstract aspects of myself, must be equally ideal and imaginary in *their* denotation. And I cannot *in* any way conce*i*ve a liv*i*ng and complex whole, like myself, to be derived from anything outside me which can only be known and named because it resembles one of my elements; when the element in question must be artificially isolated and, so to speak, killed in the process, before the resemblance can be established. Abstractions must be less real than the totality from which they are taken, and cannot thus be made levers for displacing their own fulcrum. Personality, therefore, is ultimate 'a parte ante.'"—J. R. ILLINGWORTH, *Personality Human and Divine* (Macmillan, 1894), pp. 41–43.

"The comparative failure of metaphysical thinkers in the past has been due simply and entirely, I take it, to their hav*i*ng adopted false starting-points and worked with false methods. Metaphysics, like charity, should begin at home. Though it must be metempirical in the sense of being concerned with what is not 'reducible to sensation,' it need not, and should not, be metempirical in the wider sense of the term experience, which embraces the whole of consciousness. The true beginning of metaphysics is personality, or the existence of an ego. Here we may find an immovable foundation. If it can be shown that feeling could not exist without an ego, then it is absurd to maintain, as the Positivists do maintain, that the ego cannot exist because it is not a feeling. . . .

"The denial of Personality is the denial of knowledge. Without a metaphysical ego there could be neither memory nor sensation. The attempt to disprove the existence of such an ego is only rendered apparently successful by that existence being throughout assumed. Its very negation is tantamount to its affirmation; for without this principle of permanence the concepts employed in its denial could not possibly have been formed. In other words, the personality, which should be the beginning of metaphysics, is essential to the conception and statement of every anti-metaphysical argument." — ALFRED WILLIAMS MOMERIE, *Personality, the Beginning and End of Metaphysics and a Necessary Assumption in all Positive Philosophy* (Blackwood, 1889), pp. 23, 132.

Note 17. Page 58. — "Christianity is historical in its antecedents. It is the fulfilment of Judaism, which was in its very idea definitely prospective, and only really intelligible through the end to which it led. The Covenant with Abraham included the promise of which the later religious history of 'the people,' working throughout for and in 'the nations,' was the gradual accomplishment. The call of Abraham was the beginning of the universal life of Faith. For as Christianity was the goal of the revelations of the Old Testament, so it was also the answer to the questions of the whole præ-Christian world, the satisfaction of the aspirations of the 'many nations' with whom in the order of Providence the 'people' was brought into contact.

"Chr*i*stian*i*ty is historical in itself. It is not a code of laws; it is not a structure of institutions; it is not a system of opinions. It is a life in fellowship with a living Lord. The Work and the Person of Christ, this is the Gospel, both as it was proclaimed by the Lord Himself, and as it was proclaimed by His Apostles: the revelation, the gift, the power, of a perfect human life offered to God and received by God, in and with which every single human life finds its accomplishment. The laws, the institutions, the opinions, of Christendom are the expression of the life which works through them. In Christianity the thoughts by which other religions live are seen as facts.

"Christianity is also historical in its realization. All human experience must be a commentary on the perfect human Life. The new life which was communicated to men requires for its complete embodiment the services of all men. The fuller meaning of the Faith in Him Who is the Way and the Truth and the Life is slowly mastered through the ages by the ministry of nations and by the ministry of saints and heroes through which the thoughts of the nations are interpreted. Such a process must go on unhastingly, unrestingly, irreversibly to the end of time; and if anything can make us feel the nobility of life, it must be that in Christ we are enabled to recognize in the whole course of history a majestic spectacle of the action of Divine love in which no failures and no wilfulness of men can obliterate the signs and the promise of a Presence of God." — BROOKE FOSS

WESTCOTT, Bishop of Durham, *The Gospel of Life* (Macmillan, 1892), pp. 255–257.

Note 18. Page 59. — "Thus far our task is accomplished; however briefly and hastily, the outer conditions of the life of Christ have been spread before us. But it would be an unpardonable omission, if even here special attention were not invited to the fact that these are utterly irreconcilable with the vaunted mythical theory. The ablest expositor of this theory, while admitting a certain basis of historical truth in the Christian Gospels, denies altogether their authenticity as histories, and maintains that the life which they delineate, like the ancient mythologies of Greece and Rome, is fabulous rather than historical. What seem to be facts he pronounces myths, shadowing forth certain spiritual truths, and these he labours to show were the very truths most firmly believed by the nation in connection with the expected Messiah. His avowed purpose is to prove that by the aid of their imagination the writers of the Gospels wrought up the scanty materials which they possessed into a series of fables, each containing a spiritual meaning, and that meaning always in harmony with their traditionary ideas, and even suggested by them.

"With the utmost confidence we can defy contradiction when we assert that *these* principles are incapable of being applied to that series of facts which has formed the subject of the short review we have just finished. With whatever plausibility they may be brought to bear upon other parts of the evangelical narrative, it will baffle the most dexterous criticism to adjust them to this portion of it: 'The corrupt and debasing influences amid which Jesus grew up in the village of Nazareth;' the shortness of His earthly course, and its 'ignominious close;' — 'His poverty, His humble trade as a carpenter, and His want of education and of worldly patronage,' — these are the things which we have put forward as the outer conditions of Christ's life. These were not only not in harmony with the Messianic ideas of the Jews at that time, or indeed at any time, but they were diametrically opposed to them. We make bold to maintain that they were the very last things which a Jew would ever have dreamed of connecting with the life of his Messiah. They are not Messianic; the most unscrupulous ingenuity can never construe them into myths, or make them harmonize with national and traditionary fancies. Whatever be fable, these are certainly facts, and would have been eagerly concealed, if they had not been received and undeniable facts; and these facts are all that are now demanded, as the basis on which to found an argument for the true divinity of Christ.

"Jesus was a resident in the village of Nazareth till He was thirty years of age. He died in comparative youth, when He was only thirty-three years old. He was a working carpenter; poor, unknown, untaught, inexperienced, and unbefriended. We shall go to some obscure hamlet of our land, known chiefly for the extreme profligacy of its inhabitants; we shall go to the workshop of a carpenter there, to a young man at the bench, earning his bread by the labour of his hands, remarkable only because, amid the surrounding vice, he has preserved himself uncontaminated; we shall go to this youthful artisan not yet thirty years of age, born of humble parents, brought up in a condition of poverty, associating only with the poor, in no way connected with the rich, the learned, the influential or receiving assistance, or even countenance from them; we shall go to this poor young man, who has had no intercourse with cultivated society, no access to books, no time for reading and study, no education but the commonest, and no outward advantages of any kind above others in his humble station, from his birth till that time. Such, in simple historical truth, such *exactly* was Jesus of Nazareth; and these were *the very conditions* under which He developed His future character, and rose to His future position." — JOHN YOUNG, *The Christ of History* (Robert Carter & Bros., 1855), pp. 52–54.

Note 19. Page 62. — "The argument to the Divinity of Christ from his claim, has been recently put afresh, as part of a personal experience, in *An Appeal to Unitarians*, by 'A Convert from Unitarianism' (Longmans, 1890), pp. 41–51. 'If it is not superhuman authority that speaks to us here, it is surely superhuman arrogance.' It has, however, been chiefly brought home to men's minds, in recent times, by Père Lacordaire (*Jesus Christ,* Conf. 1) and Dr. Liddon." — CHARLES GORE, *The Incarnation of the Son of God* (Scribners, 1891), p. 266.

Note 20. Page 65. — "The Church is a unit under the lordship of Christ. This thought is most fully developed in First Corinthians, where the apostle sets it in contrast with the party-spirit which prevailed at Corinth, and in Ephesians, where it is introduced as a corollary of the supreme headship of Christ over the Church. The unity and harmony of all Christians in the Church are illustrated by various figures. One of the most common is that of the members as constituting one body: 'We, who are many, are one body in Christ, and severally members one of another' (Rom. xii. 5); 'For as the body is one, and hath many members, and all the members of the body, being many, are one body; so also is Christ' (1 Cor. xii. 12); that is, 'just as the case stands with the body, that its many members make up its unity, so also does it stand in like manner with Christ, whose many members likewise constitute the unity of His body' (Meyer *in loco*). In Ephesians the headship of Christ over the Church as His body is yet more explicitly asserted in contrast to modes of thought which degraded Christ from His pre-eminent position, and which had become rife in the churches in Asia Minor, although the apostle does not here draw out the practical lessons regarding the function of each member of the body which are so fully developed in 1 Cor. xii. 12–31. Here it is a doctrinal interest regarding the nature and dignity of Christ's person, while there it was a practical concern for the harmony and peace of the Corinthian Church, which determined the course of His thought. It is the divine purpose 'to sum up all things in Christ'; that is, to unite all things under one head, in union with Christ (Eph. i. 10). Christ is the unifying bond of all saving powers and processes. God 'hath put all things under His feet, and gave Him to be head over all things to the Church, which is His body' (i. 22). It results from Christ's position and work that mankind, who were before divided into Jews and Gentiles, are now united into one body by the reconciliation which Christ has accomplished by His death (ii. 16). It follows that it is the duty of the Christian man to fulfil the function of a member of Christ, and so to promote the strong and healthy growth of the body (iv. 16; Col. ii. 19), or, disregarding the figure, to grow in likeness to Christ, to approach ever nearer to the standard of His perfectness (Eph. iv. 13, 15)." — GEORGE B. STEVENS, *The Pauline Theology* (Scribners, 1892), pp. 321–323.

Note 21. Page 74. — "In character, in spiritual insight, in knowledge of man, and of what all men feel must be the truth of God; in ability to see into the very heart of 'human life's mystery' and to penetrate the depth of humanity's need; in ability to speak the word which His own age needed and all ages since have needed, this Galilean peasant, whose youth and young manhood were filled with monotonous toil; who had never travelled; who knew few if any books; who had no teacher but a sweet and gracious mother, — has surpassed all the ideal heroes. In a public ministry of only a few months He transcended the wisdom of the philosophers, the intellectual and spiritual forces of the universities, and, more than any other, led men — all men, men of the most diverse tastes and prejudices — toward God. It is impossible for me to think that nature, even as glorious as that in which His youth was spent, taught Him all these lessons. No great poet or artist ever came from the midst of such scenery If He is explained by natural environment, the question remains, Why has nature produced no successor to Jesus? Switzerland and Thibet have contributed no names to the list of the world's intellectual and spiritual leaders, or even to that of her great artists and poets. Natural environment influences the body, not much the intellectual and spiritual environment. But around this Man the Oriental and the Occidental alike gather, and each seems to find in Him a brother, a teacher, and a friend.

"There have been many attempts to explain the character and personality of Jesus. My object is not to add another to that list, but rather to show that the data do not exist which warrant any one in attempting to classify Him with other men as a product of heredity and environment. He seems, indeed, to have been without father and without mother. Whoever He was, and whatever the explanation of His presence on this earth of ours, He was an exception among men; not in such a sense as to break the continuity of humanity, but clearly to make it impossible to account for Him as we account for heroes and men of genius." — AMORY H. BRADFORD, *Heredity and Christian Problems* (Macmillan, 1895), p. 266.

Note 22. Page 75. — "But there is another form of satisfaction which He has rendered which is even deeper and more intense than this. Jesus Christ has satisfied humanity in the relief which He has brought to it under the consciousness of sin. There is really no experience which can compare in intensity with the experience of sin. The reality of sin is not to be confused with the experience of it. The reality is universal, the experience is unequal. Some know what sin is by its bitter fruits in their own souls and bodies, or in the souls and bodies of those yet dearer to them than their own; others know what sin is only in principle, through the selfishness which has some lodgment in every heart. Now, as the experience of sin is unequal, so the satisfaction which Christ brings to sinning men *is* unequal. And no one may argue from any knowledge which he may have of sin, short of the experience of it, how great that satisfaction is which Christ can render. For he who would satisfy humanity under the consciousness of sin must be able to meet it in its lowest conditions and in its extreme possibilities. But the fact which bears its constant witness to the power of Christ is, that when the lowest conditions are reached, and the most extreme possibilities are realized, then the satisfaction is most complete. The saying of Paul is verified a thousand times with every day. 'Where sin abounded grace did abound more exceedingly.'

"It is not to our present purpose to say how this result is brought about. If it were, it might not be possible. No theory is as wide as the fact. No philosophy of the atonement can altogether explain the process by which the sacrifice of Christ finds its sure result in purity and inward peace in the heart of a penitent and believing sinner. All that we can do is to watch the phenomena which attend the method of Jesus. We know that His approach to sin is through His own sinlessness. We can see that His purity wins its way where anything short of that would falter and fail. We know something of the power of His passion for sinners, — how irresistible at times it is, working against the love of sin by 'the expulsive power of a new affection.' And we know that the method of Jesus is always sacrificial, in its deepest sense vicariously sacrificial, life for life, the cross the standard and the measure of the satisfaction which He imparts to a sinner. So much of the process we can see — and then the result." — ***The Divinity of Jesus Christ,*** by the authors of *Progressive Orthodoxy* (Houghton, Mifflin & Co., 1893), pp. 215–217.

LECTURE III

Note 23. Page 87. — "The life of the religion, then, lies in the person of its founder; all that it has done for the race is but a form of His action within and through it. He has given actuality to its theistic beliefs, has been the motive, impulse, and law to all its beneficences. The sense or consciousness of His abiding presence constitutes His Church; the emotions He awakens determine all its worship and all its desires. Even where this seems most concealed, it is yet present as the veritable seat and principle of life. The Virgin may seem to hold the first place in what may be called the more vulgar Roman worship; but she does it not as woman, but as mother; she stands there not in her own right, but by virtue of her Son. The opposite fault has been committed in many an evangelical sermon; the Son has been so preached as to hide the Father, or to deny Him by absorbing those ethical qualities which are most distinctively Divine. But here, too, the Son could not be without the Father, or the Father without the Son; both were needed to the being of either; and so the emphasis on one was only a crude way of expressing their unity. The historical fact then remains — the person of Christ has given reality to the life of the Christian religion, and actuality both to its belief in God and to the God it has believed in."— A. M. FAIRBAIRN, *The Place of Christ in Modern Theology*, p. 381.

Note 24. Page 90. — "The Christian religion is one phenomenon, a totality, a whole, of which the New Testament is only a part. We of to-day are in actual contact with a living Christianity, which has persisted through nineteen centuries of human chance and change; and though hindered, now as ever, by schism, treachery, hate, flattery, contempt, presents the same essential features which it presented nineteen centuries ago; miracles of penitence, miracles of purity, miracles of spiritual power; weakness strengthened, fierceness chastened, passion calmed, and pride subdued; plain men and philosophers, cottagers and courtiers, living a new life through the faith that Jesus Christ is God. . . . Now to construct out of the Gospels an imaginary portrait, of One who neither worked wonders nor claimed to be Divine, is to invalidate their worth, for it is to tear them literally into shreds. The conception of Christ, as superhuman, is too completely incorporate in their substance, too subtly inwoven into their tissues, too intimately present in their every line, to be removed by any process short of their destruction as a whole. Moreover, if there were an unknown Christ behind the New Testament, a Christ whom its writers unanimously misrepresented or misunderstood, it would not be on this unknown Person, but on His misrepresentation that Christianity is built. For the absolutely central doctrine round which Christianity has always moved, and which has been the secret of its unique hold upon the hearts and consciences of men, is not simply the loving Fatherhood of God, but the proof that He has given of His loving Fatherhood, by sending His only-begotten Son into the world. Faith in the Incarnation, with all that it involved, has been the sole and exclusive source of our historic Christianity. Yet if Christ were merely man, this was precisely the one point on which either He or His reporters were profoundly wrong. The case therefore is narrowed to a simple issue. Christianity cannot be due to the goodness and wisdom of a man, marred by a pardonable element of error; for it *is* simply and solely on the supposed element of error that it rests; and its missionaries, its martyrs, its holy and humble men of heart, all of strongest that human souls have done, all of saintliest that human eyes have seen, will have derived their inspiration either from folly or from fraud." — *Personality Human and Divine*, pp. 196–199.

Note 25. Page 94. — "Of itself Son of Man in Hebrew and Aramaic simply means child of man, that is, man,— with perhaps a certain poetic tinge, and with a subordinate conception of dependence and weakness. The expression is frequent in the Old Testament in this sense, and appears in the plural, just as in Mark iii. 28. But though this fundamental meaning could never be lost in any further defining of the conception, it cannot be sufficient in the case of Jesus. As we have already said, Jesus had no need to assure any one in the days of His flesh that He was a child of man; and the view that He desired — as in the Old Testament phrases, thy servant, thy handmaid (instead of I) — to paraphrase His ego in this way, is destroyed by the twofold consideration that He must then have said this Son of man, and that Jesus, as the Gospels show, did not avoid the simple I. For if, in certain cases, He makes use of the name Son of man instead of the simple I, He manifestly wishes in some way to mark what is peculiar to Himself. . . . Among all the passages in the Old Testament in which the expression Son of man appears, there is only one (Dan. vii. 13) in which *it* has a Messianic sense: 'I saw in the night visions, and, behold, one like the Son of man came with the clouds of heaven, and came to the Ancient of days, and they brought Him near before Him. And there was given Him dominion, and glory, and a kingdom, that all people, nations, and languages, should serve Him; His dominion is an everlasting dominion, which shall not be destroyed.' That this passage from Daniel must lie at the basis of Jesus' enigmatic self-designation is now recognized, not indeed universally, but by ever-increasing numbers. And really — when the Book of Enoch, that Jewish, and in part Jewish-Christian Apocalypse of the century of Jesus, has, in virtue of this passage of Daniel, directly stamped the name Son of man as the name of Messiah; when our canonical Apocalypse twice applies Daniel's phrase (I. 13, xvi. 14) to the glorified Christ, and Jesus Himself on two occasions unmistakably refers to Dan. vii. 13, when He speaks (Matt. xxiv. 30, xxvi. 64) of the Son of man coming in the clouds of heaven — it is difficult to conceive how any one can object to that origin. The fact lies clearly before us, that the same passage of the Book of Daniel, a book much read and highly honoured in our Lord's day, furnishes the conception of the kingdom of heaven, — the eternal kingdom to be received from God in the clouds of heaven, — and the conception of the Son of man, as the receiver and bearer of this kingdom. The mutual relation which we perceive, in all the declarations of Jesus, between His character as Son of man and His calling as bringer of the kingdom of God, lies before us originally in that passage of Daniel. And therewith the whole riddle is at bottom solved. The Son of man is the God-invested bearer of the kingdom that descends from above, that is to be founded from heaven; it is He who brings in the kingdom of God." — DR. WILLIBALD BEYSCHLAG, *New Testament Theology* (T. & T. Clark, 1895), Vol. I., pp. 62, 63, 64.

Note 26. Page 99. — "As regards the apostolic testimony, the ground is happily cleared in modern times by the large measure of general agreement which exists among impartial exegetes as to the nature of the doctrines taught in the several books. The old Unitarian glosses on passages which seemed to affirm the Divinity of Christ are now seldom met with; and it is freely admitted that the bulk of the New Testament writings teach a doctrine of Christ's Person practically as high as the Church has ever affirmed. For instance, it is no longer disputed by any competent authority that, in Paul and John, it is the supernatural view of Christ's Person that is given. As to John,—using that name at present for the author of the Fourth Gospel and related Epistles,—his doctrine of Christ is of the highest. This is admitted by the most negative critics, *e.g.* by Dr. Martineau, who says that the phrase 'Son of God,' applied to the pre-existing Word in the Fourth Gospel, leaves all finite analogies behind. 'The oneness with God which it means to mark *is* not such resembling reflex of the Divine thought and character as men or angels may attain, but identity of essence, constituting Him not godlike alone, but God. Others may be children of God in a moral sense; but by this right of elemental nature, none but He; He is, herein, the only Son; so little separate, so close to the inner Divine life which He expresses, that He is in the bosom of the Father. This language undoubtedly describes a great deal more than such harmony of will and sympathy of affection as may subsist between finite obedience and its infinite Inspirer; it denotes two natures homogeneous, entirely one; and both so essential to the Godhead that neither can be omitted from any truth you speak of it. It was one and the same Logos that in the beginning was with God, who in due time appeared in human form, and showed forth the Father's pure perfections in relation to mankind, who then returned to His eternal life, with the spiritual ties unbroken which He brought from His finished work.' " — *The Christian View of God and the World*, pp. 253, 254.

Note 27. Page 106. — "What fresh characteristics, then, has this new revelation to add to the Old Testament teaching about God? He is still One, the only God. He is perfect Righteousness, yet, as even the old religion knew, a God of loving-kindness and tender mercy, 'Who wills not the death of the sinner.' But more than all this, He is now revealed to man as Infinite Love, the One Father of humanity, whose only begotten Son is Incarnate and 'made man that we may be made God.' Not one jot or tittle of the old revelation of God, as a God of Righteousness, is lost or cancelled. The moral teaching is stern and uncompromising as ever. God's love, which is Himself, is not the invertebrate amiability, or weak good-naturedness, to which some would reduce it. 'The highest righteousness of the Old Testament is raised to the completeness of the Sermon on the Mount.' 'The New Testament,' it has been said, 'with all its glad tidings of mercy, is a severe book.' For the goodness and the severity of God are, as it were, the convex and the concave in His moral nature. But what seized upon the imagination of mankind as the distinctive revelation of Christianity was the infinite love and tenderness and compassion of this Righteous God for sinful man. It was this which shone out in the character of Christ. He was Very God, with a Divine hatred of evil, yet living as man among men, revealing the true idea of God, and not only realizing in His human life the moral ideal of man, but by taking human nature into Himself setting loose a power of moral regeneration, of which the world had never dreamed." — *Lux Mundi* (John Murray, London, 1890), pp. 75, 76.

Note 28. Page 107. — "The constructive thought of Paul starts with the historical person of Jesus, and his primary postulate may be said to be its truth and reality. This historical Person is to him the one and only Messiah. In the Gospels Jesus is a personal, but Christ an official, name, and the two are never interchanged or confounded; but in the Pauline Epistle Christ has become as personal a name as Jesus — *i.e.* the Person so constitutes the office and the office is so incorporated in the Person that distinction has ceased to be possible. . . . Now, it is the distinction of Paul that he made this unity, with all it involved, articulate, and it is also characteristic that the determinative idea in the system which he elaborated with so much dialectical passion came from the personality of Jesus and not from the Messianic office. That idea was His filial relation, His Divine Sonship. What was to him the primary fact in the consciousness of Jesus became the constitutive factor of his own thought. By the revelation of the Son in him he was made a Christian and an Apostle. His Gospel concerned the Son of God, who is God's own Son, His beloved, the Son of His love. This Sonship did not begin with His historical existence, but preceded and even determined it. God sends forth His Son, who exists before He can be sent forth, and comes that He may create in man the spirit of the sonship He Himself has by nature. He, though rich, yet for our sakes becomes poor. He comes out of heaven, descends from above that He may ascend with man redeemed. Hence there follows a twofold consequence, the one affecting the Son, the other the Father. As to the Son, a place and an eminence are ascribed to Him that involve rank and honour.

But so to construe Christ is to modify the whole conception of God. Abstract monotheism ceases, and is replaced by a theism which finds within the one Godhead room for both Father and Son. It is the characteristic of the Pauline theology that it is a theology of the Fatherhood which is through the Sonship. Neither can be without the other; both must be together, or neither can be at all. The ideas exist in what we may term a spontaneous rather than an explicated and formulated unity, but they exist and are co-ordinated. The divinity of both Father and Son was affirmed; later thought must determine how their unity could be conceived and expressed. The great thing gained was, Fatherhood and Sonship were as immanent essential to Deity." — *The Place of Christ in Modern Theology*, pp. 306, 307, 309.

Note 29. Page 108. — "It is remarkable that the Apostles seem to have experienced no intellectual difficulty in regard to this Trinity in the Godhead. I suppose this is to be accounted for, by the fact that difficulties in logic do not trouble us at all where facts of experience are in question. Thus we are often ludicrously at fault in attempting to give a logical account of quite familiar experiences, for example, of the inner relations of those three strangely independent elements of our own spiritual being, will, and reason, and feeling, or of the relation of mind and body. But our inability to explain facts logically goes no way at all to alter our sense of their reality. Now the Apostles lived in a vivid sense of experienced intercourse, first with the Son, then with the Father through the Son, later with the Holy Ghost, and with the Father and the Son through the Holy Ghost. This vivid experience, outward and inward, made logical formulas unnecessary. When the formula of the Trinity — three Persons in one Substance — was developed in the Church later on, through the cross-questioning of heresies, it was with many apologies for the inadequacy of human language, and with a deep sense of the inscrutableness of God. The formula was simply intended to express and guard the realities disclosed in the person of Jesus Christ, and great stress was laid on the divine unity. The three Persons are not separable individuals, so that it could be argued that what one of the sacred three does, another does not do, as we commonly argue about persons amongst ourselves, regarding each person as separate and exclusive of others. God in three is inseparably one. Thus if He creates, it is the Father through the Son by the Holy Ghost; if He redeems, it is the Father who is the fount of redemption through the Son, by the Holy Ghost; if the Spirit comes, He brings with Him in His coming the Son and the Father, for in eternal subordination and order, the three are one inseparable God." — GORE, *The Incarnation of the Son of God*, pp. 144, 145.

"If there is a true historical sense in which the clear definition of the doctrine of the Divinity of Jesus Christ must be assigned to the Councils of the fouth and fifth centuries, yet it would be a great historical blunder to state or imagine, as inference, that till then the doctrine was only held partially or with imperfect consciousness in the Catholic Church. The Church did not, as a result of those controversies, develop the consciousness of any new doctrine; the development of her consciousness was rather in respect of the shallow but tempting logic which would deform, or the delusions which might counterfeit, her doctrine, and of the perils to which these must lead. It may be a question, indeed, how far the words implicit and explicit do, or do not, represent the distinction between the dogmatic consciousness of the Apostolic and the Conciliar ages. The difficulty in determining depends solely on this, that the words themselves are used with different meanings. Thus, sometimes men are said to hold implicitly what they never perhaps suspected themselves of holding, if it can be shown to be a more or less legitimate outcome, or logical development, of their belief. If such men advance inferentially from point to point, their explicit belief at a later time may be, in many particulars, materially different from what it had been at an earlier; even though it might be logically shown that the earlier thought was, more or less directly, the parent of the later. Now in any such sense as this we shall stoutly maintain that, from the beginning, the Church held dogmatic truths not implicitly, but explicitly and positively. They who baptized into the threefold Name of the Father, and of the Son, and of the Holy Ghost; whose blessing was 'The grace of the Lord Jesus Christ, and the love of God, and the communion of the Holy Ghost'; who, living in the Spirit, lived in Christ; whose highest worship was the Communion of the Body and the Blood of Christ, and whose perfectness of life was Christ; they, so living and worshipping, did not hold the Godhead of Jesus Christ implicitly; they did not hold something out of which the doctrine of the Trinity might come to be unfolded. On the other hand, you may use the same contrast of words, meaning merely that you have, through cross-questioning or otherwise, obtained a power which you did not possess, of defining, in thought and in words, the limits of your belief, and distinguishing *it* precisely from whatever does not belong to it. You hold still what you always meant to hold. You say still what you always meant to say. But it is your intellectual mastery over your own meaning which is altered. Like a person fresh from the encounter of a keen cross-examination, you are furnished now, as you were not before, with distinctions and comparisons, with definitions and measurements,—in a word, with all that intellectual equipment, that furniture of alert perception and exact language, by which you are able to realize for yourself, as well as to define to others, what that meaning exactly is, and what it is not, which itself was before, as truly as it is now, the very thing that you meant.

"Take, for example, the doctrine of the Holy Trinity. Intellectually it is, of course, antecedent to the doctrine of the Incarnation and the Atonement. But it will be observed that it is made known to us not antecedently, but as a consequence of our previous conviction of the Incarnation. Moreover, when it is made known, it is made known rather incidently than directly. Even though it is, when revealed and apprehended, the inclusive sum of our faith, yet there is, in the revelation, no formal unfolding of it, as of a mysterious truth set to challenge our express contemplation and worship. There is nothing here to be found in the least corresponding with the explicit challenge, 'Whom say ye that I am' or 'On this rock will I build my church'; but rather indirectly, so far as our contemplation of the Incarnation and its abiding consequences requires for its own necessary interpretation to our understanding, that we should have some insight into the mystery of the distinction of Persons in the Godhead, so far, and in reference to that purpose, the mystery of the Holy Trinity grows gradually into clearness of revelation to our consciousness." — *Lux Mundi* pp. 238, 239, 245, 246.

"Through all the fierce theological and consequently political controversies that disturbed the Church for nearly three centuries after the Great Council, the Nicene Creed survived. It is still the creed of the whole vast Greek Church; with some modifications it is also the creed of the Latin Church; and in its original form and stripped of its condemnatory clauses, it is substantially the creed of universal Christendom. Under the influence mainly of Augustine, the Latin theology soon dominated the Western Church and gradually excluded or suppressed the nobler and richer thought of the Greek Fathers. The Latin theology to some extent obscured, and while seeming to affirm, almost denied, the fundamental and structural doctrine of the Incarnation, the enunciation and persistent defence of which was the chief merit of Athanasius. That doctrine, however, survived through all strife, and now, amidst the changes and even the wreck of creeds, it still survives. In its real essence, it is not an arithmetical threeness of persons inexplicably inhering in one substance, so that we have the impossible conception, — three equals one, — as it so often appears in dogmatic theology; but it is the reality of God in Christ, as the revelation and archetype of God in humanity, and the pledge of the perfect fulfilment of man's life by his perfect union with the divine, 'being filled with all the fulness of God.' It is the supreme doctrine of Christianity,—the Incarnation, the immanence of God in the realm of personality as well as in the realm of nature." — PHILIP S. MOXOM, *From Jerusalem to Nicœa* (Boston, 1895), pp. 442 ff.

Note 30. Page 117. — "So far, as it seems to me, the Christian doctrine simply takes up, extends, illuminates, the great natural Law of Evolution.

"But, as yet, we have not viewed it as distinctly Christian; we have not asked what is the bearing in this aspect of the Manifestation in the fulness of the time of the Son of God, as Son of man.

"The truth itself of that Manifestation — let us again put this clearly before ourselves, and proclaim it to the world — is the Divine mystery of mysteries, a secret of the Will and Nature of God, revealed only to faith in the word of Him who said, 'I came forth from the Father and am come into the world; again I leave the world and go unto the Father.' We should hardly dare to bring it into analogy with the lower manifestations of God to man, if we did not remember that in all analogy the higher reality necessarily transcends the lower, and that our Lord Himself in His Parables taught us to shadow out by comparison with earthly things His Kingdom of Heaven. From these lower manifestations, who could have conceived beforehand — who can even now comprehend

— the Personal Incarnation of Godhead in humanity? If it may perhaps be foreshadowed by the recognition of the power of God, as immanent in all creation, and more visibly immanent (so to speak) in humanity, yet how dim this foreshadowing, compared with the brightness of the reality!

"But in what way is its actual working in the world represented to us? It is, as we have already seen, described as a 'new Creation' — the beginning of a new spiritual Order — which yet does not break continuity with the past, but, while it brings in a Divine spiritual force before unknown, takes up and subordinates to its higher purpose all the forces of the old Creation. Clearly in this representation there is a striking analogy to all that has gone before. By what is actually in effect a new Creation — whether it be connected or disconnected with the old — we have seen at each step the introduction into the world of a new power, as we pass from the Inorganic realm of lifeless Nature to the realm of Organic Life, from the realm of Organic Life to the realm of Humanity. Now that natural progress is shown to us as carried on to a Supernatural perfection by the bringing in of a new Divine Life—at once the Light and the Life of men—entering into the humanity which is the crown and culmination of the old development, in order to raise it to unity with the Divine Nature itself. This new Creation is set forth to us as an integral element, as the highest element, of the whole Divine Order; foreordained before the foundation of the world; in some way coexisting with the lower elements in anticipatory power before its actual Manifestation; prepared for under God's Providence through all 'the fulness of time.' The Manifestation, being in a Personality at once Divine and human, is necessarily complete in itself, unique, unapproachable, begun in the visible life of Christ on earth, continued still in its completeness in the invisible life of heaven. From the nature of the case, its relation to the human personality, as a living power, is a thing supernatural, transcending the analogy on which we are now dwelling. But yet in its effect both on the individual and on the collective life of all mankind, it is clearly (to use our Lord's own comparison) a seed sown in the spiritual soil of humanity — a leaven infused into its threefold nature — a germ to be developed through the ages of a new dispensation, which is to last till its work shall come to the full possible perfection, and then to give place to a higher dispensation still, 'that God may be all in all.'

"So every way there comes out to us the conception of the development of the Life of Christ in humanity, as the supernatural crown of the great Order of Evolution; and, if this be so, Science, which has traced this order in its lower forms, thus becomes, or should become, the παιδαγωγός to lead us to the highest in Christ Himself. It is a part of this analogy, that in this highest sphere of the great Order there should be manifested a Law and a Power peculiarly its own. For in the various provinces of being, which show themselves to us as distinct, the one 'God fulfils Himself in many ways.' In one sphere Evolution is ordered through Matter and the physical forces which pervade it; in another there is added in combination with these the new force of Life, with its inner capacity of assimilation and growth; in a third there comes with both and above both the infused life of human personality, with reason, conscience, love, and freedom of will to use them. Closer and closer in each successive phase there is revealed to us, in relation to created being, the Personality of God,— not His attributes, but Himself. So in this the supernatural sphere of the great Order, the new and dominant Force should by analogy be, as indeed it is, distinctly Supernatural, in harmony with the lower forces, but distinct from all. For it is the completion of that relation of true personality — all the number numberless of human souls being drawn to the Personality, at once Divine and human, of the Eternal Son, in a communion wrought out by the Eternal Spirit of God, and restoring us to the sonship of the Eternal Father." — ALFRED BARRY, *Some Lights of Science on the Faith* (London, Longmans, 1892), pp. 128–131, 135, 136.

Note 31. Page 121. — "Lose out of faith the sense of the Eternal in Christ, fail to recognize in Him the presence of the Absolute, miss the fact that His nature is rooted in the Deity and is part of the nature of God, and we let go the sole adequate support for belief in the consubstantiation of humanity with divinity, and the consciousness that Jesus is the moral ideal for mankind. The Christ who embodies the deepest in God, who incarnates the Eternal Filial in the Infinite is essential to hold for the world the great convictions of the kinship between man and his Maker, and the presence in Jesus of the true and final standard of human life. If the difference in Christ to humanity is the difference of the very God, then we can believe that the identity in Christ to our race is the identity of the very God. But if the contrast in the Lord to mankind does not reach to the being of God, if it is not the manifestation of the Eternal, if it is only individual idiosyncrasy, the mere separate, high-coloured envelope in which His humanity comes into the world and preserves its secrets from the vulgar crowd with whom it must be thrown together, then it follows inevitably that the kinship of Christ to His brethren does not carry us to the heart of the universe, does not go beyond the bounds of space and time. Only a Christ whose antithesis to humanity means the presence of the very God can by His union with humanity assure us of union with God. Discredit the infinite difference, and we must doubt the sublime identity. This contention will be self-evident to those who see that we owe our faith in the humanity of God and in the divinity of man, not primarily to philosophy, but to the power of the historic process. Revelation is ever through life the apprehension of the Infinite Personality through the finite; philosophy comes afterwards and finds her task. If we take Christ out of the historic process of revelation, we decapitate faith in the humanness of God and the divineness of man. We must remember the rock whence our belief was hewn, the pit whence it was dug. It was not in the world prior to Christ except in the form of intermittent prophetic dream, limited religious intuition, or vague, ineffectual philosophic fancy. It was not here as the ruling force in human civilization. The consubstantiation of man with God is the accepted and moulding belief of Christendom to-day because of the revelation of the nature both of God and man made through Jesus Christ." — GORDON, *The Christ of To-day*, pp. 119–121.

LECTURE IV

Note 32. Page 128. — "The history of art shows us numbers of artists who, grouped around some greater man, imitate his processes, as in the full belief that all there is of art is process, or what is sometimes called technique. The greater man has made the dress he wears as the birds make their plumage. The imitator imitates the dress." — JOHN LA FARGE, *Considerations on Painting* (Macmillan, New York, 1895), p. 26.

Note 33. Page 131. — "Being thirty years old when He came to be baptized, and then possessing the full age of a Master, He came to Jerusalem, so that He might be properly acknowledged by all as a Master. For He did not seem one thing while He was another, as those affirm who describe Him as being a man only in appearance; but what He was, that He also appeared to be. Being a Master, therefore, He also possessed the age of a Master, not despising or evading any condition of humanity, nor setting aside in Himself that law which He had appointed for the human race, but sanctifying every age, by that period corresponding to it which belonged to Himself. For He came to save all through means of Himself,—all, I say, who through Him are born again to God,— infants, and children, and boys, and youths, and old men. He therefore passed through every age, becoming an infant for infants, thus sanctifying infants; a child for children, thus sanctifying those who are of this age, being at the same time made to them an example of piety, righteousness, and submission; a youth for youths, becoming an example to youths, and thus sanctifying them for the Lord. So likewise He was an old man for old men, that He might be a perfect Master for all, not merely as respects the setting forth of the truth, but also as regards age, sanctifying at the same time the aged also, and becoming an example to them likewise. Then, at last, He came on to death itself, that He might be 'the first-born from the dead, that in all things He might have the pre-eminence,' the Prince of Life, existing before all, and going before all."—Irenæus, *Ante-Nicene Library,* Vol. I., p. 199.

The one error against which Ignatius was most careful to warn Christians was the obscuration of

Christ's humanity. "Stop your ears therefore when any one speaks to you at variance with Jesus Christ who was descended from David, and was also of Mary; who was truly born and did eat and drink. He was truly persecuted under Pontius Pilate; He was truly crucified and truly died, in the sight of beings in heaven and on earth and under the earth" — *Epistles of Ignatius to the Trallians*, Chap. LX.

Note 34. Page 140. — "In His mother's womb the body of Christ was also already omnipresent; when He went anywhere, He was in His humanity properly there already; risen from the grave He was in His humanity still in the grave; whilst He hung upon the cross, He was also in Athens, and ruled omnipresently the world. Thus the birth of Christ, His movements, His resurrection and ascension, became only an epideictic action, a Docetism which threatens to dissolve completely the condition of humiliation, the learning and growth. At the same time, in order to preserve the truthfulness of the sufferings of Christ, they would speak also of a growing, suffering, and exalted humanity of Christ alongside of one that was from the beginning omniscience, omnipotent, and omnipresent. Thus this very energetic striving after the unity of the Person of the God-man ended rather in a double humanity of Christ, a dualism, which renewed all the problems and absolutely rent asunder again the unity of the Person." — DORNER, *History of Protes-*

tant Theology (T. & T. Clark, 1871), Vol. I., p. 365.

Note 35. Page 145. — "The Jesus who lived, suffered, and died as a real man on earth is the same personality who was before, as the Logos of God, with the Father, and was God, and by whom all things are made. This is the marvellous problem which has for eighteen centuries exercised the minds of believers.

"The Logos of God, to whom the Father gives to have life in Himself even as He has, is, as such eternal; His self-consciousness is therefore eternally clear, His knowledge eternally perfect, His will eternally fixed and holy, and His life eternal bliss.

"The man Jesus on earth, however, so certainly as His development was really human, was as an embryo and newly born infant without self-consciousness. By degrees His self-consciousness is awakened. When He sleeps it is suspended, or, at all events, reduced to a state of obscurity. And when He dies, commending His spirit into the hands of His Heavenly Father, He again loses His self-consciousness, till the moment when the Father quickens Him as to the spirit who was dead as to the flesh (1 Pet. iii. 18). Again, as Jesus was a real child, He was childlike in every respect. He acquired His knowledge gradually (Luke ii. 52, 40). Whenever He fell asleep, His knowledge of God and the world was veiled. Nor was His knowledge of the affairs of the kingdom unlimited, as He Himself testifies during the very last days of His life (Mark xiii. 32). In fine, it is a matter of course that in the hour of death He lost His knowledge together with His self-consciousness.

"The development of His will was likewise gradual. His purposes were developed gradually; His will becoming by degrees subject to, or rather identified with, that of His Heavenly Father. He learned obedience (Heb. v. 8). He was, indeed, never disobedient, even in His sorest trials, but on every new trial and suffering He resigned His natural will afresh. This He did even in the final struggle of Gethsemane. At the close of each period of His life He had attained a higher degree of holiness, but not till the close of His earthly career did He attain that perfection of holiness which admits of no further progress.

"The life of Jesus alternated between feelings of joy and grief; His soul was sometimes shaken to its very profoundest depths. Thus, after His entrance into Jerusalem, it required a struggle for Him to regain His equanimity (John xii. 17). His anguish in the garden caused Him to sweat blood; and on the cross He gave vent to His feelings in a loud complaint. Now this is the same person, the omniscient, eternally holy and blessed Logos or Jesus, who thus alternates between self-consciousness and unconsciousness, who learns by degrees, who now rejoices in spirit (Luke x. 21), and anon is exceedingly troubled.

"Again, the Logos, having life in Himself even as the Father, is omnipotent, and has shown His omnipotence by creating and governing the world; but Jesus, as a real man on earth, is not omnipotent, but a helpless babe in His mother's womb and on her breast; when a full-grown man requires food and those things to sustain life which are furnished by the air, the earthly elements, the light of the sun, etc.; in the hour of His sorest trial requests His disciples to pray with Him; works even His miracles in His Father's power; lives by the Father, as the disciples live by the glorified Son· and is, finally, laid in the grave as a helpless corpse. And yet this omnipotent Logos and this humanly dependent Jesus are one and the same person." — REUBELT, *Scripture Doctrine of the Person of Christ,* based upon the German of W. F. Gess (Andover, Draper, 1871), pp. 318–320.

"This testimony of Jesus concerning His true humanity, given by His submitting to John's baptism, is directly confirmed by God Himself, the Holy Ghost descending and abiding upon Him (Matt. iii. 16; John i. 32). If the incarnate Logos had not been really and truly man, he would not have been in need of this unction with the Spirit and power of God (comp. Acts x. 38). It was this Spirit poured out upon Him after His baptism which showed Him the ways and times of His Messianic ministry and sufferings, which led Him after His baptism into the wilderness (Matt. iv. 1; Luke iv. 1), and in whose power He went from the wilderness to Galilee (iv. 14). By His forty days' fast in the wilderness also He confesses the reality of His humanity; for only as a real man did He need to count the cost of the tower to be built by Him, preparation for victory over such an enemy proceeding only from fasting and prayer (Matt. xvii. 21). Again, the temptation of Jesus by the devil rests on the (abstract) possibility of his sinning; if it had been absolutely impossible for Him to fall like other men, Satan's temptation would have been an act of folly, not worth recording by the evangelists. And how could Matthew represent this temptation as in keeping with the designs of the Divine Spirit (iv. 1) if Jesus absolutely could not sin? For one who cannot fall, it is mere play to be tempted. Yea, even the miracles of Jesus are confessions of His dependence; for before He healed the deaf-mute, He looked up to heaven and sighed (Mark vii. 34), and at the grave of His friend Lazarus He ascribed His miracles positively to the efficacy of H*is* prayer (John xi. 41, etc.).

"With this fully agrees His declaration: 'The Father loveth the Son, and showeth Him all things that Himself doeth' (John v. 20); and again, 'Neither has this man sinned, nor his parents, but that the works of God should be made manifest in him' (ix. 3); 'Believe the works, that ye may know and believe that the Father is in Me, and I in Him' (x. 38); 'The Father, that dwelleth in Me, doeth the works' (xiv. 10). Jesus was, then, not Himself the source from which His miraculous powers flowed, but He obtained them from the Father in answer to His always accepted prayer (comp. what Peter says in Acts x. 38: 'God was with Him, whereby He was able to do good and heal all that were oppressed of the devil'). — *Ibid.*, pp. 246, 247.

Note 36. Page 147. — (1) "The Incarnation of the Son of God was no mere addition of a manhood to His Godhead; it was no mere wrapping around the divine glory of a human nature to veil it and make it tolerable to mortal eyes. It was more than this. The Son of God, without ceasing to be God, the Son of the Father, and without ceasing to be conscious of His divine relation as Son to the Father, yet, in assuming human nature, so truly entered into it as really to grow and live as Son of man under properly human conditions, that is to say, also under properly human limitations. Thus, if we are to express this in human language, we are forced to assert that within the *sphere* and *period* of His incarnate and mortal life, He did, and as it would appear did habitually, — doubtless by the voluntary action of His own self-limiting and self-restraining love, — cease from the exercise of those divine functions and powers, including the divine omniscience, which would have been incompatible with a truly human experience.

"(2) Jesus Christ, the Son of God incarnate, was and is, at every moment and in every act, both God and man, personally God made man; He is as truly God at His birth or death as now in His glory, and as truly man now in His glory as formerly in H*i*s human b*i*rth and mortal life, but the relation of the Godhead and manhood is not the same throughout. Now in His glory we must conceive that the manhood subsists under conditions of Godhead, 'the glory of God'; but formerly during His mortal life and within its sphere, the Godhead was energizing under conditions and limitations of manhood. The Son of God really became and lived as Son of man." — CHARLES GORE, *Dissertations*, pp. 94, 95.

Note 37. Page 151. — "Christ Himself expresses His transition from the state of glory, which He had with the Father before the foundation of the world, into this earthly life, in these words: 'The Father has sanctified [set apart and consecrated to reveal the divine life] and sent Me into the world' (John x. 36; comp. iii. 16, etc.); and again thus: 'I came forth from the Father, and am come into the world' (xvi. 28); 'I have come down from heaven' (vi. 38; iii. 16). The apostles also give prominence now to the one and now to the other of these points of view. Thus John: 'God has sent His only-begotten Son into the world' (1 John iv. 9), but in another place: 'The eternal life, which was with [toward] the Father has appeared unto us' (1 John i. 1, etc.), 'The Logos became flesh' (i. 14), 'Christ has come in the flesh' (1 John iv. 2), and thus Paul: 'God sent forth His Son, born of a woman, in the similitude of sinful flesh' (Gal. iv. 4; Rom. viii. 3), but also: 'God [who] was made manifest in the flesh' (1 Tim. iii. 16), 'Jesus Christ became poor for our sakes' (2 Cor. viii. 9), 'He has divested Himself, and taken upon Him the form of a servant' (Phil. ii. 7). His Incarnation is thus both His own act, and in compliance with the will of His Father. The two points of view are connected in Heb. x. 5–10, where the Son is represented as saying at His advent, 'Lo! I come to do Thy will, O God!'

"The Scriptures moreover inform us what took place in the Logos while doing the will of His Father. When Christ says, 'I came forth from My Father, and am come into the world'; again, 'I leave the world and go unto the Father; and if ye loved Me, ye would rejoice because I said, I go unto the Father' (John xvi. 28; xiv. 28), He declares that He has abandoned His intimate intercourse with His Father, and His relation to the Father has undergone a change. And when He says, 'I am come down from heaven' (John vi. 38; iii. 13), He expresses thereby the fact *of His having made Himself lower*. This is both confirmed and more fully developed by Christ's prayer, 'And now, O Father, glorify Me with thine own self, with the glory which I had with Thee before the world was' (John xvii. 5); here Christ declares as pointedly and plainly as language can do it, that at that time He no longer had His ante-mundane glory, and on comparing His declarations in Mark xiii. 32 and John xi. 41 with Mark vii. 34, there is no longer any doubt that the glory with the Father which the Son laid aside at His Incarnation, means, not only His Divine form of existence, or His blessed life in light, but also His omnipotence and omniscience.

"Of the passages from the apostolic writings let us consider in the first place John i. 14: 'The Logos became flesh.' If every kind of *becoming* is excluded in the Logos, John certainly chose a very awkward expression. Why did he not rather say: He took upon Himself flesh and blood? John certainly knew what he was about when he expressed this central point of his faith, and thought he made no blunder in the selection of his terms. He wished to say that the Logos in His Incarnation did not remain as He had been before, but that with His assumption of human nature there was a change, introducing 'days of the flesh,' *i.e.* day of need, weakness, and the possibility of suffering (comp. Heb. v. 7; 2 Cor. xiii. 4). This agrees with Christ's own words, that His coming from heaven was a coming down, a going forth from the Father, or from that intimate life-union with Him which He had sustained from all eternity" — Reubelt *Scripture Doctrine of the Person of Christ,* pp. 329–331.

"Eternity must not be conceived of as excluding all change. It is only an arbitrary and poor philosophy that seeks eternity by a flight from time. The eternity of the Father is conditioned by His aseity, that of the Son and Holy Ghost by the freedom of their life, which streams from out of the Father and is yet identical with that of the Father. The Son divests Himself of His Divine life, of His breathing of the Spirit, and of His government of the world, not because He is invol untarily drawn into subjection to time, but because He freely loves sinners. And after He has accomplished His work of love for us, He regains that of which He divested Himself. This His free entrance into time, in order to return again into eternity, is therefore a triumph of eternity over time, an exhibition of the Eternal as the king of time, which must serve Him even while He enters into its service, and which cannot retain Him after He has accomplished His work. To dispose, as a king, of time, so that it does not sustain to the super-temporal the relation of an unapproachable something, but is serviceable to it as a form,—this is God's highest revelation of His superiority to time."—*Ibid.*, p. 430.

Note 38. Page 159.—"The truth that man was 'made in the image of God' admits of two distinct developments. It may be viewed (*a*) in regard to the individual, or (*b*) in regard to the race. In both respects man was created to gain a Divine ideal. It is true indeed that neither the race nor the individual can be properly considered apart; each is dependent upon the other for the attainment of its perfection. But much is gained both in clearness and fulness of view by considering them separately.

"(*a*) It is wholly unnecessary to inquire in what exact sense man was 'made in the image of God.' We have no faculties for the investigation. There is, however, no authority for limiting the image to any particular part of his nature. For us the individual man in his complex being is one; and as man he was made in God's image to gain His likeness.

"In this work he had constant need of Divine help. As he was made he was not at once capable of union with God. To reach this consummation he required discipline and training. In the Divine order men are 'first made men and then afterwards gods.'

"If then man had fulfilled the law of his being, he would still, so far as we can see, have stood in need of a Mediator through whom the relation of fellowship with God might have been sustained, and deepened, and perfected. Nor is it easy to suppose that this fellowship could have been made stable and permanent in any other way than by the union in due time of man with God, accomplished by the union of man with Him who was the Mediator between God and man, and in whose image man was made.

"Irenæus has given a striking expression to this truth. He starts indeed from the consideration of man as fallen, but his argument passes into an absolute form. Speaking of the necessity of the Incarnation, he says: 'If man had not conquered the adversary of man, the enemy would not have been justly conquered. And again, if God had not bestowed salvation, we should not have possessed it surely. And if man had not been united to God, he could not have partaken of incorruption. For it was necessary that the Mediator of God and men by His own essential relationship with both should bring together into friendship and concord, and on the one hand present man to God and on the other make God known to man.'

"Moreover, if we regard the predestined humanity of the Son of God as the archetype of humanity light is thrown upon the doctrine of the Atonement. It becomes in this case in some degree intelligible how Christ could fitly (if we may so speak) take man's nature upon Him, and suffer for man, inasmuch as He took upon Himself a nature which was not alien in its idea, but one which in some mysterious sense was in its propriety partially an image of His own, though it had fallen.

"So far, then, the essential constitution of man suggests at least the belief that the Incarnation, by which we understand in this case the taking of sinless and perfected humanity into God, was part of the Divine counsel in creation.

"(*b*) These considerations which apply to the individual man obtain greater weight if they are extended to the race. We cannot but believe that under any circumstances, and wholly apart from the Fall, there would have been a progress in the race, as well as in the individual, towards the gradual fulfilment of the idea of humanity. All that was potentially included in man in his various relations to being would have been realized in many parts. In this way the whole conception of humanity would have been broken up and distributed, so to speak, through countless personalities. There would then have been need of some power by which at last all the scattered elements of manhood should be brought together into a personal unity. In other words, the endeavour to follow out the normal development of the human race leads us to look for that which answers to the Incarnation, by which the completed body might be brought into a final unity in fellowship with God.

"For Christ, as we are taught, supplies that which gives a common life to all the members. He is the Head of the Body. All the differences of men, so far as they correspond with a true growth, are reconciled in Him, and shown to be contributory to the manifestation of His perfection.

"In this respect the argument which was drawn from Eph. v. 31 ff., by several early writers, deserves more consideration than we are at first inclined to give to it. The main idea in the passage seems to be that the Church, the representative of perfected humanity, of that which the race would in the end have been if sin had not intervened, is related to a Head, just as in the typical record of Creation woman is related to man. The Church and woman are severally regarded as derived, and yet belonging to, the completeness of that from which they are derived, and so destined finally to be restored to perfect fellowship with it. Man ideally is not man only, but man and woman; Christ, such appears to be the thought, however unfamiliar it may be to us, unites with the Godhead the ideal of perfected humanity, and that not accidentally but essentially. The personal relation of sex regarded, in typical individuals, represents, as we should express the view, beyond itself a corporate relation which exists in respect to the race. Just as the individual union is necessary for the fulfilment of the idea of woman, so the corporate union is necessary for the fulfilment of the idea of humanity. Christ is the true Adam: the Church is the true Eve. And both these relations, the individual relation and the corporate relation, are independent of the Fall. The Fall has disturbed and disordered each, but it was not the occasion for the first existence of either.

"So far we have regarded man only, the individual and the race. We venture to go yet further, and to look upon man as the representative of Creation. This thought appears to be distinctly suggested in the records of the Creation, and of the Fall, and of the new Creation. The dominion of man (Gen. i. 28) was such that his realm shared the consequences of his sin (Gen. iii. 17). His destiny therefore has not yet been accomplished (Ps. viii.; Heb. ii. 5 ff.). But in its promised fulfilment lies the hope of the material world. For that something is in store which answers to the redemption of man's body (Rom. viii. 22 ff.).

"It will at once be obvious how this wider view of the relations of man to Creation tends to confirm what has been already said of the inherent fitness of the Incarnation in relation to the plan of Creation, as we are enabled to look upon it. In all parts of the natural order, and not in humanity only, in the very course of progress, there is constant division, dispersion, differentiation, of elements; and at the same time clearer glimpses are opened of a unity to which all the parts appear to tend. This separation, this unity, as far as we can see, belong alike to the essence of things. The separation has been, it is true, influenced by the Fall, but, as a condition of growth, it is not due to it. The idea of the Incarnation therefore satisfies the aspiration towards the vaster unity to which the full development of Creation points. The restoration of unity to man carries with it the promise of the restoration of unity to all finite being." — WESTCOTT, *Commentary on the Epistles of John*, essay on "The Gospel of Creation," pp. 306–310.

Note 39. Page 161. — "For wherein fought He? In that He took man's nature upon Him. Take away His birth of a virgin, take away that He emptied Himself, 'taking the form of a servant, being made in the likeness of men, and found in fashion as a man'; take away this, and where is the combat? where the contest? where the trial? where the victory, which no battle has preceded? 'In the beginning was the Word, and the Word was with God, and the Word was God. All things were made by Him, and without Him was nothing made.' Could the Jews have crucified this Word? Could those impious men have mocked this Word? Could this Word have been buffeted? Could this

Word have been crowned with thorns? But that He might suffer all this, 'the Word was made flesh'; and after He had suffered all this, by rising again He 'overcame.'" — ST. AUGUSTINE, *Nicene Fathers,* Vol. VI., "Sermons on New Testament Lessons," XLVIII., p. 412.

Note 40. Page 163. — "Theology has no falser idea than that of the impassibility of God. If He is capable of sorrow, He is capable of suffering; and were He without the capacity for either, He would be without any feeling of the evil of sin or the misery of man. The very truth that came by Jesus Christ may be said to be summed up in the passibility of God.

"To confine the idea of sacrifice to the Son is to be unjust to His representation of the Father. There is a sense in which the Patripassian theory is right; the Father did suffer, though it was not as the Son that He suffered, but in modes distinct and different. The being of evil in the universe was to His moral nature an offence and a pain, and through His pity the misery of man became His sorrow. But this sense of man's evil and misery became the impulse to speak and to help; and what did this mean but the disclosure of His suffering by the surrender of the Son? But this surrender, as it was the act, represented the sacrifice and the passion of the whole Godhead. Here degree and proportion are out of place; were it not, we might say the Father suffered more in giving than the Son in being given. He who gave to duty had not the reward of Him who rejoiced to do it. Though we speak but in the limited language of our own conditions, yet, may we not ask, must not the act by which the Son emptied Himself have affected and, as it were, impoverished the Godhead? The two things are coincident and inseparable; here, pre-eminently, one member could not suffer without all suffering. The humiliation of the Son involved the visible passion and death, but the surrender by the Father involved the sorrow that was the invisible sacrifice.

"And this is the Biblical doctrine: 'God so loved the world that He gave His only-begotten Son'; 'He spared not His own Son, but delivered Him up for us all'; 'herein is love, not that we loved God, but that He loved us, and sent His Son to be the propitiation for our sins.' But what do these verses mean, if not that the essence and act of sacrifice was the surrender of the Son by the Father? It was the measure alike of His love to man and the suffering He endured to save. And so we may say, without the Fatherhood there could be no Atoner and no Atonement; but with the Fatherhood the Atoner and the Atonement could not but be. By their means He, as it were, invited man to come and see sin as He saw it, and judge its evil by beholding through the eternal Son the suffering it cost the eternal Father." — Fairbairn, *The Place of Christ in Modern Theology*, pp. 483–485.

LECTURE V

Note 41. Page 175. — "I cannot but agree with those who think that the Kingdom of God, in Christ's view, is a present, developing reality. This is implied in the parables of growth (mustard seed, leaven, seed growing secretly); in the representations of it, in its earthly form, as a mixture of good and bad (wheat and tares, the net of fishes); in the description of the righteousness of the kingdom (Sermon on the Mount), which is to be realized in the ordinary human relations; as well as in many special sayings. I do not see how any one can read these passages and doubt that in Christ's view the kingdom was a presently existing, slowly developing reality, originating in His word, containing mixed elements, and bound in its development to a definite law of rhythm ('first the blade, then the ear,' etc.). On the other hand, the idea has an eschatological reference. The kingdom is not something which humanity produces by its own efforts, but something which comes to it from above. It is the entrance into humanity of a new life from heaven. In its origin, its powers, its blessings, its aims, its end, it is supernatural and heavenly. Hence it is the kingdom of heaven, and two stadia are distinguished in its existence,— an earthly and an eternal; the latter being the aspect that chiefly prevails in the Epistles." — JAMES ORR, *The Christian View of God and the World*, pp. 405, 406.

Note 42. Page 181. — "But we are met on the threshold by a modern objection to this provisional conception of the matter. Is doctrine, even in this sense, really the essential content of the Bible? Is not its content, above all, fact and history? As for Christianity in particular, is it not a life in God mediated through Jesus Christ, rather than a doctrine of divine things? The friends of Biblical theology have no wish to deny the truth which underlies these statements; but it is a half truth, and therefore liable to be misunderstood. To say nothing of the apostles, who, at any rate, taught something concerning Christ, or of Paul, who was certainly one of the greatest teachers in the world's history, the statement that 'Jesus Christ brought no new doctrine, but presented in His person a holy life with God and before God, and in the strength which He drew from that spiritual life He devoted Himself to the service of His brethren in order to win them for the kingdom of God,' is, with all the truth which it contains, one of those misleading statements that oppose things which are not mutually exclusive. No one can deny that Jesus was known by His contemporaries as a 'Master,' that is, as a Teacher. His preaching was hailed as a new doctrine (Mark i. 27), and He Himself was conscious that it was His special mission to convey a knowledge of God which was unheard of before Him, and which could not be obtained without Him (Matt. xi. 27). Certainly this knowledge is only the abstract side of the life in God which He unfolds in order to communicate;

but this new life is anything but an unconscious one; nor is it imparted by magic, but clothes itself in idea, word, and preaching, and thus becomes essentially and necessarily a new doctrine of divine things. Nor is it otherwise with the content of Holy Scripture as a whole. No doubt that content is above all things testimony, the attestation of facts of divine revelation; but in the testimony there is thought, in the fact there is idea. What God reveals of Himself is truth to be thought about and to be proclaimed; that is, of course, doctrine, or doctrinal content." — Dr. Willibald Beyschlag, *New Testament Theology* (T. & T. Clark, 1895), Vol. I., pp. 2, 3.

Note 43. Page 183. — "Preaching being the characteristic feature of the life of Christ, no true understanding of His mission can be had without a knowledge of what He preached as the truth of God. The Gospels which give us the record of His life contain also a Gospel which He preached; and this Gospel comprises not only the rules of practical morality, the lessons and precepts of humanity and religion, but the Doctrines of a Positive Theology. It is sometimes alleged that Christ taught personally none of those doctrines which are commonly set forth by the Church in her creeds as distinctive of the Christian faith, but directed His teachings to practical life, inculcating the virtues, graces, and charities that would reform, adorn, and bless society, and elevate mankind; that the doctrines of regeneration and atonement, of the divinity of Christ and the personality of the Holy Spirit, were woven out of His sayings by speculative minds among His followers, after Jesus had finished His personal testimony of truth and goodness; that such doctrines owe more to St. Paul and St. Augustine than to Christ, and belong not to the original substance of the Gospel, but to a philosophical theology that has grown up around it. This notion is somewhat favoured by a common method of teaching theology — stating doctrines in technical terms and with scientific nicety, tracing their development in the history of the Church and of schools of philosophy, and finally authenticating them by citations from the Scriptures used mainly as proof-texts. For this purpose the writings of Paul, as the logical expounder of the Christian faith, are drawn upon more largely than other portions of the New Testament — the Pauline conception being taken as the basis of the Christian dogmatics, and the words of Jesus being used to verify the statement of His doctrines in the form of theological propositions. To reverse this method is to derive the Christian Theology primarily and directly from the words of Christ — a process in which we have to do not with the creeds of the Church nor the formulas of the theologians, but imply with the principles of interpretation. So far as the very words of Christ have been preserved, these form the essence of Christianity, just as the original sayings of Socrates as preserved by his disciples are the substance of the Socratic wisdom. To the first preacher of Christianity must we look for the freshest, truest, best conception of the system. In His words we find a proper theology,—not formulated, indeed nor systematized, yet expressed in doctrines to be severally believed, —doctrines set forth with a certain gradation of time and thought, or in a certain order of development, and these doctrines interwoven with the whole texture of the precepts and promises of the Gospel."—Joseph P. Thompson, *The Theology of Christ from His Own Words* (New York, Scribners, 1871), pp. 2, 3.

Note 44. Page 185.—"His teaching, therefore from the very first, has for its background a unique self-consciousness, the incomparable significance of His person, and from the beginning was directed towards something that must be more than teaching, that must be work and deed, viz. the founding of God's kingdom. And this founding was finally accomplished, not by His teaching as such, but by His personal devotion to and completion of His life-work, by His death and resurrection. Does His teaching thereby lose its original fundamental significance, and sink down to a mere introduction to New Testament revelation? It must be said that little as the teaching of Jesus in itself, apart from the conclusion of His life, could have called into existence the kingdom of God, as little could that ending of His life have called it into being without the foregoing doctrinal revelation. This doctrinal revelation first induced that end to His life, and gave it meaning; and it alone collected that community of disciples who were able to grasp and propagate that meaning. And therefore His doctrine is not indeed His life-work itself, but the ideal reflection of it, the evidence of what He wished, what He was conscious of being and doing. His teaching, therefore, is *that* in His appearance and active life which is necessary to make that life intelligible to us, and without which the apostolic teaching about Him would only be a sum of dogmatic utterances which we could not comprehend, and whose truth we could not prove, — a result not a little awkward for that view which contrasts the 'teaching of Jesus' as Christianity proper with the apostolic 'teaching about Christ.'" — BEYSCHLAG, *New Testament Theology*, Vol. I., pp. 28, 29.

"Hat sich in der Erscheinung Jesu die volle Gottesoffenbarung vollzogen, so muss dieselbe sich auch als solche der Welt verständlich gemacht haben. Es liegt im Wesen der Offenbarung, dass dieselbe nicht nur in gewissen Thatsachen bestehen kann, sondern dass sie zugleich die wesentlich richtige Auffassung von der Bedeutung dieser Thatsachen von vornherein sicher stellen muss, und dieses kann bei der in Christo erscheinenen Gottesoffenbarung nur durch das seine Erscheinung begleitende Selbstzeugniss Jesu (im weitesten Umfange) geschehen sein. Auf diesem Selbstzeugniss Jesu ruht aber selbstverständlich und geschichtlich die Auffassung seiner Erscheinung *in* der ältersten N. T.lichen Verkündigung. . . .

Die Lehre Jesu war vielmehr ihrem wesentlichen Kern nach selbst nichts anderes als eine Lehre von der Bedeutung seiner Person und seiner Erscheinung und musste in dieser Beziehung grundlegend sein für die ursprünglichen Vorstellungen der N. T.-lichen Schriftsteller von derselben. Jemehr man die Lehre Jesu in dieser ihrer geschichtlichen Bedeutung and damit in ihrem eigentlichen Offenbarungscharakter auffasst, um so einfacher erledigt sich die Fragè nach dem Verhältniss der Biblischen Theologie zu den Thatsachen des Lebens Jesu. Soweit die Lehre Jesu nemlich auf diese Thatsachen zurückweist, um ihre wahre Bedeutung erkennen zu lassen, oder soweit sie dieselben zu ihrem Verständniss voraussetzt, werden sie auch für die Biblische Theologie in Betracht kommen und derselben durch die Ueberlieferung, aus welcher sie die Lehre Jesu schöpft, dargeboten sein. Immer aber wird nur die Lehre Jesu den Ausgangspunkt für sie bilden, weil in ihr die Auffassung der ältesten Verkündiger des Evangeliums von der Bedeutung Jesu und seiner Erscheinung wurzelt und damit die Grundlage für das Verständniss ihrer religiösen Vorstellungen und Lehren gegeben ist." — BERNHARD WEISS, *Lehrbuch der Biblischen Theologie des Neuen Testaments* (2te Auflage, Berlin, 1873), pp. 33, 34.

Note 45. Page 200. — "The philosophers and religionists of old saw truth, but they saw it in detached forms and not as a system; they also failed to connect it with a personal, divine source, and hence had no ground of inspiration and no sufficient motive to duty. In other phrase, they were without the doctrine of the Holy Spirit. Compare, for example, Abraham and Zeno; the latter had an immeasurably wider culture and range of thought, but he could not elaborate a vital system. Abraham, on the contrary, with his one idea of a spiritual, personal God, and his one principle of obedient trust, inaugurated an order that instantly became vital and endures still as eternal truth. He did not look as widely, perhaps not as directly, at life, as the Stoic, but he looked in truer directions. No truth, unless it happens to be an all-embracing truth, and no number of truths, however clearly seen, have any inspiring or redeeming power until they are grounded in an eternal Person. Mozley, in one of his sermons, asks, 'Have we not, in our moral nature, a great deal to do with fragments?' Yes, and it is the weakness of human nature when it undertakes to teach moral truth that it has only fragments to deal with. It is because Christ did not see truth in a fragmentary way, and because there was in Himself nothing fragmentary, that He teaches with power. There is no capability in man of resisting perfect truth; when it is seen, it conquers. The main thing, therefore, is to *see*, but men love darkness, and even when they begin to see, it is in a half-blind way." — T. T. Munger, *The Freedom of Faith* (Houghton, Mifflin, & Co., New York, 1884), pp. 163, 164.

LECTURE VI

Note 46. Page 213. — "Si l'on demandait à un lecteur d'intelligence moyenne, qui aurait lu les dix-huit volumes de l'histoire naturelle et sociale d'une famille sous le second Empire, ce qu'il pense de cette fameuse théorie de l'hérédité, il serait certainement dans un grand embarras: 'J'ai vu, nous dirait-il, une vingtaine de personages qui ne se ressemblent en rien, entre lesquels on m'affirme qu'il y a un fil commun que je n'aperçois pas; dont les uns sont honnêtes, les autres intéressés, celui-ci criminel, celui-là ivrogne, par suite d'une même névrose originelle. En somme, cette famille m'intéresse fort, parce qu'elle reproduit en diminutif l'image du monde, infiniment diversifié; mais je ne parviens pas à me faire une idée à peu près claire de ce qu'elle est en tant que famille; et je ne vois pas beaucoup plus de rapports entre ses divers membres et les premiers Rougon-Macquart qu'on m'a présentés qu'entre vous, moi, quelques autres et nos premiers parents, Adam et Eve.' Mais peut-être bien que si l'on poussait notre homme à la réflexion, on en tirerait autre chose; peut-être que, en procédant selon la méthode socratique, de question en question, on l'amènerait a dire: 'Ah! je vois encore ceci, par exemple! C'est que tous ces gens sont ce qu'ils sont de par une force ètrangère, sur laquelle ils ne peuvent rien, qui les gouverne et les dirige. Ils sont de simples marionnettes: je vois leurs mouvements, et je sais que ces mouvements ne dépendent pas d'eux, mais de la ficelle qui les agite et de la main qui tient la ficelle. Et je n'aperçois pas la ficelle, et je n'aperçois pas la main. Ils ne sont pas libres, j'en suis sûr; de quel tyran dépendent-ils? Je n'en sais rien.' Et notre homme aurait résumé, au point de vue qui nous occupe, tout ce qu'on peut dire de l'œuvre de M. Zola: elle n'est pas scientifique et ne nous apporte aucun renseignement sur la doctrine de l'hérédité; mais elle est littéraire et fait pènètrer en nous les consèquences de cette doctrine, qui sont la nègation radicale de la liberté et de la responsabilité humaine. En sorte que M. Zola a détruit des croyances positives qui n'étaient pent-être que des préjugés, mais n'a aucunement justifié, ni expliqué, ni prouvé les croyances nègatives qu'il s'applique à leur substituer. Le christianisme qu'il repousse, et la science qu'il prend pour religion ont entre eux ce point de ressemblance, que leur base est également incertaine, en dehors de l'observation. Pour croire à l'hérédité de la famille Rougon-Macquart, il faudrait un acte de foi pour le moins égal a celui qu'exigent les dogmes de la Trinité ou de l'Immaculée-Conception; et, après l'avoir accompli, on serait peut-être moins avancé." — Edouard Rod, *Idées Morales du Temps Présent*, pp. 80–82.

Note 47. Page 214. — "Heredity is his hobby-horse, which he mounts in every one of his pieces. There is not a single trait in his personages, a single peculiarity of character, a single disease, that he does not trace to heredity. In *A Doll's House*,

Dr. Rank's 'poor innocent spine must do penance for "his" father's notions of amusement when he was a lieutenant in the army.' . . . Helmer explains to Nora that 'a misty atmosphere of lying brings contagion into the whole family. Every breath the children draw contains some germ of evil. Nearly all men who go to ruin early have had untruthful mothers. . . . In most cases it comes from the mother; but the father naturally works in the same direction.' And again: 'Your father's low principles you have inherited, every one of them. No religion, no morality, no sense of duty.' In *Ghosts,* Oswald has learned from the extraordinary doctor in Paris who told him he had softening of the brain, that he had inherited his malady from his father. Regina, the natural daughter of the late Alving, exactly resembles her mother.

In *Rosmersholm,* Rebecca's nymphomania is explained by the fact that she is the natural daughter of a Lapland woman of doubtful morals. 'I believe your whole conduct is determined by your origin, Rector Kroll says to her. Rosmer never laughs, because 'it is a trait of his family.' He is 'the descendant of the men that look down on us from these walls.' His 'spirit is deeply rooted in his ancestry.' Hilda, the step-daughter of the 'Lady from the Sea' says: 'I should not wonder if some fine day she went mad. Her mother went mad, too. She died mad. I know that.' In *The Wild Duck* nearly every one has a hereditary mark. Gregers Werle, the malignant imbecile, who holds and proclaims his passion for gossip as an ardent desire for truth, inherits this craze from his mother. Little Hedwig becomes blind, like her father, old Werle.

"In the earlier philosophical dramas the same idea is constantly repeated. Brand gets his obstinacy, and Peer Gynt his lively, extravagant imagination, from the mother. Ibsen has evidently read Lucas's book on the first principles of heredity, and has borrowed from it uncritically. It is true that Lucas believes in the inheritance even of notions and feelings as complex and as nearly related to specific facts as, *e.g.*, the horror of doctors, and that he does not doubt the transmission of diseased deviations from the norm, *e.g.*, the appearance of blindness at a definite age. Lucas, however, whose merits are not to be denied, did not sufficiently distinguish between that which the individual receives in its material genesis from its parents, and that which is subsequently suggested by family life and example, by continuous existence in the same conditions as its parents, etc. Ibsen is the true 'man of one book.' He abides by his Lucas." — MAX NORDAU, *Degeneration*, pp. 350–352.

Note 48. Page 215. — "It has come about that the novels and stories which are to fill our leisure hours and cheer us in this vale of tears have become what we call tragic. It is not easy to define what tragedy is, but the term is applied in modern fiction to scenes and characters that come to ruin from no particular fault of their own, — not even when the characters break most of the Ten Commandments, — but by an unappeasable fate that dogs and thwarts them. Ugliness and suffering and misfortune unrelieved make a modern tragedy, and there has come an opinion that tragedy of this sort is the highest type of literature. . . . This situation has much of the tragic in it. It is nothing else than tragic to see a rosy-cheeked or spectacled young woman whose life has been mainly guarded from evil and surrounded by the sunshine of family and social affection, or a young man of considerable culture and considerable promise, whose enjoyment of life is scarcely at all abated by cigarettes and a sceptical philosophy, sit down with an inkstand and a steel pen, and on white paper sketch the blackness of life, the misery of humanity, the wretchedness of a world of damnable complications, of which neither of them can have had more than the slightest experience. But the young only follow more experienced and skilful leaders in this — leaders who are supposed in their melodramatic tales to touch the height of ancient and dignified tragedy in literature. These writers bring together a half-dozen human beings of feeble will and strong passions, ignorant, or half-educated, or æsthetically educated, who have an assortment of good and bad qualities, who cannot tell a lie, but who can break any marriage tie they have sworn to, who can murder in a helpless sort of way, who break all the social conventions of decency but have convictions of their own about morality, who violate all the laws of thrift and order and of conduct expressed by Moses or by the state, and pass their lives in misery, and are defeated in every transient aspiration for a better life, and come altogether to a pitiful and squalid end. And for this misery and this end they are in no wise to blame. They could not help themselves, poor things; they do not know that in half the cases it was the novelist who would not let them help themselves, but kept them grinding along in his circle of cruel complications. This is the romance of fatality, and if it is tragedy, it is the tragedy of fatalism.

"If we are permitted to turn to what used to be called in literature tragedy, we find that the Greek dramatists have another conception of it. In the dramas of Æschylus we see the impassioned presentation of humanity in action, and humanity in action on the basis of the poet's ethical conception of the divine government of the world. Not a mechanical fate, but a providential Nemesis, had been the lesson of Homer and the lyric poets; and this was the ruling motive of Greek tragedy,—the sense of a righteous power, the Hebraic idea of an offended holiness punishing pride and vice to the children's children, but showing mercy to the penitent. It set forth the moral law, and the tragedy flowed from its disobedience. This had the faintest relation to the Fatality of the Orient and of the modern novelist."—CHARLES DUDLEY WARNER, *Harper's Magazine*, March, 1896, "Fatalism in Modern Fiction."

Note 49. Page 216. — "There is, however, another series of speculations, which has probably contributed as much as anything to modern pessimism. If the State Socialist is trying to compress impulse and will in political society, the physiologist is fighting the old battle against free will in the individual, with what seems for the moment asbolute success. In a sense, of course, we did not need Mr. Galton and his compeers on the Continent to teach us the doctrine of heredity. Its main facts have never been overlooked, and modern science might take for its epigraph, 'The fathers have eaten sour grapes and the children's teeth are set on edge.' Still, there is the greatest possible difference between a wise man's aphorism, the precise value of which is not easily calculable, and a scientific demonstration, which shows the whole region occupied by a particular law. Fifty years ago a man's chance of extricating himself from family failings seemed an extremely fair one. The mother's influence might counteract the father's; and the man whose parents were of dubious worth might hark back to an older and better stock; or the influences of education might neutralize the inherited evil quality. All these considerations remain as true as they were, but we see more clearly than we did that everything which has once been in the race endures as a permanent influence modifying it, and that family types are apt to remain scarcely alterable for generations. Even if a particular man can flatter himself with reason that he has escaped or conquered a vicious tendency, he knows that he is doomed to see it reappear in his children. Now, the fatalism of science in this direction seems of a more hopeless kind than the old theological doctrine of predestination to life eternal or death eternal. In Calvinism the doomed man does not know his fate. Occasionally he fancies he does, and is overpowered by the horror of the situation, but, as a rule, he acts on the assumption that he may be one of the elect. On the other hand, every man knows that the furies of past generations are behind him; and that he is bound to inherit the passions and the impotencies as well as the nobler qualities of his ancestral line. In Calvinism the man's life upon earth is not necessarily affected. He may be a very excellent man to current acceptation. Besides the ordinary obligation to live well which he recognizes, he is deeply interested in his own success, as his works are a slight indication that he may have been called. The modern thinker, however, who has taken up the teaching of heredity as a faith, may easily come to look upon himself as nothing more than a compound of experiences. He is visited at every critical moment by the doubt whether it is really possible for him to escape from the character that he inherits as he inherits physical type." — CHARLES H. PEARSON, *Fortnightly Review,* "The Causes of Pessimism."

Note 50. Page 216. — "The 'religion of humanity' runs back the genealogy of man, with all his powers, with all his equipments, to the dust of the earth. I hold in my hand a genealogy which I wish you to compare with the genealogy of Luke. It is not a satire, it is not an irony. I have taken it from the pages of Ernest Haeckel. It is true, I have condensed it from perhaps a dozen pages, but in that condensation I have followed precisely the line traced by the atheistic philosopher. What is omitted is simply the detailed description of the several species in the genealogy. Let me read it:

"'Monera begat Amœbæ, Amœbæ begat Synamœbæ, Synamœbæ begat Ciliated Larva, Ciliated Larva begat Primeval Stomach Animals, Primeval Stomach Animals begat Gliding Worms, Gliding Worms begat Soft Worms, Soft Worms begat Sack Worms, Sack Worms begat Skull-less Animals, Skull-less Animals begat Single-nostrilled Animals Single-nostrilled Animals begat Primeval Fish, Primeval Fish begat Mud Fish, Mud Fish begat Gilled Amphibians, Gilled Amphibians begat Tailed Amphibians, Tailed Amphibians begat Primeval Amniota, Primeval Amniota begat Primary Mammals, Primary Mammals begat Pouched Animals, Pouched Animals begat Semi-apes, Semi-apes begat Tailed Apes, Tailed Apes begat Man-like Apes, Man-like Apes begat Ape-like Men, Ape-like Men begat Men.'"—LYMAN ABBOTT, *Christian Thought*, 1887, Article on "The Religion of Humanity."

Note 51. Page 223. — "Men do actually antagonize and overcome their vital inheritance, defy their environment, and, without dependence upon either, choose to live as if they were the children of a virtuous ancestry and subject only to refined conditions. These truths are apparently contradictory, and yet one is as evident as the other. Two boys are the children of drunken parents; their home is one room of a tenement in which a dozen other persons eat and sleep; their school is the street. All that bad blood and evil conditions can do for them is done. Some day the elder in a fit of drunken fury strikes a murderous blow. He is arrested, arraigned, tried, condemned, executed; he alone, though at the bar of God he has many accomplices. Equally, and possibly still more, culpable are the society which makes it possible for such degraded creatures to be born; the State, which allows saloons on every corner, and permits such wretched tenements as the childhood home of these boys; and the men who own those buildings, anxious rather for rent than for the welfare of human beings. The other boy, however, son of the same drunken parents and brought up amidst the same vileness, is no longer there. His evil heritage has been overcome, and his circumstances changed; he is a gentleman of wealth, of culture, of real and unaffected goodness. What has made the difference? Not society, for the surroundings of the lads were alike bad. The younger may have received from his ancestry certain good tendencies that his brother did not; but so far as can be traced the legacy has been the same. What shall we think about this remarkable and impressive contrast? I know no answer except this: in every man there is an untainted power, something which passes from generation to generation untouched by change, and that in this ultimate essence of personality rests the power of choice, which may be shut in by evil conditions and tied to a thousand evil tendencies, but which is in its nature free, and is rarely, if ever, entirely denied expression. At least it may be said that no fact in the physical series militates against the doctrine of human freedom which may not immediately be met and fully balanced by a fact in the spiritual series." — AMORY H. BRADFORD, *Heredity and Christian Problems*, pp. 89, 90.

Note 52. Page 226. — "Under these circumstances, one can leave the question open whilst waiting for light, or one can do what most speculative minds do, that is, look to one's general philosophy to incline the beam. The believers in mechanism do so without hesitation, and they ought not to refuse a similar privilege to the believers in a spiritual force. I count myself among the latter, but as my reasons are ethical they are hardly suited for introduction into a psychological work. The last word of psychology here is ignorance, for the 'forces' engaged are certainly too delicate and numerous to be followed in detail. Meanwhile, in view of the strange arrogance with which the wildest materialistic speculations persist in calling themselves 'science,' it is well to recall just what the reasoning is, by which the effect-theory of attention is confirmed. It is an argument from analogy, drawn from rivers, reflex actions, and other material phenomena where no consciousness appears to exist at all, and extended to cases where consciousness seems the phenomenon's essential feature. The consciousness doesn't count, these reasoners say; it doesn't exist for science, it is *nil;* you mustn't think about it at all. The intensely reckless character of all this needs no comment. It is making the mechanical theory true *per fas aut nefas.* For the sake of that theory we make inductions from phenomena to others that are startlingly *un*like them; and we assume that a complication which Nature has introduced (the presence of feeling and of effort, namely) is not worthy of scientific recognition at all. Such conduct may conceivably be *wise,* though I doubt it; but scientific, as contrasted with metaphysical, it cannot seriously be called."—WILLIAM JAMES, *Psychology* (New York, Henry Holt & Co.), Vol. I., p. 454.

"The most that any argument can do for determinism is to make it a clear and seductive conception, which a man is foolish not to espouse, so long as he stands by the great scientific postulate that the world must be one unbroken fact, and that prediction of all things without exception must be ideally, even if not actually, possible. It is a *moral* postulate about the Universe, the postulate that *what ought to be can be, and that bad acts cannot be fated, but that good ones must be possible in their place,* which would lead one to espouse the contrary view. But when scientific and moral postulates war thus with each other and objective proof is not to be had, the only course is voluntary choice, for scepticism itself, if systematic, is also voluntary choice. If, meanwhile, the will *be* determined, it would seem only fitting that the belief in its determination should be voluntarily chosen from amongst other possible beliefs. Freedom's first deed should be to affirm itself. We ought never to hope for any other method of getting at the truth if indeterminism be a fact. Doubt of this particular truth will, therefore, probably be open to us to the end of time, and the utmost that a believer in free-will can *ever* do will be to show that the deterministic arguments are not coercive. That they are seductive, I am the last to deny; nor do I deny that effort may be needed to keep the faith in freedom, when they press upon it, upright in the mind." — *Ibid.*, Vol. II., pp. 573 ff.

Note 53. Page 227. — "First, the humiliation of our Lord, including His Incarnation, is represented as a continuously voluntary act. His determination to become incarnate, and the act of becoming so, are certainly represented as voluntary. Its whole moral value is described as consisting in the freeness with which it was done. It thus became the act of self-sacrifice and self-humiliation that it was. 'He who was rich became poor.' 'He thought not equality with God a matter for grasping, but made Himself of no account, and took the form of a servant.' The point, however, to which I call attention is that, after the act of incarnation had been accomplished, the incarnate life of humiliation on earth is represented as still a continuous act of voluntary lowliness. Thus, in Philippians, He not only took the form of a servant and became in the likeness of men, but, being found in fashion as a man, He humbled Himself and became obedient unto death. His subjugation to law is here described as a continuously voluntary act and as the continuation of the same purpose and personal determination by which He became man. So in the Epistle to the Hebrews we read: 'Forasmuch as the children are partakers of flesh and blood, Himself also in *like manner* [παραπλησίως, "in every respect"] partook of the same.' Both the act of incarnation and all His experimental identity with man were parts of one plan of voluntary self-humiliation." — REV. GEORGE T. PURVES, *The Incarnation Biblically Considered*, p. 78.

Note 54. Page 234. — "The whole of Jesus' preaching of the kingdom of heaven is a proclamation of grace, a doctrine of salvation, and it is united with the doctrine of righteousness in the manner of the Augustinian '*Domine, da quod jubes, et jube quod vis.*' Not as though Jesus had deprived man of moral freedom. On the contrary, — and the ethical conception of his doctrine just rejected is quite right in this, — the presupposition that man is incapable of doing the will of God on account of sin is unknown to Jesus. He demands of men throughout the doing of His commandments, the doing of the divine will. He credits them throughout with the power to repent, that is, to change their mind, and become of that mind, in virtue of which one can only truly do the commandments of God in detail. And He not only credits them with this freedom, on the authority of His Word and Gospel, but also on the authority of the words of the Old Testament, the law, and the prophets. It is by no means meant ironically when He directs the scribes to the two great commandments (Luke x. 23 f.), 'Do this, and you will live'; or the rich young man (Matt. xix. 17), 'If thou *wilt* enter into life, keep the commandments.' It is said of the brethren of the rich man (Luke xiv. 29), 'They have Moses and the prophets, let them hear them' (viz. in the interest of their own conversion). The poor Lazarus, in the same parable, has heard Moses and the prophets, and in their school has developed an inner life which could bear him at death on angels' wings into paradise; and Abraham, the patriarchs, the prophets, according to Luke xvi. 22, Matt. viii. 12, have arrived there." — BEYSCHLAG, *New Testament Theology*, Vol. I., pp. 131, 132.

LECTURE VII

Note 55. Page 257. — "This new conception of God, as immanent in nature, is necessarily accompanied by a new conception of law and miracles. Rather, we are going back to the New Testament conception and definition of miracles. They are no longer regarded as violations of natural law, or even as suspensions of natural law. Indeed, in strictness of speech, in the view of this philosophy, there are no natural laws to be violated or suspended. There is only one Force, that is God; law is but the habit of God's action; miracles are but the manifestation of His power and presence in unexpected actions, demonstrating the existence of an intelligent Will and Power superior to that of man. I say that this is a recurrence to the New Testament conception and definition of miracles; for the writers of the New Testament knew nothing about nature and the supernatural, nothing about natural causes and the violation or suspension of natural laws. The words they used to characterize what we call miracles indicate their apprehension of these events. Four words were used by them: 'wonders,' 'powers,' 'works,' and 'signs' or 'miracles.' Any event attracting attention and compelling *wonder*, exhibiting unusual or more than human *power*, accomplishing a real *work*, usually beneficent, and serving as the *sign* of a special messenger and an authentication of his message, is in the conception of the writers of the New Testament a miracle. As the New Theology believes that 'all power belongs to God,' that God is immanent in the universe, and that there is no real distinction between the natural and the supernatural, that the only dualism is the material or physical and the immaterial or spiritual, it has no difficulty in believing that the control of the physical by the spiritual, and therefore of the universe by its God, is sometimes manifested by unexpected or unusual acts of power and wisdom for spiritual ends. These are miracles." — LYMAN ABBOTT, *The Evolution of Christianity*, pp. 112, 113.

"It is not of course that there is any spiritual parsimony in God, but that it is only through the comparative rarity of the gleams of light, through their contrast to common experience, that they teach us the true lesson of that common experience. If they were much more frequent,—we being what we are,—we should lose the meaning of the lesson through that frequency; just as in countries where life is excessively precarious, death does not enhance half so much as in other countries the value of life. In a land where every one was original, originality would lose its power, and perhaps become a great danger; its value being to explain the limitations of ordinary habit, not to dissolve ordinary habit. So spiritual influence is the divine comment on ordinary human wants and desires, and miracle the divine comment on law—neither of which would have the same value, if the subject of the comment were not worked into the very substance of our minds before the comment came. Miracle teaches the divine meaning of permanent law; and owes all its impressiveness to the comparative fixity and permanence of the phenomena which it interrupts. Miracle forces upon us personality, but would not force it upon us unless it were so exceptional in its mode of occurrence as to open a new mental relation between us and the Author of Nature. It is a mistake to take the uni formity of the laws of Nature as the measure of God's purposes, just as it is a mistake to take the every-day habits even of a human being as the measure of his aims. You cannot tell what they really mean — they are too wide for interpretation — till you get some light on them from the occasions on which the man himself breaks through them, and you see the reasons he assigns for doing so. And so with the laws of Nature — they are far too big for moral interpretation, too vast for our survey, till at some one point we see the reason why they are modified, and, then, that first really tells us the reason why they were ever fixed. It is not that miracle is half as wide as Nature; on the contrary, it is just because it is so much narrower, that it lets the gleam of the personal Spirit shine through it, and so throws a light on the whole structure." — R. H. HUTTON, *Contemporary Thought and Thinkers*, Vol. II., pp. 119, 120.

Note 56. Page 258. — "They were talking about miracles, and the young Doctor said: 'You know as well as I do, Stephen, that everything in this world moves in regular order. The laws of nature are what we all have to depend on, and they never change. It's certain that if you plant potatoes they won't come up pumpkins. Neither you nor any man here ever saw a miracle. You never heard of one in your life in these parts. You never heard of pumpkin vines growing from potatoes. It stands to reason and common sense that when no man in this town ever saw anything happen that wasn't in the regular course of natural law, anything supernatural, it isn't likely such things are going to happen here.'

"I looked at Stephen, as the Doctor called him.

He was an elderly man, hard-featured and sunburned. There was a shrewd twinkle in his eye, but he looked at the stove and not at the Doctor, and there was a silence for a moment while he pondered. Then he spoke in a mild, inquiring sort of way, which contrasted with the Doctor's somewhat self-opinionated tone.

"'I don't know much about the laws of natur', but I suppose you mean something like this — that when I let go that jack-knife it'll fall on the floor;' and he stretched out a long arm holding an open knife by the blade between his thumb and finger.

"'Exactly,' said the Doctor; 'that's the law of gravitation.'

"'And it's sure to fall, and I can bet my money on it, and I needn't be afraid of a miracle? Look here, Doctor, where did the law that binds it to fall come from? What made that particular law?'

"The Doctor was honest; that was evident from his reply. 'The learned men who have investigated the laws of nature have not found the origin of the laws. They will in time. It's only in recent years that science has made its great discoveries in the laws themselves. Heat, light, colour, electricity, all the great characteristics of the changing world and of matter itself, have never been understood as they are now.'

"'And you can't tell me what made the law that binds that jack-knife to fall down?'

"'No, I can't. It's enough to know as certain that it will fall. Just let go, and you'll see the certainty.'

"'No chance of anything supernat'ral; any miracle?'

"'Miracle be hanged. Let go the blade.'

"Stephen's thumb and finger separated and stood stretched out wide apart. The jack-knife was not on the floor. It was hanging to the wooden ceiling overhead, its blade buried a half-inch in the soft pine. For about ten seconds no one spoke. Stephen was looking at the Doctor.

"'Suthin' supernat'ral happened, didn't it?' said Stephen.

"'You jerked the knife up yourself.'

"'Well, that warn't nat'ral, war it?'

"The Doctor hesitated. 'Now see here, Doctor,' said the old man, 'just tell me how old is your law that the jack-knife's got to fall down.'

"'Millions of years old. Just as old as there has been anything to fall.'

"'And how old was the law that said that jack-knife must go up there and stick its blade in that white-pine ceiling? Just three minutes and a half old by the clock. Now what I want to know is where did your law that it must go down come from. You say you don't know. Well, it stands to sense, then, and you can't deny that it may come from some one that makes it go down just as I made it go up. If your science is worth a sneeze, it oughtn't to deny what it don't know nothing about. And if that's so, it's always just as like as not whoever made the thing go down will make it go up, without you or I or any one else knowing what made it go, any more than you know what made me jerk that knife up yonder. You tell me that if I plant potatoes they won't come up squashes, but you just tell me what plants potatoes, or what makes me plant 'em, anyhow. If I don't plant 'em, there ain't going to be any potatoes nor squashes. It's according to reason that if potatoes come up because I planted potatoes, squashes don't come up from them, because some one else takes care of that part of the business. I don't believe in your argiments that laws always may be depended on, when you tell me yourself that you don't know where the laws come from and how long they're goin' to last. Your science is all right, Doctor, just as long as it talks about what it knows about. But when your science says a knife's bound to fall down, and don't take into account that something supernat'ral may interfere that science don't know nothing about, sich as my sudden making up my mind to jerk it up, why your science ain't wuth any more than a last year's almanac to tell a fellow what the weather's goin' to be.'

"By th*i*s time Stephen's tone and style had changed. He was no longer humble and inquiring, but decidedly aggressive. There were some strong words, not exactly profane, adjectively applied to science in the last sentence, which I have omitted. He talked rapidly and vehemently and with pointed logic. Is logic one of the distinguishing characteristics of humanity? There are men, exceptions, sometimes men of eminence, who do not seem to have any idea of logic, but by the vast majority of men, however uneducated, logical sequence seems instinctively appreciated, and the most illiterate are very sure to detect failure in argument.

"As he talked he rose and stood up, six feet two,—a mighty frame, fit for tremendous work,—and he poured out a storm of plain and unanswerable philosophic truth, ending up in this wise: 'No miracles, but only jest steady laws? Well, accordin' to law that jack-knife will stick there till the wood rots or the steel rusts. Make your prophecy if you dare. Say what it'll do. Is there any law that'll tell you what'll come of it? or whether Sam or Timmy won't have it down and pocket it as soon as I'm gone? You don't know? Well, I do. There's just such a law, and I made it;' and so saying he reached up his long arm, seized the knife, and strode out of the door, growling as he went."—W. C. Prime, *Along New England Roads* (New York, Harpers, 1892), "A Village Discussion," pp. 35-39.

Note 57. Page 266.—"It is objected to the belief that God is personal, that personality implies limitation, and that, if personal, God could not be infinite and absolute. 'Infinite' (and the same is true of 'absolute') is an adjective, not a substantive. When used as a noun, preceded by the definite article, it signifies, not a being, but an abstraction. When it stands as a predicate, it means that the subject, be it space, time, or some quality of a being, is without limit. Thus, when I affirm that space is infinite, I express a positive perception, or thought. I mean not only that imagination can set no bounds to space, but also that this inability is owing, not to any defect in the imagination or conceptive faculty, but to the nature of the object. When I say that God is infinite in power, I mean that He can do all things which are objects of power, or that His power is incapable of increase. No amount of power can be added to the power of which He is possessed. It is only when the 'Infinite' is taken as the synonyme of the sum of all existence, that personality is made to be incompatible with God's infinitude. No such conception of Him is needed for the satisfaction of the reason or the heart of man. Enough that He is the ground of the existence of all beings outside of Himself, or the creative and sustaining power. There are no limitations upon His power which He has not voluntarily set. Such limitation — as in giving being to rational agents capable of self-determination, and in allowing them scope for its exercise — is not imposed on Him, but depends on His own choice." — GEORGE P. FISHER, *The Grounds of Theistic and Christian Belief* (New York, Scribners, 1883), pp. 69, 70.

"A physical law has nothing wherewith to resist God, who can as easily make or do a thing in another way than that of law, as by that law. A physical law is as nothing, regarding it as preventing God from acting in any special way. If this law acts, it acts; but if it does not act, some other mode does for the occasion. But it is a different thing when we come to the actual wills of real beings. The will of man is admitted (with that reserve which, as ignorant creatures, we must fall back upon in such mysterious statements), as that which has the power of resisting the will of God. Free-will is claimed as a real attribute of man — power to do or not to do. The will can resist God's will, and can stop the progress of a work of God. Is this an intricate view of Divine dealings, and does putting Divine power under such checks and conditions as a progressive revelation implies seem radically to interfere with the attribute? This is an objection which, if it be of any force at all, does not apply to a progressive revelation specially; *it* applies to the whole idea of a Deity, as compatible with human *free-will*. Human free-will is an internal modification of the idea of God, which is only prevented from interfering injuriously with the idea, by the intervention of our resort to ignorance. As ignorant creatures we are not entitled to say that apparent limitations of the Divine power are real ones, because they may be only such as the mathematical consistency of truth itself imposes; that is, only verbal restrictions upon power, and not real ones. To the intellectual conception, however, the idea of God is thus an idea with checks and conditions in it; and those who would simplify it absolutely, would establish an idol and not a God. If we invent an idol, all is plain enough; there are no enigmas in an idol; there are no reasons why individuals cannot be converted in an instant, and why the human race cannot be enlightened in an instant by an abstract Omnipotence. But if we suppose the Deity to be the Being we represent Him in our sermons, our popular treatises, our exhortations, who *cannot* do some things, and cannot change man without his own concurrence, this is a Deity who cannot give enlightenment or implant a revelation in man by an instantaneous act." — J. B. MOZLEY, *Ruling Ideas in Early Ages* (London, Rivingtons, 1889), pp. 249, 250.

Note 58. Page 268. — "And this respect of God for His creatures is seen most of all in His relation to man. He never indeed allows human freedom to disturb the main course of the world's development; to tolerate that would be to abandon the providential government of the world. But within such an area as allows man to exercise a real, though limited, freedom — to such a degree as at least may involve considerable disturbance in the divine order for the sake of the value of free, as distinct from mechanical, service — God stands aloof and respects that free nature which He has created, that image of His own freedom which He has, as it were, planted out in the heart of the physical creation. God respects His creature man. His power refrains itself. But is there, in order to leave room for man's freedom of choice, a limitation, not only of God's power, but of His foreknowledge? Is the old controversy as regards human freedom and divine foreknowledge to be solved in part by the suggestion that a limitation of divine foreknowing accompanies the very act of creating free agents? The idea has commended itself to some very thoughtful minds: to Origen, as has already incidently appeared in this discussion, and to Dr. Martineau in modern times. The accurate examination of the meaning assigned to divine 'foreknowledge' in the Bible tends to shake the traditional belief that God is there revealed as knowing absolutely beforehand how each individual will act. Nevertheless, it is at least as difficult to reject this belief as to admit it. But, whatever be our relation to it, at least we must admit that the method of God in history, like the method of God in nature, is to an astonishing degree self-restraining, gradual, we are almost driven to say, tentative. And all this line of thought — all this way of conceiving of God's self-restraining power and wisdom — at least prepares our mind for that supreme act of respect and love for His creatures by which the Son of God took into Himself human nature to redeem it, and in taking it limited both His power and His knowledge so that He could verily live through all the stages of a perfectly human experience and restore our nature from within by a contact so gentle that it gave life to every faculty without paralyzing or destroying any." — CHARLES GORE, *Dissertations* (New York Scribners, 1895), pp. 223, 224.

Note 59. Page 270. — "We must distinguish between the intelligence of Deity and His intellectuality. His intellectuality, His capacity to know, is perfect, without any deficiency or weakness; it is an element of His necessary existence, and, therefore, is wholly subjective. But His intelligence is the knowing, and is the result of the exercise of His intellectuality. Intelligence is derived from intuition, from consciousness, from inference, and from observation. Intelligence derived from intuition and necessary consciousness can never be increased or decreased. Intelligence derived from inference and observation must be derived from objectivity, but objectivity is the realm of the contingent. Intelligence of the contingent can never exist until the contingencies exist, because a nonentity can have no objectivity. That which is a present conceivable nonentity may become an actual entity. But the apprehension of a possible entity is theory, but not knowledge. We must distinguish between the intelligence of entities and the apprehension of possibles, between God's consciousness of necessary existences, and His intelligence derived from His inference and from His observation of unnecessitated things.

"Failing to make this discrimination, men infer that God's intelligence of contingencies is just as immutable as His intelligence of necessities. In the realm of necessities all God's thoughts are immutable from everlasting to everlasting; but in the realm of contingencies He can at pleasure will worlds into existence. If He will new worlds into being, He can will new conceptions, new plans, new enterprises into existence. Having the power to will new thoughts into existence, He has the power to originate new creations, new purposes for the glorification of His intelligent creatures, for the adornment of His material universe and the illustration of His own glorious perfections. His consciousness derived from necessities must be different from His consciousness derived from actual contingencies.

"In these views of the divine nature I am gratified in being supported by Dr. Dorner, of the University of Berlin, one who stands in the foremost rank of living Protestant divines. In a recent number of the *Bibliotheca Sacra* he says: 'Any view of the divine nature that excludes all distinction, movement, and change from God is incompatible with the idea of creation. The world, as a thought, was a determination given to his mind by God. He must have conceived the world as changeable, or He would not have willed it thus to be. In the divine omniscience there must be an element of growth. If there be free beings, there must be free determinations. God may have a prior knowledge of them as mere possibilities, but He cannot have a knowledge of them as actualities. This knowledge of human acts must be acquired gradually as they come to pass. This knowledge He draws from history, and it is conditioned by the action of the causalities which He has brought into existence. In His counsels, in His knowledge, and in His volitions with respect to the world, in His relations to time and space, God is not unchangeable. In these regards He undergoes movement and change, and suffers Himself to be conditioned.'" — L. D. McCABE, *Divine Nescience* (New York, Phillips & Hunt, 1882), pp. 25–27.

"The doctrine of God's perfect foreknowledge is not only unphilosophical, but also unscriptural. The Bible exhorts us to the deepest earnestness in prayer — to downright importunity — and encourages us to believe that the fervent prayer of the righteous man availeth much. No petitioner can plead with any genuine unction unless he believes that he can actually effect some change in the purposes existing in the divine mind at the time his prayer is offered. If he were convinced that everything had been prearranged from all eternity; that his tears and sighs and passionate words of longing had been present in God's mind always; that they never had exerted, and never could exert, any influence, effect any change, as there could never be a time when they would first arrest God's attention, — how could he wrestle, agonize, in prayer? It would seem but empty show to him, that he was merely playing a part. Every word he uttered would fall back dead. If he believes in God's foreknowledge, he must, while he prays, if he prays as the Bible commands, utterly forget his belief and fall into the temporary delusion that the matter is yet undetermined; that God's heart is tender, can be moved; that His purposes can be changed. He must forget his belief, must go ahead just as if foreknowledge were not true. Think you

God would force His children to such straits, to such mental stultification?

"I am now ready to answer the question, How can we reasonably hope by our petitions to effect a change in the divine purposes, and why should we plead importunately, why kindle our souls *into* such intensity of fervour? The Scriptures in enjoining earnestness need not be understood as favouring attempts to coax and tease God, as we too frequently do our earthly parents, to act against His better judgment out of some weak, short-sighted sympathy. If that be our purpose, we may be certain of flat failure. Our prayers will never induce Him to deal any more generously with us. He has always stood with outstretched arms, with overflowing sympathy, waiting impatiently to bless us. What untold wealth of deep inventive thought, what untold æons of slowly passing years, He has already lavished in His preparations for our coming, for our maintenance, for our unfolding, for our permanent weal! While our prayers will not make Him any more kindly disposed, will not noticeably increase His sympathy *for* us, they will in most marked measure increase His sympathy *with* us, will profoundly change our attitude toward Him and multiply our capacity for blessing ten thousand fold. Indeed, so radical is the change wrought, that what would have been poison before, becomes medicine now. We thus furnish God new facts upon which to act — facts of mental attitude, the unforeseen outputs of our sovereignty. That attitude is one of Christ-like love, manifesting itself in five forms,—that of willing obedience, of self-sacrificing service, of sense of divine dependence, of restful confidence, and of intensest longing. Until that attitude is attained in all these its prime essentials, God, if He should interfere by stepping outside His general providence, in which the evil and the good are served alike, to confer special favours, would be doing violence to His conceptions of fitness and of true beneficence, would work His children a most positive injury, placing a premium on qualities that stand over against these forms of love, thereby countenancing a spirit of rebellion, selfishness, self-sufficiency, distrust, and ignoble apathy. It is the fervent prayer of the righteous man that availeth much. He must be righteous and his righteousness must be on fire to fulfil the Scripture conditions. That *availing* power is something more than retroactive; it moves the arm that moves the world. As this is a moral state of the soul within the circle of its sovereignty, the product of its absolutely free choice, there cannot be, as I have shown, any sure prophecy of its coming. But when it comes, all barriers are burned away. Reserve gives place to closest, sympathetic intimacy. What more natural, when the spirits of father and son thus meet and mingle, than that the son, care-cumbered it may be, or broken with grief, or baffled in purpose, though battling still, should pour out in most impassioned utterance his deep and noble longings? Love itself would so prompt; for love casteth out fear, is the very essence of liberty. Cautious reserve cannot live in its atmosphere of holy confidence. All curtains of concealment fall instantly at the magic touch of sympathy. He could not keep his longings back. His father's tender look and tone would break the seals of silence, would touch his lips with coals of fire. The thought of trying by coaxing to melt down his stern reluctance is utterly foreign to such a scene, repugnant to such a state, and was never contemplated in the Gospel. What more natural than that God's heart should be deeply stirred by the fervid outflow of such a passion of love and longing, and that He should by direct will-power supply the deficiencies of His general providence, or by timely suggestions reveal its resources, and place them in reach to meet the needs of such a soul in such an hour?" — William W. Kinsley, *Old Faiths and New Facts* (New York, Appletons, 1896), pp. 81, 90–92.

LECTURE VIII

Note 60. Page 297.—"We can make this clear by considering that property, private property, is the condition of the best social order. The best social order results from the social union and co-operation of the highest type of men and women; and the highest type of manhood and womanhood can only be produced when men and women have the free use of property. Property is, indeed, the raw material for the development of character. It is in property, Hegel says, that my will is made real for me as a personal will. Property is the concentrated form of power, and it is in the exercise of power that my will is trained and disciplined.

"It is in the realm of property rights and obliga tions that my personality is largely shaped. Until I have learned to use property conscientiously and beneficently, I have not equipped myself for the highest service of my fellow-men. In making it the instrument of promoting human welfare, more than in any other possible way, I socialize my own will, and prepare myself to enter into helpful relations with my fellow-men. I cannot learn this lesson in the use of property which I hold in common with my fellows. It must be my own; I must be free to express my own will in dealing with it; I cannot be unselfish in the use of that which is not mine; the most direct and effective discipline in unselfishness is that which is gained in using private property beneficently.

"The fundamental assumption of socialism seems to be that if men possess private property they will use it selfishly; therefore, the socialists say, we will have no private property. The remedy would not be effectual. It is rather difficult to abolish all vestiges of private property. Hands and feet and eyes and tongues are possessions and instruments not easily alienated, and those who would use money or machinery selfishly would be quite sure to go on using all their personal powers in the same way after they were divested of money and machinery; claws and fists and elbows and teeth would still be private property, and a very unsocial use might be made of them. Unless the will has been socialized, unless men have learned how to use all their powers and possessions for the common welfare, the society in which they live will bear very little resemblance to heaven, no matter how small their personal belongings may be." — WASHINGTON GLADDEN, *Ruling Ideas of the Present Age* (Boston, Houghton, Mifflin, & Co., 1895), pp. 76–79.

Note 61. Page 298. — "Love seeks the true good of the person loved. It will not minister in an unworthy way to afford a temporary pleasure. It will not approve nor tolerate that which is wrong. It will not encourage the coarse, base passions of the one loved. It condemns impurity, falseness, selfishness. A parent, we say, does not really love his child if he tolerates the self-indulgence and does not correct or punish the faults of the child. Faithful are the wounds of a friend. Love discriminates. It admires only that which is worthy of admiration. It cannot consent to, much less approve, anything unworthy of the loved one. The more love the more condemnation of that which is unlovely. What has been said of the divine love is true of human love:

'The very wrath from pity grew,
From love of men the hate of wrong.'

Love has a high ideal of the person loved, and is devoted to the attainment of that ideal. Love seeks righteousness, and is satisfied with nothing less and nothing other than that.

"Should not one be seeking the same things for

himself that he seeks for others? Should he not have the same ideal for himself? Is not the goodness he would promote in a friend the very goodness he should be striving to promote in his own character? If I love another, I seek his perfection. But I should seek my own perfection. Therefore I should love myself. In fact, the very best way to promote the goodness of another is to cultivate my own goodness. To be of the right character gives the power and the only power of loving and serving others. Example is the best service love can render. If one is seeking the wrong things for himself, he cannot be seeking the right things for his friend, except as he disapproves his own wrongness, and is a warning to his friend. Now we understand self-love. The representation of love as including self is by no means a far-fetched and circuitous way of thinking. In the complete summary of moral law, a summary which is almost universally accepted, two great principles are laid down, one of which gives as much importance to self-love as to love for others, and even makes self-love the rule and type of love to others. 'Thou shalt love thy neighbour as thyself,' is the second of two great commandments on which hang all the moral precepts of law-givers and prophets. The comparison has respect, *not to quantity, but to quality*. It does not mean that one is to love his neighbour as much as he loves himself, that he is to give just as much time, thought, care, service, to his neighbour as he gives to himself, in as equal division as possible.

It means that one is to love his neighbour in the same way as he loves himself, in the same manner, after the same fashion, with the same objects in view, like as he loves himself. It is not the 'as' of degree but the 'as' of kind. As thou lovest thyself so shalt thou love thy neighbour. The soul's goods one seeks for himself are the soul's goods he should seek for his neighbour. Therefore one must love himself aright in order to love his neighbour aright. According to this comprehensive precept, self-love is not derived from love to others, but love to others gets its pattern and therefore its measure from love to self. This is as distinct a declaration of self-love as could possibly be made, and certainly on the best authority. The somewhat similar precept which is found both in Christian and in Confucian ethics, — to do unto others as you would that they should do unto you, — indicates the right every one has that others should seek his good, as well as his duty to seek their good, and so objectifies self as needing love and service. If one is entitled to the efforts of others for his good, he certainly is required to serve himself as he would have others serve him and as he ought to serve them." — GEORGE HARRIS, *Moral Evolution* (Boston, Houghton, Mifflin, & Co., 1896), pp. 138–141.

Note 62. Page 300. — "For, college or school, university or institute, the beneficiaries of every endowed seat of learning or of art are by their very relation constituted the heirs and the almoners of a great fiduciary trust.

"Ability is answerability — everywhere and all ways. Private possession, *all* possession is a public trust! Accountability cannot be escaped.

"There are two sorts of souls. Those who seek for themselves the advantages of things as they are, and those who seek to give themselves to the advantage of things as they ought to be, and therefore may be made to be; those who accept advancement, and those who confer it; those who would exploit the world, and those who would save it, — benefactors and malefactors, — Christ and the thieves!

"Each one of us, to the extent of that endowment which God gives him, is a legatee that he may be a steward. It is the common law of all trusts that they cannot be delegated. They must be executed or defaulted. In the court of the supreme surrogate, many a will constitutes an indictment.

"And what is true in the stewardship of crass material wealth is also true in the stewardship of mental and administrative ability. Who can, must.

"The sybarite who uses an elegant and fastidious leisure in purveying to mere literary taste, who is dainty in mere editions, a glutton in books, and who in the seclusion of a library ignores or disdains the woe of the world, makes of his knowledge a toy and not a tool. He, too, is but a miser.

"This strenuous age, wherein still the 'people are destroyed for lack of knowledge,' demands of us our all and our best.

"If shadows are to fall from the truth, and falsehood die, the times challenge and demand souls who shall be filled with the instinct of *help* and wear on helmet and brow *Ich Dien*, souls ablaze with that love which ever 'seeketh not her own,' and who, trained for resolute, aggressive, and undaunted leadership, are exemplars in interpreting every least task by the largest ideals." — M. W. STRYKER, *Hamilton, Lincoln, and Other Addresses* (Utica, 1896), "The Stewardship of Knowledge," pp. 96, 97.

Note 63. Page 304. — "It was held that a Christian should have such a desire for the glory of God that he should be willing to be condemned everlastingly if it would promote it. The futility of such a supposition is seen when it is put in the form of this question, 'Can a man so love God as to be willing, for any end, everlastingly to hate Him?' These are such unnatural issues that it would be hard to prove God could ever propose them to intelligent creatures, or intelligent creatures realize them as possible, except in the over-refinement of speculation." — JOHN KER, *Sermons* (Edinburgh, Douglas, 1885), pp. 103, 104.

Note 64. Page 305. — "These chapters of the Epistle to the Romans have been, by scholastic theology, put to uses for which they were never intended. They are not a contribution to the doctrine of the eternal predestination of individuals to everlasting life or death. Their theme is not the election of individuals, but of a people. And the point of view from which the principle of election is contemplated is historical. The writer treats of divine choices as they reveal themselves in this world in the career and destiny of nations. But still more important is it to note that in these chapters election is not conceived of as an arbitrary choice to the enjoyment of benefits from which all others are excluded. Election is to *function* as well as to favour, and the function has the good of others besides the elect in view. As the Jews, according to the Hebrew Scriptures, were chosen to be a blessing eventually to the Gentiles, so, according to the apostle, the Gentile no-nations were chosen in turn to be God's people, for their own good, doubtless, but also for the spiritual benefit of the temporarily disinherited Jews. It is unnecessary to point out that this view is in accordance with the uniform teaching of Scripture, and very specially with the teaching of Christ, in which the elect appear as the light, the salt, and the leaven of the world. It is a vital truth strangely overlooked in elaborate creeds large enough to have room for many doctrines much less important, and far from sufficiently recognized, as yet, even in the living faith of the Church, though the missionary spirit of modern Christianity may be regarded as an unconscious homage to its importance." — Prof. A. B. BRUCE, *St. Paul's Conception of Christianity* (New York, Scribners, 1894), pp. 321 ff.

Note 65. Page 306. — "Whatever else may or may not be taught in the New Testament, the twofold law of love is there given as the great commandment of the old dispensation and enforced by the obedience of Christ as of like rank in the new; as authoritative for him and for all his. The obligation to love God is stated explicitly enough. The command to love our neighbour, like to the other in its binding force, has for its interpretation the lifelong sacrifice by which Christ gave for the world's welfare all that He had to give. His whole business on earth was to express that perfect love for God's creatures which is the obverse of His perfect love for God. As if to guard the duty of beneficence against misapprehension or neglect, He not only taught human kindness as in the parable of the Good Samaritan, but in a passage of prophecy which might well be in the ritual of every church, He made the dread decisions of the judgment to turn not on doctrine but on conduct, not on the moral law in general but on the law of beneficence in particular. This is the style of His teaching who went about doing good. Well might Paul sing the psalm of 'Charity,' and John declare that God is love.

"If the law of love has such implications and such tremendous sanctions, there seems to be no escape from the proposition that every man ought to do his absolute utmost for the well-being of his fellow-creatures." — JAMES P. KELLEY, *The Law of Service* (G. P. Putnam's Sons, New York, 1894), pp. 4, 5.

"In practice under the law we have set forth, one serves God and himself, by serving his fellow-creatures. Worship, like the expression of filial affection, is natural and spontaneous. Its public forms, like the decorous customs of the household, are determined by fitness and usefulness. Its architecture and accessories are not according to the wealth and social position of the worshipper, but, again, are for fitness and use, and are limited by the economies of service. Service of fellow-creatures is the one business and study of life; service of self is incidental or indirect. Giving of mind, body, and estate is the normal process, the daily joy of life; inability or failure to give it its chief distress. Self-indulgence beyond rational use is disreputable; private display is both ungenerous and vulgar. Public spirit, with all that it implies, is the natural atmosphere of the life of service; public misfortune a personal grief, public disgrace a personal shame. The welfare of the nation, not as a jealous competing neighbour of other states, but as a generous and beneficent member of the commonwealth of nations, is the glory and pride of the Christian citizen.

"The world is grievously afflicted. The church has doctored the symptoms of its ailment empirically, in an intermittent and emotional way. According to the law of service, we are to deal scientifically with the disease itself by radical and constitutional treatment. The springs of human life must be cleansed, its processes made normal and vigorous, its activities reformed. We have reckoned on selfishness as the motive of human action; let us have the faith and courage to reckon on love. Self-seeking competition is war with all its miseries; generous service is peace with all its blessings." — *Ibid.*, pp. 142, 143.

Note 66. Page 311. — "Christ chose a small body of disciples to be in close contact with Himself, to share His work, and to receive His deeper teaching. This will not surprise us after the analogies of the prophets, the poets, the artists of the world. The saints, too, may be few, and God may lend their spirits out for the good of others. But, moreover, in the first formation of the Church we are able to watch the process of limitation, as historically worked out; and we see that it arises not from any narrowness, any grudging of His blessings, on the part of Christ, but from the narrowness, the limitations in man. Man is 'straitened' not in God, not in Christ, but in his own affections. God willed all men to be saved; Christ went about doing good and calling all to a change of heart, to a share in the kingdom of Heaven; but such a call made demands upon His hearers; it required that they should give up old prejudices about the Messianic kingdom, that they should be willing to leave father and mother and houses and lands for the truth's sake, that they should lay aside all the things that defile a man, that they should aim at being perfect, that they should not only hear but understand the word, that they should trust Him even when His sayings were hard. And these demands produced the limitations. The Pharisees preferred the glory of men to the glory which came from God; the masses in Galilee cared only for the bread that perisheth; many of the disciples turned back; and so He could not commit Himself unto them, because He knew what was in man. Not to them, not to any chance person, but to the Twelve, to those who had stood these tests, to those who had, in spite of all perplexity, seen in Him the Son of the Living God, to them He could commit Himself; they could share His secrets; they could be taught clearly the certainty and the meaning of His coming death, for they had begun to learn what self-sacrifice meant; they could do His work and organize His Church; they could bind and loose in His name; they could represent Him when He was gone. These are the elect; they who had the will to listen to the call; they who were 'magnanimous to correspond with heaven'; to them He gave at Pentecost the full conscious gift of the Holy Spirit, and so at last formed them into the Church, the Church which was to continue His work, which was to convey His grace, which was to go into the whole world, holding this life as a treasure for the sake of the whole world, praying and giving thanks for all men, because the unity of God and the unity of the mediation of Christ inspires them with hope that all may be one in Him." — *Lux Mundi*, pp. 372, 373.

INDEX